ALVAR
AALTO

Eeva-Liisa Pelkonen

ALVAR AALTO

Architecture, Modernity, and Geopolitics

Yale University Press New Haven and London

Published with the assistance of the Frederick W. Hilles Publication Fund of Yale University, the Graham Foundation for Advanced Studies in the Fine Arts, and the Kingsley Trust Association Publication Fund established by the Scroll and Key Society of Yale College.

Unless otherwise noted, all images are from Alvar Aalto Museum, Jyväskylä, Finland.

Designed by Jena Sher.
Set in Berthold Akzidenz Grotesk and Sabon MT type by Amy Storm.
Printed in Canada by Friesens.

Library of Congress Cataloging-in-Publication Data
Pelkonen, Eeva-Liisa.
  Alvar Aalto : architecture, modernity, and geopolitics / Eeva-Liisa Pelkonen.
     p. cm.
  Includes bibliographical references and index.
  ISBN 978-0-300-11428-7 (cloth : alk. paper)
    1. Aalto, Alvar, 1898–1976—Criticism and interpretation. 2. Architecture and society. 3. Regionalism in architecture. 4. International style (Architecture) I. Title.
  NA1455.F53A2355 2009
  720.92—dc22   2008045538

A catalogue record for this book is available from the British Library.

This paper meets the requirements of ANSI / NISO Z 39.48-1992 (Permanence of Paper).

10 9 8 7 6 5 4 3 2 1

Jacket illustrations: *(front)* Matti Poutvaara, aerial view of a Finnish lake landscape, from Matti Poutvaara, *Suomi Finland* (Helsinki: Werner Söderström, 1961), and Aino and Alvar Aalto, ca. 1940, National Board of Antiquities, Helsinki; *(back)* Aino and Alvar Aalto, Finnish Pavilion in the New York World's Fair, main display wall, 1939, Ezra Stoller © Esto (fig. 104).

For Ida, Mia, and Turner Brooks

In memory of my mother, Eila Marjatta Pelkonen (1924–2006)

Contents

Acknowledgments

I owe a great deal to many people since I began my doctoral studies at Columbia University in the late 1990s. My dissertation, "Empathetic Affinities: Alvar Aalto and His Milieus," was conceived as an intellectual group biography, which looked at Aalto's various social and intellectual milieus at home and abroad. Geopolitics emerged as a major theme. When Yale University Press gave me the opportunity to write a book on the topic, I decided to emphasize this aspect. The dominance of geographic themes and political subtexts makes Aalto more topical than ever. Through his architecture he confronted the world's large-scale economic and political changes.

The project has matured and evolved thanks to reviews and comments of many people. Gwendolyn Wright helped me to understand what it means to write an intellectual biography. Barry Bergdoll, Kenneth Frampton, Karsten Harries, and Mark Wigley all in different ways helped me to focus my argument. Fred Koetter, former dean of the Yale School of Architecture, allowed me to take time off from teaching for my doctoral studies. Dean Robert A. M. Stern has given me the opportunity to test my ideas through teaching.

Mia Hipeli and Arne Heporauta of the Alvar Aalto Archive helped me navigate Aalto's correspondence and library even as the collection was being catalogued. Marjo Holma, Katariina Pakoma, and Risto Raittila at the Alvar Aalto Museum in Jyväskylä and Päivi Lukkarinen at the Museum of Finnish Architecture provided crucial assistance with images. I want also to thank Beverly Lett, Tanya Alen, and Christopher Zollo, of Yale University's Arts Library, who never lost patience with my endless requests for often obscure books and magazines. My nephew Eero Nurmi was diligent in helping me locate archival images in Finnish collections.

Numerous colleagues and friends have offered important comments: Karla Britton, Jean-Louis Cohen, Roger Connah, Peggy Deamer, Keller Easterling, Britt Eversole, Romy Golan, Sarah Goldhagen, Alicia Imperiale, Sandy Isenstadt, Keith Krumwiede, Mary McLeod, Dietrich Neumann, Aino Niskanen, Joan Ockman, Ken Oshima, Nina Paavolainen, Alan Plattus, Demetri Porphyrios, Jonathan Schell, Ioanna Theocharopoulou, Lynnette Widder, Christopher Woods, and Claire Zimmerman. I am grateful to the students of my Aalto seminars for their contributions.

I thank Michelle Komie of Yale University Press for giving me the opportunity to work with her for the second time. I also thank her colleagues Daniella Berman, Heidi Downey, John Long, and Jena Sher. Eve Sinaiko's skillful editorial comments helped sharpen the manuscript's content and style. Ted Whitten proofread the final version and made some excellent last-minute suggestions.

The project has spanned the entire length of my thirteen-year marriage. My husband and colleague, Turner Brooks, has therefore, by default, read all versions of the text. I am thankful for his comments. Our two girls, Ida and Mia, were born during the process. I dedicate this book to my family, as well as to the memory of my mother, Eila Pelkonen, who died in 2006.

In this book I explore the geographic narratives and their geopolitical subtexts generated by the Finnish architect Alvar Aalto and his mentors over a fifty-year period, from the early years of Finnish independence to the end of the Cold War. In so doing I ask broader questions: How central is Finland—its history and its politics—to understanding Aalto's architecture, and how do we make sense of geography as a dominant theme in the history of modern architecture in general?

Perhaps more than any other modern architect's, Alvar Aalto's work and persona have been linked to and explained by his country of origin, Finland. An aerial view of a Finnish lake juxtaposed with an image of Savoy vases (1937) and a plan of the Finnish Pavilion at the 1939–40 New York World's Fair, which appear in Sigfried Giedion's influential *Space, Time and Architecture,* offer a shorthand argument: they suggest that the essence of Finland flows, as if naturally, into Aalto's architectural forms (fig. 1). Although the geography of Aalto's architecture has gained new readings, the idea of Aalto being a quintessentially Finnish architect still dominates.[1]

Giedion's ambiguous statement "Finland is with Aalto wherever he goes" implies, however, that both the architect's and the author's allusions to Finnish nature developed along with Aalto's engagement with the world at large.[2] In his seminal *Sources of Modern Eclecticism: Studies on Alvar Aalto* (1982), Demetri Porphyrios points out that Aalto used formal and metaphorical tropes alluding to Finnish nature and building tradition to construct ambiguous cultural and political meanings. I agree with these authors that Aalto's work and actions had a political dimension.

I started my own inquiry with a few simple questions: What did Aalto himself say about Finland and the geographic dimension of his architecture? What did he think or say about national, or for that matter, international architecture? I discovered that while Aalto certainly was not a typical Finnish architect, he was throughout his life and career preoccupied with Finland's cultural, political, and economic future, believing that his words and works could help shape the country's destiny. Finland and Finnish culture were major themes of Aalto's writings throughout his career. His books and articles include "Finnish Homes" (1922), "Landscape in Central Finland" (1925), "Letter from Finland" (1931), "Finland" (1940), "Post-War Reconstruction: Rehousing Research in Finland" (1940), "Finland as a Model for World Development" (1949), and "Finland Wonderland" (1950). The articles "Minimum Dwelling—a Social and Economic Hurdle" (1927), "Contemporary Architecture: An Interview with Alvar Aalto" (1929), and "The Housing System in the USSR" (1932) respond in various ways to international modernism. Other articles attempt to map a relationship between international architecture and society and their Finnish counterparts. These include "Finland and Scandinavia" (1939) and "An American Town in Finland" (1940). The word "geography" appears in the title of one of the key texts dealing with the relationship between architecture and geography: "The Geography of the Housing Question" (1932). It is my hope that a close reading of these and other texts will provide a new dimension to the understanding of how geographic themes became operative in Aalto's architecture and, further, an important element in his critical reception.

A review of Aalto's personal library helps to place these texts in a larger context. National architecture and culture constitute the dominant subject matter of many of the books Aalto acquired early in his career.[3] His library includes many German books on the topic, such as Paul Mebes' *Um 1800: Architektur und Handwerk im letzten Jahrhundert ihrer traditionellen Entwicklung* (1920), the volume on *Kleinbürgerhäuser* from Paul Schultze-Naumburg's *Kulturarbeiten* series (1911), and Karl Scheffler's *Der Geist der Gotik* (1922). From these he formulated various ways to understand what constitutes a national style.

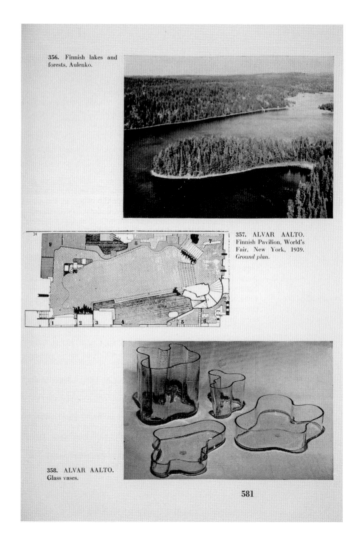

1. A page depicting Finnish lakes and forests, the Finnish Pavilion at the New York World's Fair, and Aalto's Savoy vases. From Sigfried Giedion, *Space, Time and Architecture*, 2nd ed. (Cambridge, Mass.: Harvard University Press, 1949), 581.

By the late 1920s Aalto had also been exposed to the early histories of international architecture, which promoted the emergence of a new style that transcended national particularities. These included Ludwig Hilberseimer's *Internationale Neue Baukunst* (1927), a German edition of Le Corbusier's *Towards a New Architecture,* entitled *Kommende Baukunst* (1929), and the Swedish book *Acceptera* ("To Accept") (1930). The latter was written by a group of young architects involved in the 1930 Stockholm Exhibition, under the leadership of Gunnar Asplund, to promote modern architecture in Sweden; the authors focus on the relationship between national and international architecture. Aalto also subscribed to some thirty art and architecture journals, most of them foreign, which offered multiple national perspectives on international modernism.

The library also reveals that internationalism was by no means the only alternative to the nationalism to which Aalto was exposed. His library includes the collected works of the turn-of-the-century Danish literature critic Georg Brandes and the 1923 book *Pan-Europa* by the Austrian count Richard Caudenhove-Kalergi. Both authors expressed distaste for nationalistic extremism and promoted the free movement of people and goods within Europe. In his own writings, Aalto often cited Friedrich Nietzsche and the Russian anarchist Petr Kropotkin. These ideas—Pan-Europeanism (Caudenhove-Kalergi), cultural and political cosmopolitanism (Brandes and Nietzsche), and regionalism (Kropotkin)—went much further than internationalism in promoting the dissolution of borders. Contact with Lewis Mumford in the late 1930s introduced Aalto to American regionalism, which built upon these ideas.

Aalto's library also includes books on national socialist and fascist architecture, such as one on Albert Speer's Reich Chancellery published in the early 1940s, as well as Agnoldomenico Pica's *Nuova architettura italiana* (1936) and the pro-fascist Finnish magazine *Nordlicht* (1942). Although it is unlikely that these books reflected Aalto's own political inclinations, they are, however, examples of the various shades of nationalism and national architectural expression that dominated the early part of the twentieth century, and which no active architect or theorist could ignore. All in all, Aalto's library bears witness to his participation in the larger discussion about geography—a dominant theme within twentieth-century architectural modernism and the culture at large.

Despite architectural historians' frequent use of geographic and national attributions in the literature of modern architecture (for example, "International Modernism," "Italian Renaissance"), we have not done a very good job of defining what we mean by the national and geographic dimension of architecture. While the historiography of the geography of architecture is still waiting to be written, Thomas DaCosta Kaufmann's *Towards a Geography of Art* (2004) offers a helpful overview that engages art as well as architecture and helps us understand what it means to link art and architecture to a particular locale. Kaufmann points out that when making the link between architecture and a particular location, architectural discourse has tended to emphasize a quasi-phenomenological understanding of placeness. Christian Norberg-Schulz's influential though problematic *Genius Loci: Towards a Phenomenology of Architecture* (1979) exemplifies this reading: geographic locations are reduced to psychophysical essences that flow, somewhat miraculously, into material artifacts. Norberg-Schulz uses symptomatically vague terms to define the process: architecture simply "embodies" or "reflects" nature, culture, and society.[4]

I would argue that Aalto offers a particularly rich case study for redefining the geography of modern architecture, not least because of Finland's complicated history, which has often been overlooked by Aalto scholars. Because of Finland's perilous location between East and West, the country's history has been turbulent. Its borders have changed often since it became a politically administered territory under Swedish rule in the twelfth century. By 1809, when Russia conquered the country during the Napoleonic wars, its eastern boundary had already changed many times over during the recurring wars between the two countries. The boundaries would be redrawn several times in the twentieth century, first after Finland's independence in 1917 and twice more during the Second World War, when Finland lost a big part of its eastern territory to the Soviet Union—in 1940, after the Winter War, and again in 1944, in the final peace treaty after the Continuation War (fig. 2).

Aalto's writings and library reveal a parallel between his preoccupation with geographic narratives and the historical events that marked the most volatile period in Finnish history, from the independence in 1917 till the end of his life in 1976, when the Cold War dynamics forced Finland to renegotiate once again its status between East and West. There is no doubt that Aalto's life and career were affected by these events. I therefore believe that to understand Aalto and his historical role we must consider his participation in the complex political life of Finland and its geopolitical representations. I will emphasize that from an early date Aalto's life and career transcended national borders, and that he was well aware that nations, particularly Finland, could not be understood in isolation from one another. The contemporary sociologist Anthony Giddens has noted that nation-states cannot be considered self-contained and static entities. Rather, they "exist in systemic relations with other nation-states. . . . 'International rel-ations' is coeval with the origins of nation-states."[5] Architectural geography as conceived by Aalto and his contemporaries is therefore in this book viewed as a discursive practice that produced terminology, representations, and spatial products whose goal was not only to understand and reinforce the unity of national culture, but also to conceptualize relationships to other countries.

Significantly, Aalto did not take architecture's relationship to a particular place as given but used a number of narratives and concepts to explore architecture's ties to geographic locations at different historical moments. In the immediate aftermath of the Declaration of Independence, Aalto used the expression *national architecture* to reinforce the uniqueness of Finnish culture. The country was seen as an entity with its own architectural sensibility, even when subject to external influences. The idea of international influence developed in the late 1920s, specifically through an interest in international modernism as Aalto became more and more aware that Finland needed to establish reciprocal relationships with other countries. He associated internationalism with what today we would call a network—a system of linkages and exchanges with many nodes. At the same time, around the mid-1920s, Aalto became exposed to the pan-European movement and started to emphasize unhindered mobility across, even the dissolution of, national boundaries. Europe was here conceived as a unified dynamic field where national differences would eventually start to blur. Contact with American regionalists helped him to take a pragmatic approach to geographic questions emphasizing management of economic, human, and natural resources during the period of postwar Finnish reconstruction, which laid the foundation for the future economic prosperity of the country. The spatial idea behind regionalism is a nested

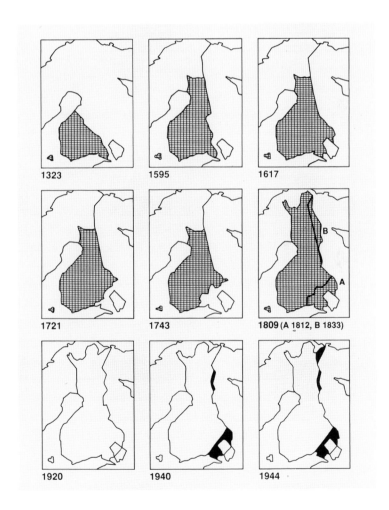

2. Changes to Finland's borders since 1323. From Anssi Paasi, *Territories, Boundaries, and Consciousness: The Changing Geographies of the Finnish-Russian Border* (London: Wiley, 1996), 88.

network in which the country's internal infrastructure, settlement, and production networks are supported by and connected to the larger global networks of international commerce. After the Second World War, as Aalto became a self-described universalist and humanist, he started to invest his architecture with formal and semantic ambiguity. This correlated with Finland's attempt to avoid being drawn into further international conflicts.

Indeed, we should not take Aalto's geographic narratives at face value. In addition to complex cultural and political motivations and biases, his work was influenced by—and had an influence on—the popular ideas and images of Finland depicted in literature, art, and the media, both at home and abroad. These cultural expressions reflected both how Finns understood themselves as a nation and how they chose to represent themselves to the rest of the world. As Benedict Anderson has pointed out, nations are "imagined realities."[6] Ideas and images established in the late nineteenth century laid the foundation for Finland's national self-image during Aalto's life: Finland as an innocent nature reserve with plentiful forests and lakes; Finns as innately fiercer and more creative than their western European counterparts; and Finland as the site of confrontation between East and West.

We can also look to maps for expressions of Finnish identity. Although we might consider them to be raw blueprints of a physical territory, maps are, in fact, mediated representations rather than disinterested factual documents. Cartography, as the visual representation of geography, reflects ideas about physical, political, and ethnic affinities and territorial interests. The earliest existing maps depicted Finland as the tail end of Europe, while during the early years of independence Finns tended to see themselves as part of a larger tribal network that spread deep into the Soviet territory.[7] During the Cold War foreigners commonly depicted Finland part of the Soviet camp.[8] Such a broad range of cartographic representations leads one to wonder how Finland's constantly shifting boundaries have shaped the national imagination, including its intellectual and artistic formulations.

When the full spectrum of a nation's representational products, from objects of art to maps, is taken into account, it becomes clear that one cannot talk about the geography of a country in the abstract. The discussion must be grounded in an actual historical moment, together with its politics, discursive practices, spatial products, and representational techniques, all of which contribute to the social construction of a territory. In this book I endeavor to show that when Finland's geopolitical location, its complicated historical events, Aalto's individual actions, and the full range of discursive practices and representational strategies are taken into consideration, a whole new way of understanding Aalto's architecture —and modern architecture in general—emerges.

I have chosen the monographic format because I believe it can transcend the essentialism that often accompanies discussions about national architectures to reveal the complexity of historical events as actual people imbedded in real-life situations experienced them. Aalto is here seen as an active agent whose ideas about architecture's geographic dimensions evolved in particular historical moments. Göran Schildt's three-volume biography of Aalto has provided important information about his life and career. That Schildt knew Aalto personally and was able to interview the aging master allowed him great insights into his complex personality. Schildt's biography can be credited for emphasizing Aalto's friendships and travels abroad and for recognizing that there were, in a sense, multiple Aaltos: architect, writer, artist, businessman, wartime propagandist, cosmopolite, and so on.[9]

This book is not a comprehensive survey of Aalto's life and career but rather an exploration of geographic themes, both within his work and as evidenced in the political nature of his career and persona. The three parts of the book each present a different geographic narrative put forward by Aalto and speculate on the geopolitical subtext. Part 1, "Making of a Nation," examines the period from the early 1920s through about 1930. It deals with Finland's and Aalto's search for national identity and, subsequently, national style, uncovering the racial, cultural, and geopolitical sympathies and antipathies within Aalto's proposition. Part 2, "New Geographies," covers the early 1920s to the mid-1940s, when Aalto started to engage various theories of internationalization and key figures within the modern movement. In each chapter I explore a different approach to transnational relationships—namely cosmopolitanism, pan-Europeanism, internationalism, and regionalism—that link to various ideas and scenarios about Finland's foreign policy and economic future. In Part 3, "Formal Registers," I consider the period from circa 1930 to the mid-1970s and take a close look at the geopolitics behind Aalto's formal ideas and his critical reception.

Aalto's intellectual and personal malleability emerges as a dominant theme in this story. By constantly seeking out new places and people—and in the process appropriating new ideas and images—Aalto embodied three key ideas of modernity: change, progress, and dynamism.[10] His architectural ideas changed often, depending on the intellectual and political context he was operating from. He was a statecrafter par excellence, intuiting, as it were, a suitable geopolitical strategy before the country's leaders did. Reading *Modernity and Self-Identity,* in which Anthony Giddens calls modernization and individual actions the "two extremes of extensionality and intentionality, which define modernity," convinced me that what appear merely to be Aalto's personal traits are actually symptomatic of modern subjectivity at large.[11] For Giddens, modernity is not reducible to an abstract economic or social superstructure; it must be understood as a condition that forces individuals to make choices, take risks, and thereby to transform existing conventions; in other words, modernity as condition gains meaning and is understood only through individual actions.[12] Stylistic questions aside, this ability to act out and represent various large-scale historical and geographic narratives as they were unfolding makes Aalto in my mind one of the most modern architects of the twentieth century.

Making of a Nation

National culture was a major theme in Aalto's writings and architectural projects from the beginning of his career, in about 1920. His earliest articles, published in both professional magazines and newspapers, discuss the architecture and art of Finland and its neighboring countries and address, albeit indirectly, the key theoretical problem of architectural geography: What constitutes national style and, subsequently, how do qualities in a particular geographic location transfer to formal and aesthetic registers? Aalto's first buildings were a part of this exploration.

The foundation was laid at the Polytechnic Institute during Aalto's tenure as a student in 1916–21, the years surrounding Finnish independence. Armas Lindgren (1874–1929), a former partner in the leading architectural firm Gesellius-Lindgren-Saarinen (1896–1905), played a central role. As a historicist, Lindgren taught his students how to communicate cultural meanings through architectural style. With his early National Romantic–style buildings he used rustic tectonic details and ornamental motifs depicting Finnish flora and fauna to suggest an indigenous national style, although he never veered far from the typologies common to Western architecture. His history lectures traced a regional "ethos" within Finnish, eastern Baltic, and Scandinavian architecture. His studios taught students to view Finnish architecture and culture within this immediate regional context.

At the same time, Lindgren opposed national isolationism and saw Finland as part of a larger European cultural sphere. He was convinced of the universal applicability of historical styles in architecture, believing that an imported motif would quickly acquire its own character within each nation, and that national character played a decisive role in determining which styles were adopted. He considered medieval Gothic the first true Northern style, which, born of the "Northern soul," spread to different countries and gained its "own character" in Finland.[1] Lindgren's *Building and Decoration Styles* (1914), which Aalto studied, helped make sense of the spread of neoclassicism in Finland during the nineteenth century by asserting that "Empire-style and neo-classicism became then the preferred cultural form, [because their] clarity and plain simplicity best suited the Finnish mentality."[2]

As a historicist, Lindgren saw style as a vehicle for communicating cultural values, and his own preference for classicism was politically motivated: the idea of Finland having a distinct mentality capable of appropriating foreign influences gave the nation a right to exist, and an inclination toward classicism proved that the country belonged to the West. As a corollary, hostility to all things Russian had defined Finnish art and architecture since the late nineteenth century. The famous late nineteenth-century painting by Edward Isto titled *The Attack,* in which a white-gowned young Finnish woman defends her country's law, as an emblem of its independence, against the Russian Eagle, still looms large in the national psyche (fig. 3).

The situation intensified when Aalto came to Helsinki in 1916 to study architecture. The city was an epicenter of events that led Finland to declare independence from Russia in November 1917, only to be drawn into a civil war the following spring. The war pitted the Red Army, consisting of landless peasants and factory workers who wanted to join the Bolshevist revolution, against the White Army, backed by the newly founded, pro-German government of Finland. After a brief but bloody war, the Whites were victorious, yet rifts persisted for years to come.[3] Aalto had joined the White Army at age eighteen and was involved in some crucial battles.[4]

The debate surrounding national style intensified accordingly. By drawing attention to certain precedents and overlooking others, architects and architectural historians took part in the national debate over Finland's cultural and political relations to other countries. The dominant pattern in Finnish foreign policy in the years after independence was expressed in architectural discourse by teaching Scandinavian and Baltic architecture and by eliminating Russian examples. One architect had this to say about window types: "Why should we not use the 2-, 4-, 6- and 8-pane windows, which have long been known to be good? No one should have anything to say against them. We only have spoilt tastes to thank for extensive use of the tripartite windows I have experienced. This prob-

3. Edward Isto, *Hyökkäys* (The Attack), 1898. Oil on canvas, 200 × 140 cm. Finnish National Gallery, Helsinki.

ably originates in Russia, a country with which we probably do not need to have too much in the way of intellectual or cultural links."[5]

An essay from 1926, "Traditional Finnish Architecture," by the influential historian and critic Carolus Lindberg (1889–1955), one of Aalto's beloved teachers and the editor in chief of the Finnish architecture review *Arkkitehti* between 1921 and 1928, characterized the quest for national style as important because it was an actualization of historical events and geopolitical tensions:

Geographically speaking, Finland belongs to the eastern European continent; the Baltic Sea and its bays separate the country from Western Europe. But here, like elsewhere, the sea has rather connected than separated [us from the West]. Finland gained contact with Christian civilization through the Baltic Sea. The same source gave birth to our science and art.

The highly stylized architecture of Eastern Europe, with which Finland came into contact both in peace and in war, had little influence in Finland. The roots of Finnish civilization and national art can be traced to the West since the Middle Ages. We can therefore conclude that Finland has always been, and will continue to be, the easternmost abode of western civilization.[6]

Despite the length of the land border between Finland and Russia, and the presence of Finnish tribes deep in Russian territory, Lindberg made a case for closer cultural affinity between Finland and the western European countries separated from it by water. Relative to the development of Aalto's ideas about national style and architectural geography, it is important to note that Lindberg considered national style an outcome of historical processes, whereby a nation takes its destiny into its own hands by choosing certain cultural affinities over others.

Aalto elaborated this approach by shifting from the analysis of buildings to the search for the broader, more ineffable reasons that certain buildings were perceived as significant in the national consciousness. He became drawn to the mystical qualities of architecture that he believed not only embodied values of the culture that produced them but could also further a sense of belonging to a nation.

The article "Painters and Masons," from 1921, found this intensified emotive experience in the idea of *Gesamtkunstwerk,* or "total work of art," which could subsume a person or a communal body completely, as only a building could. In response to Victor Hugo's dictum "this killed that," Aalto writes: "In the days before printing, people needed—as symbols of their spiritual aspirations and to fulfill their longing for beauty—large and, above all, beautiful buildings. Temples, cathedrals, forums, theatres and palaces communicated history with greater clarity and sensitivity than old rolls of parchment ever could. There was but one art in the world, the art of building." He saw the Middle Ages as the last moment when the unity of the arts reflected the historical role and aspirations of a community.[7]

In believing that architecture represents the highest cultural achievement of a nation, Aalto followed the legacy of Finnish architects who, in about 1900, started to investigate the country's domestic building tradition in an effort to define what made it and the culture behind it unique. They focused on Finland's medieval stone churches, even though these simple rectangular buildings with steep gable roofs were a far cry from the more elaborate medieval churches on the continent. Most were made of fieldstone, with only the most significant ones of brick. The gables were ornamented with brick lacework, and vaulted ceilings were painted *a secco* on an often unevenly plastered surface. Lindgren was an expert; he did measured drawings with his students and ended up restoring many of the churches.

In order to define the origins of a distinct national style that would support their bid for increased autonomy from Russia, some architects relied, like Lindgren, on cultural taxonomies traceable to Goethe and Romanticism that distinguished between southern and northern sensibilities. They saw these churches as bearing witness to the "silent Nordic soul" that "did not produce forms for form's sake, decoration for decoration's sake—as the southerners like to do—but used decoration only to represent a certain idea."[8] An ink drawing accompanying Lindgren's article "About Our Medieval Art," from 1901, depicted a dark mass rising from the bare fields. Its monolithic quality made it appear as if it was part of the earth's crust, grounded to its particular geographic place (fig. 4).

Aalto also tackled this topic, albeit through painting. His 1918 gouache of the Porvoo Cathedral, built between the thirteenth and fifteenth centuries, depicts in heavy brush strokes a bold, luminous form against a dark background that produces a dialectical reading: light triumphing over darkness while matter fights the settling into form (fig. 5). Importantly, Aalto tries to capture the essence solely

4. Armas Lindgren, sketch of the medieval Hattula Church. From his "Något om Vår Medeltida Konst" (About Our Medieval Art), *Ateneum*, 1901.

through form, texture, and color. It marks the beginning of a nascent modern sensitivity that invests the aesthetic object with a kind of spiritual torpor and inner will that, like a religious experience, had power not only to represent people's aspirations but to move people, and even change their behavior.

Focusing on the immaterial freed Aalto to consider stylistic changes and make a call for a new style for a new era. In "Painters and Masons," written a few years later, Aalto talked about architecture's ability to "reflect the prevailing spirit of the age," a complex notion originating from the Romantics that refers to an ethos of an era.[9] Importantly, he saw national style as a local actualization of the larger spirit of the time, and subsequently world history. The two existed in a dialectical relationship. The question of how to modulate between them became his project.

Like his teacher Armas Lindgren, Aalto was a progressive rather than an insular nationalist, believing that the nation's future lay in cultural, political, and economic connections with other western European countries. The travels that

5. Aalto, Porvoo Cathedral, ca. 1918. Gouache. From Göran Schildt, *Alvar Aalto: The Early Years* (New York: Rizzoli, 1984), 104.

he chose to make reflect his political and cultural attitudes. I will show that rather than settling into a particular locus, however, Aalto's affinities changed in time.

Aalto's first study trip abroad, in 1920, took him to Stockholm and Copenhagen. Growing up in a Swedish- and Finnish-speaking family, he was naturally inclined to promote the idea of a culturally unified and politically strong Nordic region, so much so that he believed that Nordic peoples shared a visual sensibility. Ragnar Östberg's (1866–1944) Stockholm City Hall, built between 1909 and 1923 (fig. 6), and Martin Nyrop's (1849–1921) neo-Gothic Copenhagen City Hall (1892) were the two modern must-see buildings of his generation. Both drew on contemporary eclectic international architectural ideas of the revival of great past styles—the Greco-Roman, the Gothic—but employed new materials and new building methods. Historical revivalism had been the trend in architecture in Europe before World War I, and many architects continued to draw on that tradition well into the 1920s. It is sometimes forgotten that architects who practiced historicism at that time did not view it as backward or conservative. Rather, as it was passed down through generations from the nineteenth century on, historicism was associated with European learnedness.

The Stockholm City Hall was a typical example of this fairly late historicist and eclectic trend, which allowed the building to communicate cultural and historical values, and accommodate historical motifs, even as it formulated a new stylistic idiom. The building was made of brick and dominated by a tower that linked it to a long tradition of Gothic-style city halls, and which alluded to the political and social coherence of a medieval city-state. A close-up view revealed ornate window and capital details reminiscent of Venetian Gothic columns, recalling the Palazzo Ducale in the Piazza San Marco. Ornaments and mosaics derived from

6. Ragnar Gunnar Östberg, Stockholm City Hall, 1909–23. Swedish Architecture Museum, Stockholm.

MAKING OF A NATION

Swedish and foreign mythologies and from different periods bear witness to the deep and geographically expansive roots of the country's culture. The impression was at once eclectic and stylistically pure as all the elements merged into an ideal Gesamtkunstwerk of urbanism, architecture, and decorative arts. The word "complete" comes up in Aalto's exuberant review of Östberg's building when it was still under construction. "Young architects of the north, who dream of a cool, classical, linear beauty, may not always approve of Östberg's Venetian magnificence, but we must all admire him nevertheless. He is the only man who, in the midst of our chaotic era, has succeeded in producing something complete. Martin Nyrop [who designed the Copenhagen City Hall] and Ragnar Östberg—these are the two men who represent the first phase of the early Nordic Renaissance."[10]

His praise went here to the architect as a great visionary and leader, one who was able to crystallize cultural forces, past and present, into unified architectural form. Merely copying historical forms was not enough. Emotional intensity and complete immersion were the ultimate measure not only of architecture but also of the vitality of the individuals and, by extension, the nations who produced it. Aalto used all his rhetorical skills to convey the strong emotional sensations triggered by the building: "This is one of the rare places where 'the greatness of simplicity' wholly overcomes the visitor (at least myself) in an almost physical way. If the City Hall, through its proportions and beauty of detail, can be said to represent this country's present level of civilization, generations to come will have a beautiful testimony of 20th century Sweden." Aalto reads Östberg's ability to abstract and simplify as a sign of Sweden's cultural sophistication and the moral stature of the Nordic people as a whole.[11]

This paragraph shows that by graduation Aalto had become a well-versed historicist who knew his stylistic periods and believed that historical styles could be used to communicate cultural and political aspirations. Historicism, which was a dominant force in Finland's architectural heritage, promoted the circulation and appropriation of styles and forms from varying sources both past and present, challenging any narrow geographic definition of national style. An architect could choose to appropriate different cultural references and even facilitate a shift in cultural affinities, both promoting his or her own ideas and expressing the nation's political aspirations.

By drawing a parallel between Stockholm at the beginning of the twentieth century and Venice in the fifteenth, Aalto demonstrated that, while he was a historicist, his view of history was Hegelian: historical events unfolded in predetermined cycles—a period of social confusion was always followed by one of order. As the Middle Ages had been followed by the Renaissance, so would the nineteenth century's era of confused values, which had culminated in the First World War, be followed by a period of order and prosperity. The idea of a new "Nordic Renaissance" suggested that, like Venice, the Baltic cities could spearhead a new era and become major cultural and political players. One could continue to speculate that Östberg's chosen period, the Venetian Gothic, was appealing to northerners because it marked the point when the supposedly murky Northern Gothic was followed by a more refined Venetian iteration, the first sign of the emerging Renaissance sensibility. The transitional style celebrated culture and style in the making, something that Aalto must have found appealing from the Finnish perspective. The site strategy supported the role that buildings played in this cultural and political process: the big, dramatically prominent building on Kungsholmen Island was a potent symbol for the shared ideals and aspirations of the population.

The review also reveals Aalto's familiarity with contemporary German art-historical scholarship, which emphasized lines and contours as formative elements of design and vehicles of cultural analysis. Johann Joachim Winckelmann, who presented Greek antiquity as the highest ideal for civilization and Greek art and architecture as a yardstick for all artistic production, had laid the foundation in the eighteenth century. Winckelmann's theory was based on the idea of universal beauty; he was not interested in either cultural or aesthetic diversity. Later art historians like Heinrich Wölfflin, while accepting the idea of normative classical beauty, invested forms additionally with anthropological, psychological, and cultural significations measured against the norm. Even Alois Riegl, often considered the main proponent of artistic formalism, believed that art was a product that could be used to access the collective psyche of a particular nation or region. Riegl famously sought what he called the *Kunstwollen,* or "will to form," in the lesser arts.

Winckelmann, Riegl, and Wölfflin were formative voices for aestheticians and critics before and between the world wars. Not surprisingly, Aalto, following his teacher Armas Lindgren, thought about style along similar lines: forms were not beautiful in themselves but because they bore witness to the values and aspirations of the culture that produced them. Like Wölfflin's and Riegl's, Aalto's and Lindgren's formalism had a national and regional subtext. Geography was used to support psychological and anthropological models, and vice versa. Geographic (north versus south), formal (simple versus ornamented), and psychological (calm versus flamboyant) taxonomies corresponded with one another. Aalto's close study of the Stockholm City Hall was thus not motivated simply by the fact that he thought it a beautiful, well-composed building, but by his belief that every line in it offered access to the culture that had produced it.

Aalto's admiration for Östberg's City Hall had a domestic political subtext as well. In praising the building he was by implication endorsing Finland's alliance with Sweden, its prosperous western neighbor and former ruler, from the twelfth century to 1809. The relationship with Sweden was, however, very complex. Despite long historical and cultural connections—including a Lutheran faith shared by 90 percent of the population—close ties to Sweden were controversial among many Finnish speakers. The relationship hit rock bottom around 1921 owing to the territorial dispute over the Swedish-speaking Åland Islands, located between the two countries. Although the problem was resolved in favor of Finland, nationally minded Finns had difficulty overcoming their negative attitude toward Sweden.

Finland's first president, Kaarlo Juho Ståhlberg (1865–1952), for example, never visited Sweden because, as he put it, it was "difficult [for Stockholm] to accept Finland as a state on an equal footing."[12]

One of Aalto's first architectural commissions, the exhibition grounds for the Tampere Industrial and Craft Fair of 1922, is an instance in which the architecture can hardly be understood without knowledge of the contemporaneous political situation and how fast it could change (fig. 7). At first glance there seems to be nothing Finnish about these buildings, some of which had half-timber frames and thatched roofs. They are more akin to Danish architecture, to which Aalto had been exposed during a visit to Denmark in 1921. Yet, thatched roofs were also characteristic of the region of Ingria, around St. Petersburg, whose local population, the Ingrians, were Finnish-speakers and Lutherans (fig. 8). During a brief period in the late teens the Finnish government backed the short-lived Republic of North Ingria and had high hopes of eventually absorbing the region into its territory. The issue was resolved when the Treaty of Tarto of 1920 settled the border issues and reintegrated Ingria into Russia. The particular tectonic motif, a thatched roof, could be thus read as making a case for continuing cultural and political alliance among all of the Baltic countries. Finland, in this case, was poised as a link between its eastern- and westernmost regions.

The idea that Finns were somehow unique and certainly not to be confused with Swedes started to influence Aalto's thinking about Finnish national identity and how it was being expressed in art around this time. He chose to write about contemporary painting, which, relative to architecture, is a much quicker indicator of cultural trends. In 1922 he reviewed an exhibition of Tykö Sallinen (1879–

7. Aalto, display booth at the Tampere Industrial and Craft Fair, 1922

1955), Finland's first expressionist painter, notorious for his depictions of rough, robust peasants. By endorsing Sallinen, Aalto rejected the use of historical motifs practiced by the so-called National Romantic artists and architects, in favor of a more immediate expression of national sensibility through painterly means. "Sallinen cannot be simply considered a 'contemporary artist,' but a colorist who continues the legacy of old monumental art and whose racial instinct has guided him to the right historical sources where he has found the right precedents. To be sure, the so-called national style traditionally derives from the past, but has so far limited itself to depiction of mythological themes. Sallinen sees 'national art' also as a search for painterly values. Learning from the old church art has introduced a new backbone to our contemporary art."[13]

In his attempt to define national style, Aalto faced the challenging question of how collective national traits are channeled through individual artistic production. He was influenced by the dominant art-historical theories of his time, according to which people in different nations and regions produce different types of art, driven by the different mindsets that emerge from racial traits. Such reasoning played an important role in early twentieth-century critical theory, which held that every race had its own optical culture.[14] Aalto, for example, described Sallinen as a quintessentially Finnish artist who through "racial instinct" had reached a "national art." Importantly, Sallinen did not represent just Finnish landscape or Finnish people, but rather, according to Aalto, captured the national essence or soul without attempting to beautify or idealize the country. "Sallinen sees the beauty in Finnish landscape itself, its geology and its topography. Destroyed woodlands, suburban settlements—in all these he finds painterly values. In addition he is able to analyze the soul of the landscape and to discover its monumental, characteristic shapes" (fig. 9).[15]

The piece on Sallinen illustrates that Aalto, while interested in fostering cultural connections with other countries, nonetheless celebrated the Finns' unique identity, both aesthetic and racial. His pseudoscientific ideas about national

8. Traditional house of West Ingria. From Artturi Kannisto, ed., *Suomen Suku I* (Family of Finns) (Helsinki: Otava, 1924), 282.

sensibility were symptomatic of a broader trend in the 1910s and 1920s: a desire for international collaboration that dominated the realms of politics and economics and converged with an "introspective nationalist atmosphere" in the realm of culture in order to make a claim for sovereignty.[16] The leading Finnish aesthetician, Erik Ahlman (1892–1952), captured the sentiments of the post–World War I era in *The World of Values and Means* (1920). Nationalism, he wrote, was a basic human sentiment and needed an outlet in art. "From its most primitive stages onwards artistic production is an outcome of the special characteristic of a nation," he insisted. "The *Volksgeist* gains its strongest expression in the work of a poet."[17] In Ahlman's formulation, as soon as the subject turned to nationalism, artistic creation became primitive and impulsive; art was a product of an urge rather than of skill and erudition.

As the bilingual Aalto was surely aware, Finns were a heterogeneous population and hardly in agreement about what constituted national expression. Nor was the notion of "racial instinct" necessarily a unifying factor. Early twentieth-century racial theorists considered Finns a so-called "mixed race"—half Aryan, half Mongolian, in the terminology of the day. This caused concern among Finns who wanted to stand on equal terms with Swedes and other presumably Aryan western Europeans.[18] This racial profile supported the convergence of internationalism and nationalism that came to characterize Finnish politics and culture: Aryan blood in the Finnish genetic heritage guaranteed that Finns belonged to the Occident, while the Mongolian strains made them unique and somehow more exotic.

Aalto used the idea of Finns as a hybrid race in his essay "Motifs from Past Ages" to put forward an idea of an equally hybrid national architectural style. He discusses Olkkala Manor, a neoclassical country estate probably designed by Charles Bassi (1772–1840), an architect of Italian origin commissioned by the Swedish crown to be the first building superintendent of Finland. The house

9. Tykö Sallinen, *Kevättalvi* (Early Spring), 1914. Oil on canvas, 49 × 46.5 cm. Finnish National Gallery/Central Art Archives, Helsinki.

was built between 1843 and 1845 and is exemplary of a type: it was built by a Swedish-speaking family, the af Hallströms, who belonged to the landowning elite. The fairly modest main building was designed in the Swedish Empire style and built of wood. It had two stories and a long symmetrical main facade divided in three bays, with rusticated pilasters painted white. The horizontal wooden siding was painted ochre yellow (fig. 10).

In discussing this house Aalto surely was suggesting that the Aryan race was (putatively) responsible for the most important cultural developments in Finland. At the same time, he differentiated this Finnish example of classical architecture from its Western counterparts, focusing on the small dining room, which was lined with Doric pilasters. The title page of his article shows their somewhat tacked-on quality: half-columns alternate with urns in shallow relief, set on an awkwardly low dado (fig. 11). While his teacher Lindgren had considered classical architecture well suited for northerners because of its simplicity and harmony, Aalto, on the other hand, was attracted to the quirkiness of the outcome when the style was appropriated by the northern countries of lesser means. He wrote about the "almost Tuscan ornamental columns" of the Olkkala dining room and

10. Charles Bassi, Olkkala Manor main building, 1843–45, in 1920. National Board of Antiquities, Helsinki.
11. The small dining room at Olkkala Manor. From Aalto, "Motifs from Past Ages," *Arkkitehti* 2 (1922).

the "almost ludicrously insignificant double staircase in the castle of Vadstena, of which Professor Romdahl spoke with such enthusiasm, as the first harbinger of the Renaissance in the North."[19]

The article demonstrates that when attempting to define the future of national culture and style, the country and its culture should not be solely determined by the racial traits of its people. Aalto was equally interested in how the house spoke of the desire of its builders to overcome any limitations imposed by remoteness from the centers of Western civilization. He concludes that "all such phenomena in our early art are as Nordic and as Finnish as one could wish, but they also reveal the *internationalist artist* hidden in our forefathers."[20] Thus his reasoning behind the Nordic version of classicism differed radically from Lindgren's. Whereas his teacher drew a correlation between the idea of a stable national essence and formal harmony, Aalto saw form as an index of collective inner drives and unconscious motivations. For him it was this inner striving and will that made the buildings—often found in the middle of nowhere—so moving. He was fixated on the export of "stylistic motifs": "These stylistic motifs [Tuscan ornamental columns] are so few and far between in our old architecture that this alone is reason enough to prize them, but this is not all there is to them. They crystallize the remoteness of our country, our distance from the centers of culture; and their artistic value is not diminished by the meaningless label of 'provincialism.'"[21]

Aalto's own explorations into classicism, conducted after his move to Jyväskylä in 1923, must be viewed within this framework. The idea of Finnish architecture being both a result of its geographic limitations and an embodiment of the internal drive to overcome them was put into practice in the buildings Aalto designed for the Jyväskylä Singing Festival in 1924 (fig. 12). The barrel-

12. Aalto, Jyväskylä Singing Festival entrance arcade, 1924

vaulted entrance arcade was executed in simple vertical wooden boards, without any attempt to reproduce the complicated detailing characteristic of the eighteenth-century Empire Style that served as a model. The structure speaks also of the geographic and social differences within Finland. Olkkala Manor was certainly much more elaborate than structures built in the Finnish-speaking heartland. The Seinäjoki Civil Guard Building (1924–29, fig. 13), his first major commission, exemplifies how these complex geographic and racial narratives enter into the architectural object. Like Olkkala Manor, it was a symmetrical two-story building. However, it had no entrance portico, and its board-and-batten siding, common to the area, gave it a more explicitly local flavor. The 1927 meat inspection building in Jyväskylä offers a somewhat humorous example of how classical language could be used to elevate even the most banal activities. A loggia with a straight entablature gave the simple structure a dignified, classical appearance (fig. 14).

Aalto's bell tower for Kauhajärvi Church (1921, fig. 15) suggests that he had been studying Finland's seventeenth-century wooden churches, which had been built by local craftsmen, often following stylistic guidelines sent from Stockholm. Some of the most spectacular of these, such as Petäjävesi Church (1763–65), near Aalto's hometown of Jyväskylä, skillfully mimicked the appearance of Gothic groin vaulting in their wooden ceilings (fig. 16). These churches were stylistically eclectic, combining allusions to Gothic structural elements with a centralized Renaissance plan, and, scattered as they were across the countryside, were even humbler versions of their continental counterparts than were the manor houses. For example, the exterior walls were often tarred and the interior decorations executed with simple pigments. With its absurdly stubby base and pointed spire not quite brought to conclusion, Aalto's church emphasized how the formal idio-

13. Aalto, Civil Guard Building, Seinäjoki, 1925. Museum of Finnish Architecture, Helsinki.
14. Aalto, Meat Inspection Building, Jyväskylä, 1927

syncrasies of these traditional structures could be seen as desirable by-products of the translation process.

All in all, these early works and writings can be considered a summary of Aalto's ideas about national style. He accepted that international influence was both a historical fact and a manifestation of a desire to overcome the geographic distance from Europe's great cultural centers. Further, he believed that national idiosyncrasies were both an outcome of limited resources and of particular national traits, including race. Importantly, Aalto did not list the exact ingredients for a national style based on such factors. Instead, he suggested that both analysis and creation depended on the sensitivity and emotional investment of onlooker and architect alike. In so doing, he left the door open for something new and unpredictable. At best, the early articles, such as "Motifs from Past Ages," masterfully capture the spontaneous groping of a young mind seeking the particular formal and emotive nuances of the building. "A portal: even as an idea, a bold venture for Finland in those days. Not just living stone, but living forms. Style. Here we met with architecture. It was a work of style as seen by a particular northern architect, the portal's designer. This was no longer the inherited skill of the master bricklayer taking pleasure in a job well done; it was the artistic creation of an architect."[22]

15. Aalto, Kauhajärvi Church and bell tower, 1921

This aspect of Aalto's early consideration of what constitutes national style recalls Wölfflin's words: "Technical factors cannot create a style; . . . the word *art* always implies primarily a particular conception of form."[23] The word *style* here refers to the moment when a work reveals the creative energy and forward-looking trajectory of its maker and the era. In other words, style is understood as the nonmaterial essence of architecture, which can only be directly experienced and felt. This departs from the idea of a constant national essence or style. In order to emphasize this more active and dynamic idea of the creation of forms, Aalto referred to the "living form," a concept that can be traced to Schiller's notion of *Lebensform* (life form) and *lebende Gestalt* (living form). According to Schiller, such artistic creation and aesthetic experience unified inner vision and outer reality in a single elemental moment.[24]

Aalto's early mastery of these key aesthetic questions and theories—dealing with how forms come into being, how they are experienced, and what links them to the culture that produces them—can be credited at least in part to the high level of Finnish aesthetic theory in the first half of the twentieth century. Yrjö Hirn (1870–1952), an internationally known professor in the department of aesthetics and comparative literature at Helsinki University from 1910 to 1937, was a leading influence in Finland and on Aalto. A historian of literature, a cultural critic, a sociologist, an aesthetician, a political figure, and an author all in one, Hirn emerged at the turn of the century as the main critic of speculative aesthetics, favoring instead a psychological and sociological understanding of art and beauty.[25] He argued that art was an essential, everyday human activity and should be discussed as such. For him there was no disinterested art; both the "art-impulse" and the "art-sense" were always informed by a practical or psychological interest.

Hirn's theories helped reconfigure the relationship between art and society at a time when Finns were defining their cultural affinities by shifting focus from the communication of images with fixed meanings—as exemplified by the failure of National Romantic architects and artists—to the idea of using art as a tool for triggering feelings. For example, Aalto's emphasis on the character of lines

16. Petäjävesi Church, Petäjävesi, 1763–65, view from the southwest in 1978

and textures over subject matter when discussing Sallinen bore a resemblance to ideas expressed by Hirn. In *The Origins of Art* Hirn wrote, "Physiological counterparts of distinct emotions may be, so to speak, translated into lines and forms, by which the emotion is reproduced in other minds. Thus even an object of handicraft—a vase, for instance—may, by the suggestiveness of its shape, affect our emotional life in an almost immediate way."[26]

Although Hirn did not explicitly address the issue of national or regional art— he strongly opposed cultural chauvinism and national extremism of any kind— his version of empathy theory contributed to a new way of understanding the geography of art. Instead of the "soul" of the people or the landscape giving birth to a particular style without human mediation, the relationship between art and the culture that produced it emphasized the perceptions people had about their culture, their fellow countrymen, and how they felt about other cultures. Art and architecture no longer carried fixed meanings about a country or its culture but called forth a mental response and the will to see in the mind of the onlooker. As a consequence, art and architecture were able to transfer emotions and trigger responses that were unstable, even unpredictable. Since Hirn's fundamental premise was that all artistic experience was collective experience, art and architecture could lead to the creation of new cultural patterns.

"Motifs from Past Ages" integrated questions of national style with theories about the nature of aesthetic experience, proposing something similar: that art and architecture not only embody a preexisting national essence but affect the senses directly. To describe how this happens Aalto used the technique of immersing himself in the experience of a work and letting himself be drawn intuitively to those aspects of it that express pathos or bear witness to individual and collective longing: "When entering our old churches, gazing at a Gustavian country manor or examining a century-old work of rural handicraft, we are seized by emotion. No doubt this is partly due to the trace of human handwork on the surface, the artistic purity of building materials or the simple lines adapted to our landscape; on the other hand, it also has to do with the signs of wear and centuries of patina in the building material."[27]

Aalto's first efforts to define a national style thus drew upon a number of influences—political, cultural, and intellectual—current in Finland in the late 1910s and early 1920s. From the beginning of these explorations he was surely aware that national culture and style were contingent upon many factors: the mindset of the people (perhaps even their racial traits), individual talent, the country's history and geopolitical location, and the cultural and political aspirations that had through the centuries opened Finland to multiple external influences.

Aalto's version of national style was therefore bound to be mutable and unstable. His writings suggest that he believed that art and architecture were both influenced by, and able to influence, changes in the political and cultural climate. Because of this, Aalto would take positions only to adjust them in response to his changing context.

Aalto decided to return to his hometown, Jyväskylä, the provincial capital of central Finland, in the fall of 1923, two years after his graduation. The move made sense. It was far easier to start his own architectural practice in a small town, where there was less professional competition and where he had family contacts. In Jyväskylä he was a big fish in a small pond, a hometown boy with a much-coveted university degree. As we will see, returning to his roots also had far-reaching implications for how he envisioned architecture's cultural role.

Aalto's social and intellectual milieu changed radically after the move. He traveled less and had less contact with colleagues, leading artists, and intellectuals. In fact, most of his intellectual and artistic influence now came through books and magazines. During the next six years of semi-isolation Aalto built his first major buildings, married Aino Marsio (1894–1949), and had two children. Aino, who came to Jyväskylä first as an employee in Aalto's firm, became eventually an important collaborator. Ideas they developed in Jyväskylä about national culture originated from their mutual discoveries and intellectual exchange.

The city itself redirected Aalto's thinking. The town had been far removed from the battlefields of the Finnish civil war and did not have a large working class. As a haven of the rising Finnish-speaking middle class, it offered a vantage point from which to observe where the culture was heading. The post-independence recession was soon followed by prosperity, which by the mid-1920s allowed the young architect ample opportunity to start testing his ideas in practice.

Despite receiving an increasing number of architectural commissions, Aalto continued to write articles for local newspapers, and occasionally for the national professional and popular press. But his tone had changed. He had come to believe that something was wrong in Finnish culture and society, and that a change was needed. His ideas about what constituted good and bad architecture became more assertive, and his understanding of the role of the architect more ambitious. He took on the grand task of raising the level of national culture overall, addressing in his articles the steps by which this could be achieved: proper individual conduct, care for domestic space, and the beautification of cities.

The concept of culture, which comes up repeatedly in his writings from this period, is a key for understanding the links Aalto makes between aesthetic and social ideas. A complex idea, *culture* had many conflicting meanings for him. He used it in the early 1920s predominantly to refer to the body of values and customs carried from the past by select members of society. This use of the word is tied to the notion of *Bildung,* a German concept of personal education and self-cultivation. Aalto, for example, often divided Finland's citizens into those who were cultured and those who were not. Naturally he saw himself as belonging to the former group: the leaders and teachers who brought culture to the less educated. In Aalto's usage the word *culture* had strong class associations—the upper classes were presumed to be more cultured than the lower.[1]

Aalto's writings suggest that he also believed that culture grew organically from the people and the soil. Indeed, the term has its roots in the word cultivate.[2]

Friedrich Nietzsche, a widely read philosopher among young architects of Aalto's generation, believed that a "true culture" could not be built upon the positivist education of book knowledge but had to grow from life and be practiced.[3] Culture depended on shared customs and could be acquired only through experience, so a person could be cultured simply by maintaining the organic traditions of a place. Aalto's writings and projects in the mid-1920s indicated a broad interest in domestic and other everyday spaces, which followed this line of thinking about how to advance national culture.

Both meanings of the word had geographic implications. The first implied that Finns were less cultured than were people in continental Europe and the rest of Scandinavia. In his "Motifs from Past Ages" Aalto talked about Finland's "distance from the centers of culture," by which he meant the great European metropolises (Paris, Berlin, and Vienna) and historically significant cities (Rome, Florence, and Venice).[4] Tellingly, the adjectival form of the Finnish word *kulttuuri* is *sivistynyt, which* translates as *civilized.* This suggests that culture was, at least in part, thought of as something *civil* and essentially urban in nature.

If one were to apply the same geographic criteria, similar hierarchies could be detected within Finland: the more urban south was more cultured than the less populated north, and cities were more cultured than the countryside. This geographic structure coincided with social and racial hierarchies. The country was divided between a Swedish-speaking, racially Nordic minority in the coastal and urban areas that formed the economic and intellectual elite of the country, and a mostly Finnish-dialect-speaking majority in the countryside, most of whom belonged to the peasant class.

Aalto's writings from early 1920s bear witness to such racial and geographic stereotyping. The "Gustavian country manor" from the southern coastal area, which Aalto discussed in "Motifs," was likely to be occupied by Swedish-speaking landed gentry, who were typically blond and tall. Aalto considered them the importers of culture to the presumably uncultivated Finnish-speaking interior. Those depicted by Sallinen in *The Laundresses* (1911, fig. 17) were eastern Balts from Carelia, the territory shared by Finland and Russia. They had darker complexions and were generally shorter than members of the Nordic race. Sallinen's painting is telling: the features of the two women are as rough as the paint strokes that depict them.

Despite the obvious difference between elitism and populism, both usages of the word *culture* implied that national culture was something tangible and could therefore be practiced. The term thus held in it a latent promise that race alone did not define a nation. Belonging to a nation required shared aesthetic preferences and traditions, which bound people as a community. Old ones should be fostered and new ones could be learned and shared. The idea that national culture was something that could develop and change was more in tune with the Finnish social reality than the notion that each nation had an inherent national ethos with a predestined outcome. The goal was that all Finns, independent of

their social status, could find a common ground, although the bloodshed of the civil war was still fresh in memory. It would take World War II to mend the rift in relations.

It is perhaps no surprise that a desire to establish a common national culture preoccupied a person like Aalto, who, although he was bilingual, lived in an enclave of the increasingly dominant Finnish-speaking middle class. Aalto's linguistic identity in part explains his investment in the birth of a new cultural identity. Even though his mother tongue was Swedish, his education and career were integrally linked to this new class and its eventual rise to power.

The foundations for the emergence of the Finnish-speaking middle class were laid by educational reforms introduced in the late nineteenth century, which made elementary-school education available to the masses. The transformation took place in small towns and farming communities throughout the country. Aalto and his family were products of these changes. He had been seven years old in 1905 when the family moved to Jyväskylä, which at that time had only some three thousand inhabitants. Despite its small size, the town was a center of the social restructuring. With its roots in the surrounding farming community, Aalto's family was a typical example of this new class, many of whom had improved their social status through education. His father, a surveyor, was the first member of the family to earn an academic degree. His mother was a Swedish-speaker with some claim to aristocratic pedigree, which raised the family's status above that of an average Finnish family.

17. Tykö Sallinen, *Pyykkärit* (The Laundresses), 1911. Oil on canvas, 154 × 136 cm. Finnish National Gallery, Helsinki.

They had come to Jyväskylä from the small town of Kuortane in Ostrobotnia, on Finland's west coast, known for its hardworking, independent farmers (*talonpoika*) as well as for religious fanaticism. The Aaltos were drawn to Jyväskylä by its reputation as a center of education—the first Finnish-language teacher training college, founded in 1863, was located in town—which had earned it the nickname the Athens of Finland. From 1908 to 1916 young Aalto attended the famed Jyväskylä Lyceum, the first Finnish-language school in the country, founded in 1858, which defined its task as the education of a new Finnish-speaking elite. His parents were sympathetic to the founding principle of the school, according to which national culture would benefit if students were exposed to western European culture. As a result, the school emphasized the study of languages—Aalto studied Russian, French, German, and Latin, besides the two domestic languages—and world literature. Students also learned practical subjects like home economics, woodworking, and handicrafts.

Aino Marsio's path into the professional middle class offers an interesting comparison. She was born to a working-class family—her father worked on the railroad—and grew up in the Ruoholahti district near downtown Helsinki, in a progressive housing cooperative named Alku, founded in 1888. Carpenters and other skilled laborers lived there. The community fostered a strong work ethic, frugality, independence, and mutual aid. It had a theater, and youth and music groups. Many future cultural and political figures of national stature grew up in the community, notably Väinö Tanner, the leader of the Social Democratic Party and prime minister; Väinö Vähäkallio, one of the most successful Finnish architects of the early twentieth century; and of course, Aino Aalto.[5]

The idea of national spiritual and cultural growth through education and hard work had been introduced to the country by J. V. Snellman (1806–1881), a philosopher and an educator, later a senator, a stout supporter of the Finnish language, and a pioneer of public education. He distinguished two levels of cognitive processes: the first, emotional and instinctive, and the second, reflective and based on the accumulation of intellectual knowledge. In his thinking, individual spiritual awakening led to national awakening; when individuals were able to take their destinies in their own hands, national independence would follow. Snellman fostered hope among Finns who had become used to seeing themselves as inferior to their Western counterparts.[6]

Snellman's ideas were introduced to the public by Zacharias Topelius' hugely popular *Book of Our Land* (1875), which every child educated during the first half of the twentieth century, including Aalto, read at school.[7] Topelius blended Snellman's idealism with racial and geographic arguments. He accepted the prevalent idea that Finns had come from Asia, which explained their physical characteristics and character, but did not believe that race alone explained behavior or determined the destiny of the nation. Education and exposure to other, more advanced cultures were equally important influences. Topelius also accepted the idea that Finns were of mixed race and that Finland was a multicultural and multilingual country. A large part of the book is devoted to the description of the different regions in Finland and the particular characteristics of the landscape and people of the area. Topelius, himself a Swedish-speaker, wrote the book in order to foster love for the land and a sense of community among the diverse populations. He talked about a shared "national character," insisting that "it is only natural that everybody who has lived in the same country, under the same laws under the same living conditions, would share a lot of commonalities, despite their diversity."[8] Topelius was also an internationalist who believed that countries depended on one another for their wellbeing. In the chapter "Our Country and the World," he writes, "What one country lacks the other possesses and provides. This is the command of almighty God, that countries and nations need each other, because if every country possessed everything, none would need the others, and each would live separately, minding its own business. But now people must learn to know and help each other, so that peoples from different countries may consider each other brothers."[9]

The idea that local cultures were threatened gained potency after World War I. Oswald Spengler's widely read *Decline of the West,* published in 1918 as a manual for would-be German leaders, was a key book in an era marked by disillusionment with the modern world. Spengler, who followed the thinking of nineteenth-century German philosopher Gottfried von Herder, believed that great cultures grew organically from a particular place, while their decline was marked by the advent of a "civilization" based on abstract laws and social organizations. Like Mebes, Spengler located the watershed for European civilization in the year 1800: "*Culture and Civilization*—the living body of a soul and the mummy of it. For western existence the distinction lies at about the year 1800—on the one side of that frontier life in fullness and sureness of itself, formed by growth from within, in one great uninterrupted evolution from Gothic childhood to Goethe and Napoleon, and on the other the autumnal, artificial, rootless life of our great cities, under forms fashioned by the intellect."[10]

Spengler yearned for more truthful times, when individuals existed in harmony with the world around them. Informed by Herder's emphasis on individual emotional investment in the phenomenal world, Spengler used the notion of milieu to emphasize the oneness between people and their surroundings, which he considered essential for vital cultures. Architecture and art formed, not surprisingly, a central focus of Spengler's book. The aesthetic experience was able, at least momentarily, to yield such oneness. This was true particularly of buildings, as they envelop the viewer completely. Most important was architecture's ability to communicate ineffable values and traditions and carry them on from generation to generation, a hallmark of organic culture and community. Typical is this passage on patina: "Patina is a symbol of mortality and hence related in a remarkable way to the symbols of time-measurement and the funeral rite. It corresponds to the wistful regard of the Faustian soul for ruins and evidences of the distant past. . . . It is not the Classical status, but the Classical torso that we really love. It has had a destiny: something suggestive of the past as past envelops it, and our imagination delights to fill the empty space of missing limbs with the pulse and swing of invisible lines."[11]

Aalto disagreed with what he considered Spengler's cultural pessimism, but the idea of authentic culture, the attention given to a particular kind of aesthetic experience, and the importance of shared traditions carried over to his thinking.[12] The 1921 essay "Our Old and New Churches," which distinguishes "good" and "bad" architecture based on their ability to embody a sense of tradition and trigger emotive investment, is exemplary. He makes the case by comparing an eighteenth-century wooden church to a nineteenth-century neo-Gothic brick church, both located in the small town of Keuruu in central Finland (figs. 18, 19). Like Spengler, Aalto wanted to distinguish the profound from the superficial. He dismissed the new church as a product of the cultural degeneration of the nineteenth century: "The new church is made of brick, it has a high tower, and the whole building stands out of the landscape. This church does not speak, it shouts, like a person who doesn't want to hear other voices. We see no trace of a devoted master's love of his work here, we do not see the consideration of a sensitive eye for the surrounding natural environment. This church is like a glossy picture cut out of a German picture book. It is bad architecture."[13] He considered the eighteenth-century church, by contrast, a product of a more moral and truthful time. Here Aalto came close to Spengler in that he did not merely analyze the visual but looked for the poetic essence of culture and the mental rapport established between people and material objects. He too ends up focusing on patina as the symbolic essence of the building: "The old church is built of wood. Its color is black, a strikingly beautiful shade of black. The homely tar sealant has darkened over the years into a wonderful patina. The tower has a noble design; the whole church is well proportioned. It reflects stylistic forms from faraway, civilized countries, but seen through the eyes of a Northerner. Its style is quite simply homely. . . . Every mark of the knife [*puukko*] speaks of work that was dear to the carpenter. Every form reveals its author and bears witness to the fact that he did his best."[14] It is easy to sympathize with Aalto's assessment. When walking into any of the eighteenth-century wooden churches, like that at Keuruu, one feels the effort and inventiveness invested by the local carpenter in making the most from limited resources, while there is no magic or mystery behind the brick wall of the nineteenth-century church. The literalness of its execution leaves no room for imagination or awe.

Aalto's project of fostering national cultural revival through architecture was informed by two other German books: Paul Schultze-Naumburg's *Kleinbürgerhäuser* (Petit-Bourgeois Houses) (1911), the fifth volume in the Kulturarbeiten series, and Paul Mebes' *Um 1800: Architektur und Handwerk im letzten Jahrhundert und ihrer traditionellen Entwicklung* (Circa 1800: Architecture and Crafts of the Last Century and Their Traditional Development) (1908).[15] What made the Aaltos and their fellow Finns susceptible to Mebes' and Schultze-Naumburg's ideas in

18. Antti Hakola, Keuruu Old Church, interior, 1758, in 1984. National Board of Antiquities, Helsinki.

19. Theodor Granstedt, Keuruu New Church, 1892, in 1984. National Board of Antiquities, Helsinki.

particular was the suggestion that the word *culture* could no longer be applied only to the great civilizations. On the contrary: while many of them had already fallen, Finnish culture had yet to reach its full bloom.

Like Schultze-Naumburg and Mebes, Aalto believed that the future of Finnish architecture and culture was in the hands of the common man. Therefore, instead of studying important monuments, architects could learn from ordinary, every-day buildings built by individuals uncorrupted by foreign stylistic influences. As a sign that cultural revival was in part based on the rediscovery of a simple life, and with it the most basic human emotions, Aalto gave his wife a copy of Paul Gauguin's *Noa Noa* (1902), a story of the discovery of a paradisical island where indigenous people lived in an uncorrupted simplicity.[16] The choice demonstrated that new members of the middle class, like the Aaltos, desired to distinguish themselves from the general populace not only through their learning but also through psychological emancipation and self-knowledge.

Subsequently, Aalto saw his role as an educator teaching the common people to appreciate their domestic building and craft traditions. The opening paragraph of Aalto's 1922 article "Motifs from Past Ages" reads as a mission statement: "'Popular education,' which aims at educating public taste and is indeed one of the architect's responsibilities, seeks to draw the attention of the general public to our historic building culture and, by emphasizing its ideals and aesthetic values, to prepare the ground for contemporary architecture."[17]

The emphases on education, national and spiritual awakening, and modern individualism complemented one another. It was indeed very modern to believe that national culture was not predestined but depended on each and every individual. The way one lived, dressed, and behaved mattered. This led to a growing interest in family life, hence the proliferation of how-to books, such as *Kotiruoka* (Home Cooking), published in 1908 and still in print. Several magazines focused on home decoration. *Kotitaide* (Home Art), founded in 1902, had a mission to educate the public in matters of interior decoration and general aesthetic judg-ment. Even *Arkkitehti* magazine was subtitled "A Magazine for Architecture and Decorative Arts" in the 1910s.

As a sign that Aalto wanted to reach laypeople, many of Aalto's early articles and projects were published in one of the magazines that promoted grass-roots cultural revival, *Taide-Käsiteollisuus* (Arts-Handicrafts). It is in this spirit that Aalto in 1922 wrote the article "One's Own House: Why Does It Need to Be Beautiful?" which made a plea for people to contribute to national culture by beautifying their immediate surroundings (fig. 20). Aalto begins by asking: "Where can one see the level of culture of a nation?" He goes on to argue that, unlike a statistic or numerical fact, culture is tangible and visible. Aalto puts particular emphasis on the physical environment: "A keen-eyed observer can decipher every-thing from the physical environment. When we see the work, we know the author. We have in front of us not only the product of today's labor, but also that completed before and even earlier. It's the most concrete and precise form of

Käsiteollisuus

N:o 2   1922

Toimitus:
Fredrikinkadun 14:ssä   Kuudestoista vuosikerta   Konttori:
Museokadun 18:ssa

OMA TALO.

MIKSI SEN TÄYTYY OLLA KAUNIS.

Mistä parhaiten voimme nähdä kansan sivistystason? »Näemmehän sen tilastotaulukoista, näemme kansan valtiollisesta elämästä, yhteiskuntajärjestöstä, sen maailmanhistoriaan piirtämistä merkeistä, sen tieteitten ja taiteitten tasosta ja lopuksi sen yksilöistä sellaisina kuin ne joutuvat henkilökohtaisen arvostelumme alaisiksi.» Näin kai kysymykseen voi vastata tarvitsematta pelätä, että mitään tähdellisempää näkökulmaa olisi jäänyt pois luettelostamme, mutta jos alleviivaamme sanan »nähdä», muuttuu kysymys paljon enemmän henkilökohtaiseksi ja vastaus sen mukaan vaikeammaksi.

Ymmärtäkäämme kysymys aivan kirjaimellisesti ja koettakaamme tosiaankin selvittää itsellemme, mitä silmillämme on kertoma kanssaihmisistämme ja heidän muodostamistaan kokonaisuuksista — kansoista. Kuvitelkaamme, että meidän on lähemmin tutkittava esim. jotain vierasta maata. Mitä silloin

PIENVILJELIJÄN ASUNTO

LÄMMIN PUOLEINEN PÄÄTY

teemme? Tietysti ensi töiksemme matkustamme tähän maahan, tarkastellen siellä kaikkia ja kaikkea, mikä eteemme sattuu, tutkien toisaalta maan asukkaita ja toisaalta sitä kehää ja ympäristöä, jonka se aikain kuluesa on itselleen luonut. Tulemme silloin myös pian huomaamaan, miten arvokkaaksi lähteeksi juuri tämä viimeksimainittu, »ympäristö», meille muodostuu. Sehän kertoo tarkkasilmäiselle tutkijalle itse asiassa kaikki. Kun näemme työn, tunnemme jo suurelta osalta sen tekijän. Tässä on meillä edessämme ei vain tämän olevaisen päivän työ vaan lisäksi kaikki, mikä ennen ja sitäkin ennen on tehty. Se on historiaa havainnollisessa ja pilkulleen tarkassa muodossa. Me näemme siitä ei ainoastaan tämän kansan nykyisen kehitysasteen vaan samalla kaiken sen, mitä esi-isät ovat tehneet, ja vertailujen kautta saamme siitä esille »kehityksen diagrammin» kaikessa tarkkuudessaan.

20. Aalto, "One's Own House: Why Does It Need to Be Beautiful?" *Taide-Käsityö* 2 (1922)

history lesson. We don't therefore only see the current level of culture but everything achieved by the forefathers, and comparing it all we can see the 'diagram of development' with all its precision."[18] The article includes an image of a model home designed by architect Oiva Kallio for the Finnish Craft Association. The house was a simple rectangular structure with a few decorative elements, such as a carved entrance portico and shutters. The title image depicted a winter scene with a man and dog approaching the house from the back, with a birdfeeder on the left and a snow-covered tree on the right—architecture embedded in the landscape and routines of everyday life. Aalto's architectural "diagram" had three trajectories. First, a single piece of architecture was meant to work like a kaleidoscope that merges cultural influences, past and present; second, architecture's main task was to serve both individual and public good; and third, individual buildings should be considered part of a larger "environment and circle" (*ymparistö ja kehä*) consisting of "cities, fields, roads, railroads, villages and private houses, churches and even the most modest shelters."[19]

At the same time, Aalto saw architecture as a highly complicated symbolic system whose goal was to communicate meanings and values. As such it had two audiences: it gave the foreign visitor access to the culture that produced it, and it reminded Finns that the development of culture required everyone's contribution. "The beauty of home has to do with responsibility," he wrote. "From the exterior a home should not only bring pleasure to ourselves but also provide an example and support for others, and every one of them should help to give a positive impression of our Finland and *strengthen our own belief in Finnish culture*."[20]

After analyzing the problem for his countrymen, Aalto provided a solution. A small advertisement that he placed in the Jyväskylä newspaper in 1923 stated: "We beautify churches and make homes look civilized." The small print above this statement read: "Finland is undoubtedly a civilized Scandinavian nation, yet unfortunately, everybody who has seen Finnish bourgeois homes must stop and wonder if that is really so. Homes are filled with second-rate German decorative and functional objects. The low artistic level of the country is not convincing about the level of Finnish culture."[21] As a founding member of the German Werkbund, Hermann Muthesius, had done a few years earlier, Aalto aimed to foster domestic craft traditions, seeing that this would ultimately raise the country's international status and economic prosperity. And, like Muthesius, Aalto assessed the level of domestic craft production unfavorably.

Even as Aalto engaged the debate about cultural revival Finns continued to have a hard time defining Finnishness, which carried both positive and negative associations. In addition to its domestic conflicts, Finland suffered from a major image problem: few foreigners had heard of the country, and those who had probably thought of it as a primitive territory, an outpost of Russia or Sweden, a nature reserve inhabited by fierce, robust natives. While a few years earlier Aalto had celebrated Sallinen's depictions of Finnish peasants, he now saw very little positive in such representations, however romantic. Also, as Finland was beginning to establish itself in the international arena, it was harder, and even unde-sirable, for Finns to continue seeing themselves in isolation. The question became: How is it possible to foster the idea of a distinct, even idiosyncratic, national culture in a diverse population, while simultaneously communicating to the world an image of Finland as a civilized Western country? And further, how could Finland overcome being simply an importer of culture and become a producer of culture on par with other western European countries? This required a geo-graphical paradigm shift: instead of being viewed as a country on the fringes of western Europe, Finland needed to be considered a valid member of the club.

Aalto realized that in order to effect this shift in geographic affinity, a case needed to be made that the country and its culture had ties to the origins of Western civilization. So Aino and Alvar Aalto honeymooned in Italy, the cradle of that tradition. In so doing they followed a recent interest in classical culture among Swedish and Finnish architects, such as Håkon Ahlberg, Gunnar Asplund, Hilding Ekelund, and Erik Bryggman.[22] Aalto's generation of architects were drawn to Venice, Pompeii, and the small hill towns in the north. Their interest was less in grand monumental architecture than in places that bore witness to everyday life—domestic buildings and urban squares.[23] The couple probably traveled by plane to Vienna and from there by train to Innsbruck, Verona, Florence, Padua, and Venice, stopping in smaller towns in between, as well as in Pompeii, and staying four to six weeks.[24]

They joined a long line of northern pilgrims to the great southern source of classical and Romantic cultural ideals, particularly the Germans, from Dürer to Goethe. One could make the case that Aalto was viewing Italy partly through the eyes of Goethe, especially through his 1829 *Italienische Reise,* an ode not only to the physical beauty of the country but to the way Italians lived, which Goethe, like Spengler after him, considered the height of culture. Like Goethe, Aalto and his contemporaries were drawn to the *architettura minore,* the vernacular domestic buildings and streets of Italian towns, especially those of the early Renaissance, where the life lived was still tangible. They were attracted to forms that resisted perfect geometries and compositional order: off-center piazzas that fitted into the organic fabric of medieval towns; facades that were almost, but not quite, symmetrical.

Traces of the Goethean model can also be detected in how Aalto started to reassess the relationship between native work and foreign influence. Famously, Goethe had gone to Italy to look for the *Urpflanze,* the mother of all plants. Likewise, Aalto's mission seems to have been to sample Italian building types and urban typologies, which, like plant species, could adapt to different con-ditions while maintaining some of their original characteristics.[25] A private house of his design, Casa Laurén (designed 1925, built 1927–28, fig. 21), can be inter-preted as such. The most distinctive element of this two-story, two-family house is the exterior staircase with a covered loggia at the south end of the building, common in Venetian palazzos. Rather than replicating stucco walls, Aalto made

the building out of wood, with vertical board-and-batten siding. The exterior was meant to be tarred, a typical way to seal vernacular wooden buildings in the country until paint, an expensive luxury, became more common in the early twentieth century among wealthier Finns.

The unbuilt atrium house that Aalto designed for his brother Väinö in about 1925 was based on a courtyard typology, in this case a Pompeiian house (fig. 22). From its name, Casa Aalto, to its decorative classicizing frieze to its central sunlit atrium, the design embraced the Pompeiian architectural forms that had inspired architects since the rediscovery of the buried city two hundred years earlier. Aalto seems to have been charmed by the traces of daily life still to be seen there; thus, he added a whimsical clothesline in the background of a sketch of the house, as if to suggest that such a typology could facilitate a Finnish way of living.

The early Renaissance provided another reference point for Aalto's work during this time. The sense of incompleteness of that period clearly appeared more attractive to him than did the greater formal unity of the high Renaissance. The delicate columns of Filippo Brunelleschi's Ospedale degli Innocenti (Foundling

21. Aalto, Casa Laurén

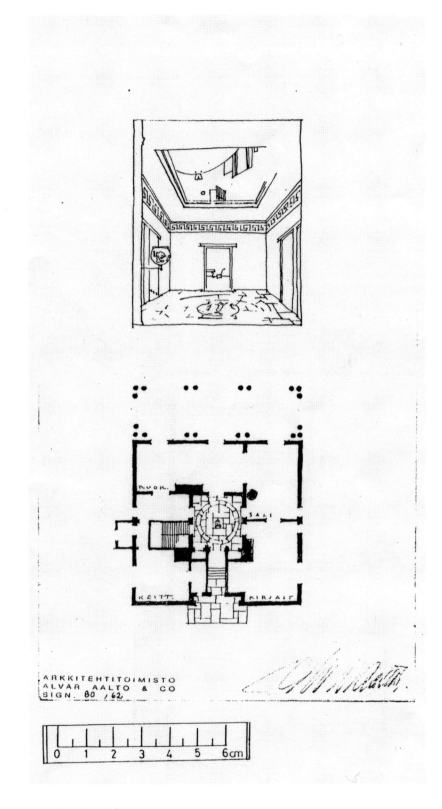

22. Aalto, Casa Aalto, project, 1925

Hospital, 1419–28) in Florence found their way into a project for a funeral chapel in Jyväskylä from 1925. Similarly, Leon Battista Alberti's church of Sant'Andrea in Mantua (ca. 1470), which has what Nikolaus Pevsner called a "curiously pagan facade," appears in a competition entry for a church in Jämsä, as well as in a project for an old people's home, both from 1925 (fig. 23).[26]

A series of articles on Italian architecture and urbanism, written before and after the trip for the local newspapers *Sisä-Suomi* and *Keskisuomalainen,* discusses a set of building and urban types, variants of which existed in every culture: domestic buildings, churches, market squares, houses, bathing facilities,

23. Aalto, Säynätsalo Old People's Home, project, 1925

streets, and so on.[27] Aalto focused on the adaptability of these typologies: since Finnish culture was young and Italian old, the Finnish versions were naturally less developed than those found in Italy. Finns could thus learn how to develop these typologies and in so doing foster the customs associated with them.

Aalto also admired the way Italians integrated buildings into the landscape—another dimension of typological adaptation. As discussed earlier, the idea of architecture being part of a larger environment was central to his project of cultural revival. The improvement of Finnish nature was the subject of a 1925 essay, "Landscape in Central Finland": "Pure, original nature, with all its magic power, cannot surpass a vista where one can detect a human touch, whenever this 'human stamp' has added a harmonious, enhancing factor. We Northerners, especially we Finns, are very prone to 'forest dreaming,' for which we have had ample opportunity up to now."[28] In order to qualify as contributing to culture, "original nature" had to be perfected into "landscape"—that is, something shaped and developed that could be appreciated as a harmoniously composed picture consisting of topographical accents, trees, and carefully placed buildings. In an article a year later, "Architecture of Landscape," Aalto calls for "aesthetic criteria" when siting buildings in the countryside and scorns the purely "emotional" and sentimental approach to nature. Aalto complains that Finnish literary culture has emphasized nature at the expense of culture:

It has often been remarked that the love for pure nature and, in general, admiration for nature, is a special characteristic of the Finnish national soul. . . . A Finnish youth infused with philanthropic knowledge writes his first piece of poetry about a pathetic little pond in the forest. But it is questionable whether he is able to show equal admiration about material objects, which form the basis of culture. (All culture is material.)

Isn't it so that although we are prone to admire nature, this admiration, as soon as it must be extended to areas, which require a bigger effort and more care than an emotional outburst, soon runs out?[29]

The statement that "all culture is material" suggests a radical revision of the idea that culture is merely a visible manifestation of an invisible essence, which dominated his idea of national style. Cultural revival was based on the notion that all material objects—including architecture—are shaped by us and, in turn, shape us. It is important to note that Aalto does not consider nature inherently Finnish, just because it grew in Finnish soil. It had to be tended by Finnish people and identified by them as being quintessentially Finnish.[30] The Taulumäki Church competition of 1927 captures what Aalto imagined this new "cultural" landscape would look like. The proposed building emerges from the topography as if growing from it (fig. 24). Even nature itself, the only thing that was literally, physically rooted to a particular place, needed to be given form in order to contribute to national culture.

Most of all, Italy taught Aalto to appreciate *kaupunkikulttuuri,* or urban culture, as the highest level of development a civilization could attain. Spengler's dictum, "What the house is to the peasant, a symbol of 'the settled,' the town is to the man of culture," helps to characterize Aalto's growing interest in urban culture from the mid-1920s.[31] Aalto made this association even though only about 20 percent of the Finnish population lived in towns, and most of these were very small. Recognizing this, he was particularly drawn to the medieval hill towns of Italy, and he believed that Jyväskylä could learn from them. The goal was to copy neither their architecture nor their way of living but to identify Italian traditions and typologies and then discover comparable ones in the Finnish towns.

A 1925 newspaper article, "A Beautifying Measure Undertaken in Our Town, and Its Chances of Success," makes manifest that early in his career Aalto saw urban design as part of the architect's mission and a key element in cultural renewal. The article began with an apology: "Like most of our towns, Jyväskylä is so extraordinarily young that it has been almost entirely deprived of culture. Its aesthetic aspects have not been fostered. In this it reflects Finland's young culture as a whole."[32] Aalto identified the aspects of his city that he believed could give rise to urban culture if supplemented by lessons learned from Italy. First was the better use of the city's natural topography, which had been undermined by the nineteenth-century gridded urban plan. Aalto proposed to revise the street plan with a flight of open-air stairs leading to a belvedere at the city's highest point, a forested hill adjacent to downtown. The sauna was another such undervalued tradition: "The Finnish cultural sauna could survive for centuries, just as the Roman baths did, becoming a national attraction cherished by all. There is only one problem, and that only in the eyes of weak people—it has no precedent."[33] The point was clear: Finns did not understand how to raise their local assets to the level of culture.

Since culture was something shared and practiced by a group of people, Aalto was particularly interested in urban culture and the moments when a custom—for example, going to a street market to buy and sell produce—was performed according to a commonly understood, if unspoken, set of social rules. "One of the surest criteria that enable us to evaluate the level of urban culture of a modern town is its market square," he wrote in the 1925 article "Urban Culture." "Arriving at daybreak in a town in which we have never been before, we realize that there must be laws, traditions, customs and details in this hustle and bustle which, just like the other phenomena of our day and age, are not just the movements of atoms, but energy directed into these channels and supervised by more advanced individuals."[34] In other words, human activity did not in itself constitute culture. As in nature, activity had to be given form.

The market square was a particularly poignant example of the relationship between the city and the country—its role was to draw people from surrounding areas and organize them into a coherent social and spatial system. So conceived, a city had a similar kind of influence over its region. Jyväskylä, for instance, was

PERUSTUS, KOILLISESTA.

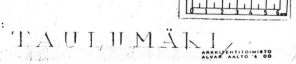

TAULUMÄKI

ARKKITEHTITOIMISTO
ALVAR AALTO '& CO

24. Aalto, Taulumäki Church, competition entry, 1927

a center for a large swath of central Finland and thus was responsible for the region's growth and development—and by extension for the whole of Finnish-speaking Finland's.[35] Cities were spiritual, cultural, and geographic centers—visible manifestations of the cultural progress of a region or, indeed, a whole nation. Conversely, the size and quality of a region determined the power of the city at its core.

We get a first sense of Aalto as an urbanist around this time. In 1924 he created a design for a market square in front of the Jyväskylä Lyceum, with a monumental well for horses to drink from and a columned market hall on one side. In 1926 he added a baroque garden next to it and designed two other squares, one next to the City Church, with mosaic paving (fig. 25). The diagonal street leading downtown from northwest, Puistokatu, was to be turned into an avenue leading toward Taulumäki Hill.

25. Aalto, Church Square, project, 1924

Aalto never realized these early urban plans. However, his Jyväskylä work was active and successful, consisting mainly of typical institutional and public commissions of the early independent era—churches, defense-corps buildings, a workers' club, and government buildings—executed in a classical idiom. A practice that started with an occasional design or renovation of a private house or villa in the early 1920s was, by 1926, a busy firm: in a two-year period Aalto designed some twenty-five buildings and projects and entered some dozen competitions.

Aalto's ideas about cultural revival culminated in the Muurame Church (1926–29, fig. 26). It is executed in Nordic classicism, a kind of domesticated version of international classicism that spread to Finland from Sweden. It is based on Italian typologies and consisted of a campanile, a loggia, and an unbuilt walled garden. The 1926 article "From Doorstep to Living Room" summed up many of the themes central to Aalto's ideas about cultural revival that were included in the church. The article uses Fra Angelico's fresco *The Annunciation* (Florence, ca. 1441), showing the Archangel Gabriel and Mary nestled in a corner loggia—architecture that clearly influenced the design of the building—as the title image. On the left is a garden with Adam and Eve lurking in the background, naked. Aalto describes the painting as follows: "The picture provides an ideal example of

26. Aalto, Muurame Church, 1926–29

'entering a room.' The trinity of a *human being, room and garden* shown in the picture makes it an unattainable ideal image of the home. The same smile that plays on the face of the Holy Virgin is seen in the delicate details of the buildings and in the brilliant flowers in the garden. Two things stand out plainly: the unity of the room, the external wall and the garden, and the formation of these elements so as to give the human figure prominence and express her state of mind."[36] The painting sets the tone for a discussion about architecture's cultural role. Adam and Eve are depicted as sinners—until, that is, they encountered civilization as represented by classical order. The loggia acts as a mediator that ties the individual body to a larger social order and cultural values.

The image also works as a metaphor for most of Aalto's clients at the time, who wanted to distinguish themselves from the peasant class. The article was published in *Aitta,* a new Helsinki-based illustrated magazine tailored to young, educated urbanites who followed continental fashions and trends.[37] The elitism is obvious as he announces in the article that he is mainly interested in discussing "private houses, country manors, villas, etc., which stood freely in their surroundings and where good taste and artistic ambitions have to some extent prevailed."[38] On one level the article functioned as a decoration manual instructing its readers in how to construct an elegant apartment and display good taste—in other words, how to be cultured in the way that the upper classes of European metropolises were cultured. Interior photographs from mainly Swedish projects projected the aura of upper-class living, which the middle class aspired to share. The rooms featured high-quality items sparingly placed against white walls and enjoyed by elegantly dressed people. The spatial narrative of these flats—hall, living room, and patio—was designed around public functions: the living room was not so much a place for the family to gather as a stage on which to receive guests in a grand manner.

Aalto clearly identified himself with a new type of Finn—urban and upwardly mobile—and believed that Finland's future lay in the hands of this elite group. An outer environment in tune with the inner psyche would make them prosper. "The point of contact between the structure of a house and some intimate feature," wrote Aalto, is that "no architectural creation is complete without some [personal] trait; it will not be alive," adding with a pinch of salt that "perhaps the reader should not immediately start cultivating the clothesline between the marble columns of his hall." The statement, "It is enough to be aware that 'the open visor' is and will remain the true mark of the modern gentleman, and his home reflects this attitude,"[39] can be read as a wider reflection on the modern man, who is sensitive, potentially even vulnerable, and thus able to adapt and change.

By this time Aalto had been exposed to the idea of modern subjectivity from Nietzsche's Scandinavian disciples, writers such as August Strindberg, Henrik Ibsen, Knut Hamsun, and Georg Brandes. Their books promoted the individual's ability to challenge conventions and strike new paths. Overall, Aalto's milieu considered the ideal Finn to be an upwardly mobile urbanite, well educated and well versed in foreign languages and literature. Unlike a peasant (the favorite subject matter of the National Romantic painters), such an individual was self-aware and able to shape his own destiny, and by extension that of his or her immediate surroundings.

Therefore, while Aalto was still working in the classical idiom, these statements demonstrate that he had already appropriated the key aspect of modernity: namely, the idea of the modern subject, which both influenced and was influenced by larger social changes. It followed that after the subject of architecture had changed, architecture had to change, even at the risk of challenging a stable national architecture and culture. A series of images accompanying the article "From Doorstep to Living Room" singled out spatial flow as the most important architectural technique to calibrate the relationship between an individual and the world. They include a house in Pompeii with an open courtyard surrounded by columns; the loggia-like entrance hall of Erik Bryggman's Atrium Housing in Turku (1925–27); an unidentified Swedish residence with a vast living room opening onto a garden through a floor-to-ceiling window; and the open living room of Le Corbusier's Pavillon de l'Esprit Nouveau, an experimental housing unit designed for the 1925 Exposition des Arts-Décoratifs that extended the living room out-doors via a large terrace. The historical trajectory culminates in the modernist con-ception of domestic space, marked by fluidity between inside and outside. The idea that instead of settling into a cozy interior when arriving home, the modern man is, as it were, thrown right back into the world, speaks about the porous relationship between the modern individual and his or her environment.

Aalto arrived at these ideas about architectural space and modern subjectivity after reading Gustaf Strengell's (1878–1937) three influential books, *The City as a Work of Art* (1922), *The Home as a Work of Art* (1923), and *The Building as a Work of Art* (1928).[40] Following vitalist philosophers such as Henri Bergson and Jean-Marie Guyau, Strengell argued that contemporary architecture must embody the change from the static to the dynamic worldview that was charac-teristic of modernity. The boundary between inside and outside and the progres-sion from closed toward open space was a potent emblem of man's changing relationship to place. Greek architecture's emphasis on static physical presence and human scale was about a palpable connection to a particular place, while, in Strengell's words, "western man's sense of space is boundless, and reaches beyond the visible to what is only imaginable, absolute, abstract."[41]

It comes as no surprise that once Aalto gained access to the core ideas and images of the emerging modern movement he decided in 1927 to relocate his young family to the coastal town of Turku in the southwestern corner of Finland. Winning first prize in a competition for an agricultural cooperative building in the town helped make the decision. Yet, apart from the practical wish to be close to his biggest building site to date, Aalto surely yearned to be back in a large city, where he could experience and participate in modern dynamism and change firsthand.

"Is Turku the Most Modern City in Finland?" asked the Helsinki-based literary magazine *Tulenkantajat* (The Torch Bearers) in 1930. Indeed, by the late 1920s the city, located in the southwestern corner of the country, had become the capital of Finnish modernism and was far more au courant than Helsinki, let alone Jyväskylä, awash with the latest continental trends. It is no accident that it was also the city closest to Sweden. Turku's reputation as Finland's most modern city rested on a vivid modern art and theater scene and, later, after Aalto's move there in June 1927, its modern architecture.

Unlike Jyväskylä, a regional governmental center, Turku was a commercial city that relied on contacts with the outside world. The city, the former capital of Finland under the Swedish regime (ca. 1200–1809), had for centuries served as a gateway to Scandinavia and western Europe, a transit point through which people, goods, and ideas came into the country, first by commercial sailing ships, then through regular steamship links, and, beginning in 1927, by an air connection that allowed easy travel to Stockholm and thence to continental Europe. The Swedish-language newspaper *Åbo Underrättelser,* which catered to people engaged in seafaring and foreign trade, was often the first in the country to report on important foreign events. Aalto's decision to resettle there, at the age of twenty-nine, supported his intellectual and professional ambitions: Turku was Finland's window to the world in the cultural sense as well. After five years of living in relative isolation in a provincial town, he was excited to be in a city with a vivid social and intellectual climate. He immersed himself in discussions of new aesthetic and social ideas, befriending artists and intellectuals and traveling frequently to Stockholm to gain even more direct exposure to new ideas as they emerged in Europe's cultural centers. His office, still small, included two Norwegian employees, which further speaks to his desire to open himself to the outside world.

Turku also gave Aalto a new vantage point on national culture and politics. While in Jyväskylä he had preoccupied himself with the creation of cohesive national culture in a relatively homogeneous small town. Turku presented a more challenging political environment, revealing that ten years into independence, Finnish society was still full of tensions among different groups. This state of affairs was perhaps more pronounced in Turku than elsewhere. The city had a large, rather conservative middle class. A powerful but shrinking Swedish-speaking community dominated politics and culture, but a growing working class was becoming increasingly vocal. Aalto experienced this firsthand, moving to the city just in time for the national dockworkers' strike of 1928–29, which paralyzed the city, whose livelihood came from its harbor. Six daily newspapers—a remarkable number for a population of only fifty thousand—catered to these different social and political groups, as did various schools, theaters, and sports clubs.[1] Indeed, there were many parallel Finlands, and Turku exemplified this problem.

Turku was thus a testing ground for national unity. At best, its diversity led to a healthy dialogue among different constituencies. It was home to two universities, the newly founded Turku University, led by the ardent nationalist Rafael

Koskimies, which served the city's Finnish speakers, and the Åbo Akademi, the country's oldest institution of higher learning, a bastion of the city's Swedish-speaking intellectual culture. (Helsinki had only one university and Jyväskylä still none.[2]) The coexistence of Turku's universities provided an intellectually dynamic context for the exchange of ideas, and a forum for dialogue between the Finnish- and Swedish-speaking communities, whose relationship had been strained by the civil war.

Aalto's first strategic move was to establish a design partnership with the architect Erik Bryggman (1891–1955). The two men complemented each other in many ways. Aalto was sociable, Bryggman more introverted and studious. While Aalto was a newcomer to the city, Bryggman was Turku-born and well established in the city's tight-knit social scene. And while Aalto was at the time of his move still fairly ignorant about continental modernism, Bryggman was already well versed in the latest architectural trends. Books and magazines in Bryggman's library offered Aalto a window into the architectural debates on the continent.[3] Although their partnership was short lived and limited to only a few buildings, they became known as the arbiters of Finnish architectural modernism. Covering the annual rowing race between the two universities in 1928, a journalist of *Aitta* noted that even though Turku was a historical city, "it has the kind of buildings no one in Helsinki has even dreamed of [those of Aalto and Bryggman], and two universities, and now the rowing race between the two."[4]

Aalto's ability to grasp and adapt to this complex new social terrain is demonstrated in his articles from late 1920s, which he wrote for three of the city's newspapers: the leftist Finnish-language *Sosialisti,* the politically independent *Åbo Underrättelser,* and the Finnish-language *Uusi Aura.* His articles contrast starkly with those written in the Jyväskylä years. This time Aalto was receptive to his readership and open to new political ideas and forums. For example, for *Sosialisti* he wrote an article on the housing problem—something previously unthinkable for someone of his upbringing and family background. The article, "Minimum Dwelling—a Social and Economic Hurdle," was published in 1927, during the upsurge of communism and labor unrest. Aalto indirectly acknowledged the country's growing social and economic disparities by focusing on the lack of decent housing for the urban working class.[5] The discussion of economies in building construction—for example, the use of standardized steel windows at the Agricultural Cooperative Building—and an emphasis on social housing (Aalto cites Le Corbusier's 1922 Ville Contemporaine as an example) differ sharply in tone from that of "From Doorstep to Living Room," written just a year earlier. Yet Aalto was neither an ideologue nor an idealist; an awareness of the professional opportunities in housing design certainly played a part in triggering this new interest.

If the articles written in Jyväskylä were based on the assumption that national cultural revival is grounded on the taste and habits of the new middle class, which Aalto saw consisting ideally of enlightened individuals, the articles in Turku acknowledge the emergence of modern mass society. Finding ways to engage this audience became Aalto's new project.

Yet modernity and modernization meant different things to different constituencies. While for the cultural avant-garde the terms might have meant the influx of modernist art and lifestyle, the majority of the urban population experienced modernity as a new socioeconomic condition marked by increasing urbanization and industrialization, which came with their own problems. In Turku, Aalto realized that the civil war had not erased the concerns of the working class, as non-socialists had hoped. For anyone interested in the creation of a unified national culture, like Aalto, it was important to be assured that the sympathies of the working class were directed to building a single homeland rather than to establishing international class solidarity—in other words, to the Soviet Union. In this climate Aalto started to see the quest for a national culture and architecture as integrally linked to the creation of a collective body that would feel a sense of commonality more powerful than class, language, or local loyalties.

Aalto's projects from the Turku years are thus focused on the question of how architecture could engage and provide for the collective body. Aalto's first mass housing project, the Tapani apartment building, was designed and built in 1928 for Juho Tapani, an owner of a prefabricated concrete building-units factory (fig. 27). Conceived as a prototype, the design demonstrates that Aalto was aware

27. Aalto, Tapani apartment building, Turku, 1928

of German housing experiments, such as those carried out by Ernst May in Frankfurt-am-Main.[6] The simple slab building had steel windows, regularized floor plans, and prefabricated, reinforced-concrete construction. The design suggests that at this point Aalto still saw the masses in a homogeneous and purely numerical light; society needed to produce a certain number of dwelling units for a certain sum of Finnish marks to satisfy the housing needs of a certain number of families. Each family was housed in identical units, and the buildings had no common areas. The link between architecture and new mass society was defined in purely quantitative terms.

Aalto made a major leap toward the formulation of a richer relationship between architecture and society in the article "On the Latest Trends in Architecture: The Key Questions Concerning the Essence of Art and the Problems of Our Times; What Is the Aim of the New Realism in Building Art?" published in the January 1928 issue of *Uusi Aura*.[7] It grapples with finding an alternative to the two basic tenets of continental modernism: Corbusian rationalism, which sought to distill universal typologies, and German dogmatic functionalism. The article combines the two under the title "modernism," which is considered, like "traditionalism," to be just another form of superficial aestheticism. These are contrasted with New Realism, a concept Aalto appropriated from the Danish architect and critic Poul Henningsen (1894–1967), the editor of *Kritisk Revy*.[8] That Danish magazine embraced many of the aesthetic stances of modernism—attention to function and technology, rejection of shibboleths of taste—but was supposedly based on more precise study of actual daily life and the functioning real world.[9]

Two buildings from the Turku period, Turun Sanomat Building, consisting of editorial office and printing facilities, and Paimio Sanatorium exemplify what Aalto might have meant with "new realism." The former was designed in spring 1928 and completed in 1930.[10] The client was the local Finnish-language newspaper, founded in 1904 as mouthpiece for the Young Finnish Party, which advocated for social reforms and programs. True to this progressive legacy, the new owner, Arvo Ketonen, wanted to modernize the publication by moving away from Gothic typeface and building a modern facility. Designed in an elegantly modernist idiom—with white walls, metal-strip windows, and a roof terrace—the building soon became the emblem of Turku's embrace of modernity as a condition that produces new types of experiences (fig. 28). Therefore, while the building has been heralded as Aalto's first "functionalist" or "*sachlich*" building, a closer look reveals that Aalto was just as invested in its atmospheric qualities, which culminate in the almost sacred expression of space and light in a large basement hall dedicated to an industrial process: the printing room (fig. 29). The sculpted columns that widen as they reach the ceiling make the physical forces manifest in form, while the shimmering light on their glossy white surfaces renders the heavy structure weightless.

With the building's exterior Aalto aimed to engage the public (fig. 30). The main facade, facing Kauppiaskatu, is dominated by a large, 7.5-meter-high window

„Tuntuu kuin Euroopan kansat olisivat yksi suuri suku; vierailulla käynnit vain perhekutsuja”

(YRJÖ KILPISEN HAASTATTELUSTA „UUDESSA SUOMESSA" 19. 3. 30.)

Tulenkantajat

No 6

Hinta 5 mk.

Onko Turku Suomen modernein kaupunki?
Miksi valtaa realismi taas teatterin?
(«Matkan päin» tekijäin vastaus)
Kuka on Parisin suurin vampyyri-näyttelijätär?
LUKEKAA VASTAUKSET NÄIHIN KYSYMYKSIIN TÄSSÄ NUMEROSSA

28. The cover of *Tulenkantajat* 6 (1930), with Aalto's Turun Sanomat Building

29. Aalto, Turun Sanomat Building, printing room, 1931
30. Aalto, Turun Sanomat Building, street facade, 1931, rendering

through which one could view projections of newspaper front pages. Next to it was the entrance door and, above it, a band of slightly slanted address signs lit by electric lights.[11] Vitrines lined the street to the right. When compared to Aalto's earlier designs, the real break had less to do with style than with Aalto's decision to make the building a mediator between the producers of information and their audience, as the building invited the viewer to engage and construct meaning from a multitude of information and effects.

Turun Sanomat building shows that as soon as Aalto came into contact with continental modernism he realized that his building should endorse not only the new formal idioms but also the new types of experiences brought by modernization; in this case produced by industrial processes and new media. It is important to note in this context that Aalto was by no means the first Finnish modernist. That honor belongs to the editors of the literary group Tulenkantajat (Torch Bearers). Their magazine, which carries the same name, started publishing in 1928, and Aalto was a subscriber.[12] From Tulenkantajat and their magazine he learned to appreciate modernism as part of a larger cultural movement that sprung from Europe's more cosmopolitan centers. At the center stood a new type of modern subject willing to break boundaries, to expose oneself to new types of experiences, and, ultimately to change.

Paimio Sanatorium, designed in 1929 and executed between 1930 and 1933, gives another example what New Realism meant for Aalto in practice: splash-free sinks, door handles that would not catch the sleeves of doctors and patients, and low windowsills to benefit the bedridden. Functional lighting was also a major concern. The operating rooms were semicircles that faced north in order to create diffuse light conditions. The operating table in the middle of each room rotated and was lit by a round skylight.[13] Paimio also paid particular attention to the building's relationship to the nearby pine forest, an important factor for a tuberculosis sanatorium, in which fresh air and sunlight were considered therapeutic necessities. The more "realistic" a building was, the more it was about a particular place, time, and people. A realist approach could therefore be understood as truly Finnish because it responded to the particular light conditions and programmatic needs.[14]

The commission to design a facility to cure tuberculosis, a sickness associated with urban congestion and poverty, surely changed Aalto's outlook on the social role of architecture. In the era of mass society one could no longer assume that national culture would be based on stable social ideals, such as conventional family values. Architecture could contribute to building a unified nation by helping people meet their basic needs, such as housing, and battle even the most unpredictable side-effects of modern society as they emerged.

Another series of built and unbuilt projects from the Turku years—a theater and some set designs, a fairground, a choir stand, a movie theater, and a stadium—suggests that Aalto realized that architecture's sole function was not limited to programmatic needs. Citizens needed to share joy in their cultural achievements.

Aalto used these projects to further explore the possibilities offered by new media and representational strategies and to pose questions about how the new mass aesthetic experience differed from the conventional individual aesthetic experience.

The emerging mass media arrived in Finland in the 1920s, not only through an explosion in journalism (newspapers and magazines in Finnish and Swedish) and the accompanying rise in advertising, but also in the spread of broadcast media, such as radio and film. The 1920s also witnessed a huge movie theater boom. The founding of Yleisradio, Finnish national radio, in 1926 was a milestone. It allowed a vast number of citizens, independent of their social status, language, or location, to share experiences and information about domestic and world events in real time. It became a major agent for social change as it helped Finns to understand themselves as a nation—sometimes through such simple means as the playing of the national anthem at the end of the broadcast day. Aalto's projects from late 1920s demonstrate that he had come to realize that architecture could benefit from lessons learned from the emerging mass media if it wanted to contribute to the creation of a national identity.[15]

Like many thinkers, Aalto saw the new art forms as based on completely different perceptual and experiential paradigms. Old art forms (such as painting and sculpture) required individual contemplation, whereas new ones, like film, fostered an experience of being part of a social whole. Thus, at the very time when Aalto was endorsing aesthetic modernism, he also became aware that to be modern demanded a radical transformation of the individual subject, a willingness to give up some of one's individuality. Aalto's projects that housed collective bodies of people embraced a modern conception of subjectivity, in which the individual exists in a porous relationship with his surroundings.

The first attempt to create what could be called "mass architecture in service of national unity" came in 1927, when Aalto worked on a competition entry for a monument to commemorate the tenth anniversary of Finnish independence (fig. 31). In a letter to a newspaper he wrote about how new media were altering human experience: "What of modern man's scale of values? Whereas the 'public image' might previously have been enormously meaningful, deserving respect, modern man's retina is beleaguered with images (photographs, printed matter, street advertisements, cinema) from morning to night." The new experience meant, he realized, that any attempt to create a permanent, stable value system—a key part of the project of cultural revival—was in vain. "Modern man" had changed, and a completely new type of aesthetic experience was emerging as a result: modern people experienced everything in a state of distraction and immersion. Consequently, national unity could no longer be based on shared, enduring traditions and permanent values, but rather must be founded on the creation of a new subject through immersion in mass events and collective experiences.

In the letter discussing the monument, Aalto concluded that a building would be more appropriate than a statue, because a functional building would better be able to meet the new social function: "A statue might be beautiful in itself, but unable to fulfill its 'social' function as a monument.... The monument to independence in 1927 cannot be conceived as a free, plastic art, nor as a building, structure or statue devoid of real significance [*reaalifunktio*]. It would be inartistic and would not reflect our time (when independence was achieved) and it would not perform its social function as a monument and a unifying symbol of a nation."[16]

His rationale was that, by engaging visitors in activity, a functional building eliminated the contemplative distance that characterized traditional art forms. A stadium was particularly well suited to this, since it housed the collective experience of a sporting event. Sports were popular in Finland at this time—the runner Paavo Nurmi's success in the Paris Olympic Games of 1924 had given them a favorite national pastime. In proposing a stadium as a national monument Aalto was suggesting that national cohesion required buildings that would house activities that triggered collective sentiments, such as the national pride elicited by a sports hero.

The programmatic focus did not eliminate the need for a monumental dimension. This is evident in the perspective drawing, which depicts the running track as a simple disk hovering just above the treetops of Tähtitorninmäki, or Observatory

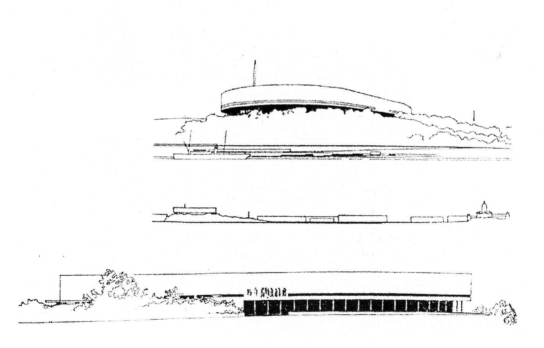

31. Aalto, Memorial for the tenth anniversary of Finnish independence, competition entry, 1927

Hill, overlooking the Helsinki harbor. The building was designed to loom over downtown Helsinki like a large oval *Stadtkrone*—or city crown, to use Bruno Taut's concept—functioning as the symbolic center of the town.[17] Although formally different from its expressionist precedent, it shared many of the same goals. The architect's task was to become an active builder of a new society based on the idea of *Gemeinshaft,* or community, that would transcend political disagreements and social differences. One could even read the project as an attempt to depoliticize the socialist working class by focusing them on new national passions—sports and entertainment.[18]

Aalto's theater designs from the late 1920s present an interesting parallel on how to construct collective experience. Instead of depending on monumental expression for effect, they consist solely of interior spaces. Multisensory spaces constructed of light and sound eliminated perceptual distance altogether. The first project is a prototype for a movie theater entitled "The Rational Cinema," published in Henningsen's *Kritisk Revy* in 1928 (fig. 32). After making a distinction between old art forms ("unique" and "monumental") and new art forms ("reproducible" and "anti-monumental"), Aalto drew links between film as a

i filmens väsen är medtaget som realitet.

Alvar Aalto.

Der findes ikke anden Klasses Kunst, men kun anden Klasses Kunstnere.

32. Aalto, project for a prototypical cinema, perspective toward the screen, reproduced from "Rational Cinema," *Kritisk Revy* 3 (1928)

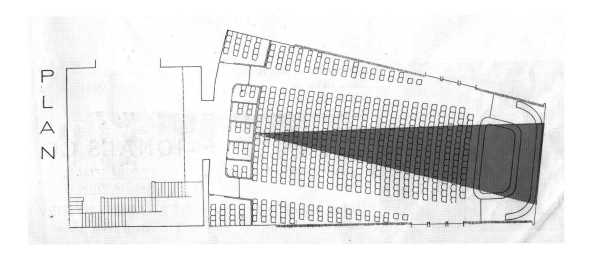

medium, the psychophysical conditions of viewing, and architectural space.[19] Film was the mass aesthetic experience par excellence, since it was based on collective absorption in the ever-flickering images; even the movements of the audience's retinas became synchronized. Aalto considered the architectural, technological, and psychological aspects as homologous and designed the new cinema to expose the "actual system comprising the auditorium and the technical and psychological aspects of film showings."[20]

Because film is a technological art, Aalto's reasoning went, architecture had to have an equally sophisticated technological apparatus. Perfect lighting was essential. Aalto used various tectonic strategies to achieve this: complete darkness during the screening, and ambient lighting during intermissions (figs. 33, 34). A nonreflective wall cladding consisting of thin metal slats, which ran vertically on both side walls, mediated the relationship between the audience and the screen. The side of the slats facing the screen was painted black to eliminate reflection, while the side facing the audience was painted different colors in order to provide reflected light during intermissions.[21] The section drawing shows a version of PH light fixtures (named after their designer, Poul Henningsen) along the balcony balustrades just under the film projector. They too consist of slats, in this case located in concentric circles, to create well-distributed lighting across the room from ceiling to seating.

In addition to enabling a completely new sensory experience, the use of electric light brings many key themes of modernization to bear on the project. Like many of his contemporaries, Aalto saw lighting as a means to improve the human living environment. He had probably read Henningsen's article "Room Lighting" in *Kritisk Revy* the previous year and the articles by Finnish lighting expert H. Kjäldman in the *Finnish Architectural Review* and the magazine *Valo ja Voima* (Light and Power) in the late 1920s. Electric light was more than conve-

33. Prototypical cinema, plan

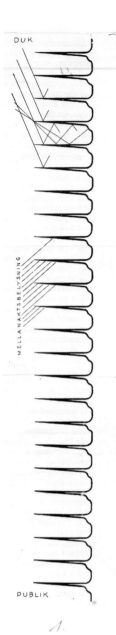

nience; it was the ultimate means as well as symbol of modernization. In 1928, when Aalto was starting to design his prototypes, lighting had just become more available in Finland. The Finnish company Airam started to make lightbulbs in 1925, and Finland's biggest waterpower plant opened in Imatra in 1928. Although it took well into the 1930s for the electric grid to reach rural areas, lighting was seen as a means of launching a major cultural and social transformation, as well as a source of national pride. It played such a big part in the national economy that when the Phoebus cartel (consisting of General Electric, Philips, and Osram, and established in 1924), aimed to control the sale and manufacture of light-bulbs, the move triggered patriotic sentiments throughout the Nordic countries.[22]

Some of Aalto's lighting ideas found their way into the design of the theater for the Southeastern Finland Agricultural Cooperative, which opened in 1929 (fig. 35). The auditorium was stripped of decoration, and the walls were painted an intense, symbolic red, which further intensified the interiority of the space and the experience of being part of a collective body. As Aalto had already acknowledged in his "Rational Cinema" article, the "lighting technique in a theater auditorium is more of a psychological problem, a question of the right relations between the stage and the public."[23] He called it a "people's auditorium" (*kansa-invaltainen katsomo*) and wrote that "during a theater performance, the auditorium is always lighted to a greater or lesser extent.[24] Even if the light is directed entirely towards the stage, reflected light on the audience fulfils an important psychological function. The contact between actors and audience will be better if the stage and auditorium convey the impression of forming, as it were, a single space."[25]

Aalto's first exposure to international modernism had, in fact, been through theater and cinema rather than through modern art and architecture; theater, in particular, was far ahead of architecture and other visual arts in introducing con-tinental ideas into Finland.[26] Books on avant-garde theater in Aalto's library attest to his interests and include Ernst Stern and Heinz Herald's *Reinhardt und seine Bühne: Bilder von der Arbeit des Deutschen Theaters* (1919), László Moholy-Nagy's *Die Bühne im Bauhaus* (1924), and Erwin Piscator's *Das Politische Theater* (1929). Stern and Herald describe the influential work of the impresario Max Reinhardt in terms that must have struck a chord with Aalto: Reinhardt's wanted to "estab-lish a unity between the three elements: script, actor and audience," and make theater a "popular" (*volkstümlich*) art form.[27] Piscator took the thesis further, argu-ing that actors and audience ought to occupy the same space mentally and physically, so that the audience would engage in "political activity."[28] All in all, the goal of avant-garde theater was to define a more socially engaged public.

Nobody captured the nature of the collective aesthetic experience better than Aalto's future friend, the Bauhaus artist and writer László Moholy-Nagy (1895–1946), who wrote about it from an epistemological standpoint. He emphasized the need for theater to move away from a focus on speech and narrative, and

34. Prototypical cinema, wall detail

from "values based on logic and thought" (*logisch-gedanklichen Werte*), to a total psychophysical experience. The goal was to produce a human being complete as a "living psycho-physical organism."[29] Moholy stated that theater must be an "activity that doesn't allow the spectator to sit in silence, that does not only stimulate the soul, but grabs the spectator and forces him to engage and to merge with the highest level of exploding ecstasy produced by the action on stage."[30]

The different techniques used in the stadium and in the two theater projects—programmatic, formal, and atmospheric—converged in Aalto and Bryggman's collaborative project known as the Turku 700th Anniversary Jubileum Exhibition (aka Turku Exhibition). It was a trade fair that opened on June 15, 1929, and stayed open only a little more than a week, during which time it hosted some thirty thousand visitors. Such fairs had become common since independence. Their function was to promote national—and, in this case, regional and municipal—industry. Like the world fairs, the national fairs boosted global commerce and tourism. Aalto had already participated in designing two of them: the First National Fair of 1921 and the Tampere Industrial and Craft Fair of 1922, both of which had relied on eclectic styles to convey ideas about cultural affinities.

35. Aalto, Turku Finnish Theater in the Southeastern Finland Agricultural Cooperative building, Turku, 1928–29

Turku Exhibition was different. As Aino Aalto acknowledged, "It used many modern means in lieu of earlier decorative and ornamental means" to convey a "festive happiness (*juhlailoisuus*)."[31] Significantly, she talked about the importance of creating atmosphere rather than relying on formal idioms. The architecture was intentionally simple: the fairgrounds consisted of low, long slab buildings situated on Samppalinna Hill in an orthogonal plan (fig. 36). The buildings had a wood frame clad mostly in fiberboard, painted white. Most of the pavilions were open kiosks or bazaars that invited viewing of displayed wares. Advertisements played a big role in the overall design: they were painted on the siding and on the masts that rose over the pavilions (fig. 37). The apex of the plan was a round restaurant

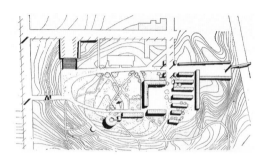

36. Erik Bryggman and Alvar Aalto, Turku Exhibition, 1929. From *Arkkitehti* 6 (1929), 100.
37. Turku Exhibition, advertising masts, 1929

pavilion, set on the highest point, which had a panoramic view over the whole exhibition area. Additional small kiosks were located in the city.

It is difficult to determine the exact division of labor between Aalto and Bryggman. The latter most likely drew up the plan of the exhibition grounds in 1928. Tellingly, the plan was drawn from a bird's-eye view, which highlighted the homogeneity of the rational building systems, similar to those he had studied in Germany. Aalto can be credited with introducing a symmetrical entrance sequence leading to the round restaurant (fig. 38). The fan-shaped inclined plaza consisted of a broad set of stairs, which was divided in the lower area in order to make room for a fountain. The plaza was framed by open kiosks and two round ticket booths where the split stair became one. Thousands of visitors were channeled through the plaza during the ten days the fair was open.

Bryggman and Aalto's teamwork was thus based on their discrete strengths: Bryggman was interested in rational building techniques, while Aalto drew on his interest in an experience of modernity. As in many of his other projects from this period, Aalto's efforts were focused on amplifying and celebrating collective experience. The project used multiple strategies toward this end: urban typology (for example, the plaza or a street); scale and elements normally associated with monumental buildings (symmetry, broad stairs, procedural organization of

38. Turku Exhibition, entrance plaza, 1929

function); and, finally, modernist formal tropes in the form of white, flat-roofed kiosks and advertisement posts, which stepped up with rhythmic staccato on both sides of the plaza. The latter were densely covered with Aalto-designed company logos in a manner that mimicked the abundance of images in a metropolitan environment. The crisscrossing texts were not meant to be read but, rather, absorbed through a kind of omnisensory osmosis. This use of text mimics Moholy-Nagy's layouts for the *Bauhausbücher* series, of which Aalto owned several, which invited the viewer to engage in nonlinear reading and to actively construct meaning from bountiful information.[32]

One of the most remarkable structures at the exhibition grounds was the choir stand Aalto designed for the Turku Singing Festival (fig. 39). It consisted of a sloped surface and an arched acoustic backdrop, both made of wood. The choir was placed against the wall on steps, and between the audience and the choir was a long proscenium—an empty, sloping surface area. While often pictured without people, the architectural expression was completely dependent on the crowd on the stage and in the audience (fig. 40). Its goal was to distribute sound toward the audience, which sat on simple benches. The political function of the sloping stage was even more explicit than in the stadium and the exhibition area: singing festivals had become a powerful emblem of national unity since the late 1870s, when they were first imported from Estonia.[33] The idea of a unified nation was embodied in the powerful sound produced by the choir and aided by the architecture, which was, in effect, the reversed theater form used in both the Turku theater and the Rational Cinema projects. In both cases, repeated elements—slats, seats, and concentric circles—communicate the rhythmic energy and self-generative power of lines that can go on forever. Rays of light and sound depicted in the drawings laid a scientific foundation for an invisible energy creating atmosphere and effects, crafting spaces along the way.

Turku brought Aalto also into the orbit of Stockholm, where he befriended a group of young modernist architects involved in the planning of the 1930 Stockholm Exhibition and the parallel Stockholm Housing Exhibition. The architects all shared his interest in collective experience and energy. The group included the architects Gunnar Asplund, Wolter Gahn, Sven Markelius, Eskil Sundahl, and Uno Åhren, and the art historian Gregor Paulsson, the superintendent of the exhibition and head of the Swedish Slöjdföreningen (Werkbund). Aalto followed the planning of the exhibition during his frequent visits to Stockholm from 1928 onward, which explains the commonalities between the exhibitions in Turku and Stockholm, even though the latter took place a year later. The influence went both ways—Gunnar Asplund (1880–1940), the main designer of the Stockholm Exhibition, visited the Turku exhibition and praised its festive joyousness.[34]

In many ways the Stockholm Exhibition can be considered the fulfillment of a dream of urban, collective modern experience as imagined by Aalto and his Swedish colleagues. Located near the Stockholm zoo, by the bay of Djurgårds-viken, its focal point was a large terraced area, with the main restaurant, tellingly

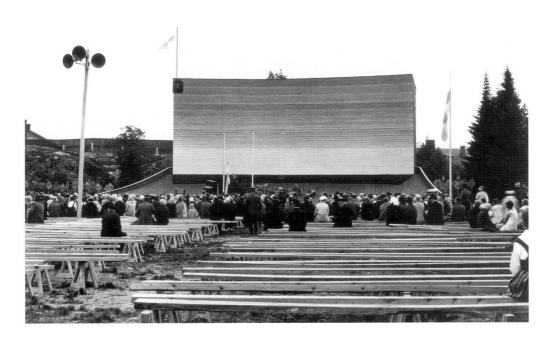

39. Aalto, choir stand for the Turku Singing Festival, 1928
40. The choir stand

NATIONAL IDENTITY IN THE AGE OF MASS CULTURE

called the Paradise, and a tall advertising mast. Visitors arrived there along an avenue called the Corso, lined with exhibition pavilions executed by different architects (fig. 41). Asplund's achievement was to invest modern architecture with unprecedented gaiety and joy. Great attention was given to such extra-architectural elements as flags, colorful awnings, advertising masts, flowerbeds, and water fountains. Asplund personally designed the electric lighting. The colorful renderings showed crowds of people as an integral part of the architecture. This was particularly evident in the illuminated night views of the large glass wall of the restaurant, which made people inside the buildings visible. Besides seeing exhibitions, visitors could eat in more than ten restaurants, visit an amusement park, go swimming, promenade on the Corso, or visit an aquarium.

The ethos of this hugely successful exhibition, which drew four million visitors over three months and triggered a lively public debate about modern architecture, can be considered in many ways the ultimate modern phantasmagoria of happiness and communality, a stark contrast to anything that had been seen on the continent, including the Weissenhof Siedlung Exhibition in Stuttgart three years earlier. Asplund and his younger colleagues, who had done buildings for the Stockholm Housing Exhibition, examined the wider architectural and social implications of this dream in their manifesto the following year. The title, *Acceptera* (To Accept), was meant to encourage openness to the new socioeconomic conditions of modernity, and, by extension, modern architecture.[35] The changing individual experience in the age of modernity was a dominant theme of the book—in fact, the authors of the individual essays did not identify themselves, emphasizing the collective nature of their work and thinking. The title indicated the need to accept industrialized mass society and reevaluate the role of the individual in it. The title page showed a handsome Swedish man in front of an anonymous urban crowd (fig. 42). The caption read:

The individual and the mass?

The personal or the universal?

Quality or quantity?

Insoluble questions, for the collective is a fact we cannot disregard any more than we can disregard the needs of individuals for lives of their own.

The problem in our times can be stated as: Quality and quantity, the mass and the individual. It is necessary to solve this problem in building-art and industrial art.[36]

The message was clear: in a modern mass society the individual could no longer be understood in isolation. In fact, the emphasis on individuality in Western societies was seen as a negative condition. The nuclear family as the basic social unit was rejected in favor of collective forms of social organization, which the authors traced to tribal and nomadic societies. The Russian anarchist Petr Kropotkin (1842–1921) was widely read among the group. Not only did he prioritize basic needs over large-scale economic transformations, but he provided, through

[opposite] 41. Gunnar Asplund, Stockholm Exhibition, 1930, view along the Corso. Swedish Architecture Museum, Stockholm.

42. Title page, Gunnar Asplund et al., eds., *Acceptera* (Stockholm: Tiden, 1939)

his theory of "mutual aid" among all species, an alternative to Darwin's theory of the survival of the fittest, which was embraced by the proponents of American-style free-market capitalism.[37] Aalto captured the altruistic and communal principle of modernism when he reviewed the book and the exhibition for *Arkkitehti* magazine. He celebrated the Swedish architects' ability to see the world through the eyes of the man on the street by using the German expression *aussersichgehen,* to "go outside of oneself."[38]

Acceptera put forward the argument that new technology and modern mass media fostered a sense of community among people living in different parts of the country, and subsequently among different nations. The book included pictures of people talking on the telephone and listening to the radio, sharing information about personal and world events. Like Aalto, the authors of *Acceptera* considered the image of a darkened cinema, where individuals formed an autonomous mass, emblematic of modern collective experience. Viewers were united in a trancelike state of absorption, feeling the same feelings, united in collective synergy. A quote from Karl Scheffler's (1869–1951) *Italien: Tagebuch einer Reise* (1913), cited in *Acceptera,* was telling. Here a social idea (collective synergy) was combined with a programmatic idea (the ancient Roman Arena in Verona) and an aesthetic concept (the simplicity of repetitive form). The emphasis was on a complete homology between aesthetic experience and collective sentiments:

Irresistibly triumphant is the impression made by its enormous objectivity and purposeful simplicity, its grandiose manifestation of reason, the power of its will and the self-evident character of its form. One is gripped—at this one spot in Verona—by the rhythm of the organic. Involuntarily one imagines this wonderfully proportioned curved oval with all its stone ledges filled by people and sees in the mind's eye how the architectonic whole endows the masses with order and with tempo. Involuntarily one links this building with life and movement, while one always links Renaissance architecture to historical ideas alone.[39]

43. Image from Karl Scheffler's *Italien*, reprinted in *Acceptera*

Two photographs depicted the rhythmic articulation of seats in an unnamed arena, which seem to go on forever, expressing the manifestation of collective experience: formal repetition, simplicity of form, and a scalelessness that arises from a lack of detail (fig. 43).

In the years of cultural ferment following World War I, Aalto and his generation were drawn to the energy and excitement of the idea of the emerging mass culture. A number of writers and thinkers early in the century had shared this interest and absorbed its underlying principles: the playwright August Strindberg, one of Aalto's favorite authors, was interested in occult experiments aimed at transmitting thought waves.[40] William James, the American Pragmatist philosopher, argued that the only way to attain true supremacy and higher consciousness was to lose one's self by breaking down the confines of personality, pointing to the "immense elation and freedom [one feels] as the outlines of confined selfhood melt down."[41] Leo Tolstoy, in his popular 1898 book *What Is Art?*—a key book for Finnish modernists until the 1930s—had claimed that art's main function was altruistic and its main task to make us love our fellow human beings.

Aalto, like many in his generation, was attracted to these ideas just at the moment when the European countries were emerging from war. The communal idealism that had preceded the events of the First World War, even if easily dismissed as naïve idealism, had by then led to real political experiments, such as the workers' movements and internationalism. Yet the approach to the masses was a crucial yet polarizing issue: as Aalto had experienced during the riots that preceded the Finnish civil war, the masses had the power to destabilize society. In this light it is no surprise that not everybody was enthusiastic about mass events. Gustave Le Bon's hugely popular 1895 book *Psychologie des Foules* (the Finnish-language *Joukkosielu* [Group-soul] was published in 1912) offers perhaps the most famous discussion on this problem.[42] Generalizing from existing theories of mass reception, Le Bon emphasized the automatism that can underlie collective experience, which made crowds more prone to manipulation and persuasion than individuals.

During the late 1920s and early 1930s Aalto seemed still to have been unaware of the dangers behind the convergence of nationalism and mass culture. Both concepts were presented as foundations for a healthy society, as opposed to one torn by internal hatreds. It is, in fact, at times hard to distinguish between Aalto's architecture from the late 1920s, which promoted a benign form of nationalism, and buildings that housed mass rallies organized around the same time by the German Nazi government. Aalto's simple, elegant stage for the Turku Exhibition reminds us that the modernist ideal of collective experience could be applied to various political and social ideas, and that only a hair's breadth distinguished between architecture being part of a government-led propaganda machine and having the noble goal of supporting solidarity among human beings.

New Geographies

During Aalto's student years, Helsinki had little in common with the predominantly rural, Finnish-speaking inland territory. The city, situated at the southern tip of Finland, had been established under Swedish rule in the seventeenth century as a commercial rival to Tallinn, just across the Baltic Sea's Gulf of Finland in Estonia. The first wave of the city's population came from nearby Swedish-speaking coastal areas and from Sweden itself. In the eighteenth century, trade and manufacturing around the Baltic increasingly connected it to other Baltic cities, as "merchants and artisans moved fairly extensively between cities such as Lübeck, Danzig, Vilna, Riga, Narva, Stockholm, Reval, and St. Petersburg, and some people also settled in Finland."[1]

Remnants of this cosmopolitan, business-oriented culture were still present in the late 1910s and 1920s. The population consisted of Swedish-speakers, Russians, Germans, and relative newcomers from the Finnish inland. Public architecture, which from the nineteenth century had sought to convey worldliness and grandeur rather than insular national culture, added to Helsinki's cosmopolitan flair.

The city's architectural character was established during the early nineteenth century, when the Russian tsar Nicholas II hired the German-born architect Carl Ludwig Engel to improve the city, making its design and appearance competitive with those of the major neighboring Baltic countries. Thus the student Aalto strolled along the Bulevardi, an elegant avenue lined with linden trees and neo-Renaissance buildings built in the 1870s (fig. 44). The street flowed into equally grand Esplanaadi, where Aalto could sit in cafés and view art, including Sallinen's, at Gallery Strindberg. These were grand urban gestures fostering grand urban lifestyle, considering that the city had fewer than fifty thousand inhabitants at the time they were built. Helsinki offered the young architect important lessons in architecture: architecture is tied to history, politics, and power, and, perhaps most of all, it could affect people's behavior, even change their outlook on the world. One of the most potent dreams that Aalto began to share with the leading Finnish practitioners of the nineteenth century was that Finnish culture and architecture could be opened to international, and particularly European, influence.

To be sure, the internationalist aspirations of the earlier architecture were in tune with the most burning political question of the day: how to foster international unity and collaboration after the birth of the new nation-state. In his early career he was particularly attracted to large metropolises—Stockholm, Copenhagen, Riga—with cosmopolitan, polychromatic cultures and multiple constituencies. Although Aalto did not go as far as to endorse the cosmopolitan ideal that all humanity belongs to a single community undivided by national boundaries, his writings from this period started to question the idea of a nation as a stable cultural and political entity with definite physical boundaries and a unified *Volk*. Furthermore, through his frequent travels he saw his own life unfolding within a larger transnational territory. These sentiments were most pronounced around 1930, when Aalto often celebrated the idea of an ethnically and linguistically mixed population, and even world citizenship.

Therefore, despite his commitment to Finnish national culture and its development, it would be fair to say that Aalto was an internationalist throughout his career. This international-mindedness can be traced to his liberal, bilingual family, from whom he had inherited a distaste for the nationalist extremism that had plagued relations between Finland's two linguistic communities since the late nineteenth century. His parents' library included the collected works of the Danish literary scholar and devout Nietzschean Georg Brandes, who was critical of the shortsightedness and insular thinking of Scandinavian and Finnish nationalist groups. In his essay "Thoughts on the Turn of the Century" (1900), Brandes had argued that the political map of Europe supported pan-Scandinavian unity; the individual countries were too small to react effectively to a foreign threat in politically unsettled times. Brandes was scornful of what he described as the "hateful fight between the Finnophiles and the Swedophiles, representing two ancestries and two languages, but only one fatherland and one Nordic culture. The two parties, weakened by strife and without any mutual solidarity, very easily became the prey of superior power."[2] The observation that "Swedish culture has its northernmost beginnings up in Finland and Danish culture's southernmost home is in Schleswig" promoted the idea of a common Nordic cultural heritage.[3]

Brandes' position was shared by Finnish architects Sigurd Frosterus (1876–1956) and Gustaf Strengell (1878–1937), who emerged at the beginning of the century as the most vocal critics of the dominant National Romantic style and of the insular national culture it promoted. Their joint 1904 manifesto, "Architecture: A Challenge to Our Opponents," was written two years after they lost the

44. View of the Bulevardi, ca. 1920. Postcard. National Board of Antiquities, Helsinki.

Helsinki Railway Station competition to the architecture firm Gesellius-Lindgren-Saarinen, whose proposal was still anchored in nineteenth-century eclecticism. Frosterus and Strengell were critical of the chosen design, which was based on the National Romantic style pioneered by the firm; it had stone walls, eight bears lined up above the main entrance, a tall tower, and many smaller towers. In contrast, Frosterus' proposal had called for a more modern expression and drew from continental examples; it highlighted the vertical load-bearing elements, made of reinforced concrete, which allowed large panes of glass between them. Large Sullivanesque entryways on three sides emphasized fluid movement of people in and through the building.

It was understandable that Frosterus and Strengell were concerned about the appearance of the capital's central railroad station: a rail terminus represented the new era of increased mobility. Therefore, although the city still had fewer than one hundred thousand inhabitants at the time and one could take a train from there only to a limited number of locations in southern Finland or in Russia, a magnificent monument to rail travel in itself celebrated this era of growing internationalization. Most important, the authors disapproved of the insular national thinking represented by the Gesellius-Lindgren-Saarinen approach: "The fact that this country is not a leading center of civilization should not discourage us from profiting by the gains of culture. Even in Finland we do not live on hunting and fishing, as in the old days, and decorative plants and bears—to say nothing of other animals—are hardly representative symbols of the age of steam and electricity. . . . WE WANT INTERNATIONALISM ON THE BASIS OF WHAT IS COMMON IN WESTERN CULTURE."[4]

Frosterus' and Strengell's ideas about internationalism should not be confused with later notions of international modernism. Rather, the origins of their thinking can be traced to Weimar and to the atelier of the Belgian art nouveau architect and designer Henry van de Velde, where Frosterus worked in 1903 and 1904. The manifesto was written upon his return to Finland. Van de Velde had exposed Frosterus to the intellectual debates around the German Werkbund and the Nietzsche archive, in which Nietzsche's ideas about the New Man merged with van de Velde's notion of New Style, both conceived as dynamic and evolving entities. Based on Nietzsche's idea of a complete openness between inner and outer worlds, both men condemned anything stable and fixed, including national identity and bourgeois mentality. Van de Velde translated these principles into buildings, which took the flow of movement as a leitmotiv.[5]

What could be called Frosterus' and Strengell's "proto-internationalism," envisioned before the establishment of international organizations, was rooted in Nietzsche's radical condemnation of nationalism and patriotism, which he formulated in the wake of German unification as the Second Reich in the late nineteenth century. In the chapter "Peoples and Fatherlands" from *Beyond Good and Evil* (1886), Nietzsche writes: "What I think of the Germans: they belong to the day before yesterday and the day after tomorrow—as yet they have no today."[6]

Nietzsche's idea of dynamically evolving transpersonal and transnational identity was in sharp contrast with the notion of insular nationalist thinking. According to Nietzsche, national identities, like individual identities, evolved with time. The world was a vast, constantly unfolding ecology rather than a static, closed system. A nation had to be open to transnational exchange, just as an individual had to be open to transpersonal exchange. Nietzsche considered nationhood something made, rather than something born or innate, and a national soul as a dynamic "social structure of the drives and affects."[7] A German soul, for example, was "manifold, of diverse origins, more put together and superimposed than actually built."[8] Transnationalism occurred as a consequence of the mutability of this fluid, dynamic spirit. In fact, there was no such thing as innate national culture to start with.

The first expression of this new type of metropolitan architecture started to appear in Finland the year Aalto entered architecture school, when Frosterus, now working on his own, won the competition for the Stockmann Department Store (1916–35). The building was reminiscent of Alfred Messel's Wertheim Department Store (1896–97) in Berlin, making the point that the new international architecture was a product of the vibrant new metropolitan lifestyle. The perspective drawing for it depicted a building with a strong vertical articulation of alternating columns and windows and a slightly curving roofline, somewhat in the style of van de Velde, which added to its dynamism (fig. 45). Although Helsinki was still a far cry from a continental metropolis, the tramlines on the street signified a new and dynamic world order, brought about through technology and com-

45. Sigurd Frosterus, *City 1920*, competition entry for the Stockmann Department Store, 1916, reproduced in *Arkkitehti* 3 (1916). Museum of Finnish Architecture, Helsinki.

merce.[9] The building occupied a whole block at one of the busiest intersections in Helsinki, between Aleksanterinkatu, Esplanaadi, Keskuskatu, and Heikinkatu (now Mannerheimintie). The uninterrupted columns suggested what was inside: a six-story-high sky-lit atrium, surrounded by open sales floors; the effect was of a temple of capitalism. Like van de Velde's, Frosterus' approach to structural expression was more expressive than literal: the focus was on the dynamism of the lines created by structural members and other architectural elements. The overall effect was dominated by the staccato of marching pilasters and the rhythmic vertical calibration of bricks and window frames. Just a few years later, Frosterus would be dreaming of skyscrapers in downtown Helsinki (fig. 46).

Even the work of Armas Lindgren, Aalto's teacher at the Polytechnic and a former partner in Gesellius-Lindgren-Saarinen, had by the late 1910s moved from National Romanticism toward a more dynamic visual and structural expression, the trademark of metropolitan architecture. The break is evident in Helsinki's new center, if we compare the railway station, which he had designed ten years earlier with Saarinen and Gesellius, with his Kaleva Insurance Company Building (1911–14; fig. 47) and the neighboring Seurahuone Hotel and restaurant, designed some ten years later. Like the neo-Renaissance buildings of the late nineteenth century, which line Bulevardi and Esplanadi and introduced continental flair and lifestyle into Helsinki, this new architecture—marked by repetitive elements and bold continuous surfaces—brought an aura of continental *Grossstadt* into the city by capturing the dynamic tempo of the twentieth-century metropolis. One can

46. Frosterus, skyscraper project for downtown Helsinki, 1922. Museum of Finnish Architecture, Helsinki.
47. Armas Lindgren, Kaleva Insurance Company Building, Helsinki, 1911–14

already detect the emphasis on rhythmic structural elements, large surfaces of glass, and uniform streetscapes that rendered individual buildings as components of the city, and the city as an ever-expanding matrix.

As we have seen, Aalto too grew up to believe that at the deepest level the Finnish soul was dominated by the desire to overcome the limitations of Finland's remoteness. The challenge was to determine how art and architecture were to express the idea of a nation that was adaptable and constantly evolving. Aalto's 1921 thesis project at the Polytechnic Institute, "The Finnish National Fair," demonstrates that he shared Frosterus' and Lindgren's desire to turn Helsinki into a metropolis (fig. 48). The facade had a repetitive vertical articulation of its structural members. Also here a tower dominated the massing. Similar, too, was the grand urban scale: the drawing presented the proposed building in a scene that depicted the whole block.

Aalto's choice of architectural language departed radically from the National Romantic sensibility of the executed version of Finland's First National Fair, which was built in the same year and on which Aalto had worked. The architect was Carolus Lindberg (1889–1955), Aalto's beloved teacher in the department of urban planning at the Polytechnic Institute, and who became the professor of Finnish and Scandinavian architecture in 1925. His design, reflecting his commitment to the more insular idea of a national culture and architecture, was an eclectic mix of quasi-Finnish and Nordic stylistic allusions. Located on the corner of Sepänkatu and Fredrikinkatu in what is now called the Sepänpuisto, the fairgrounds consisted of individual pavilions executed in an eclectic mix of styles, and a gate designed by Aalto, which somewhat humorously depicted a silhouette of what looked like a church with a cut-off human figure (fig. 49). Its stage-set quality was a sign of how Aalto thought of the fairgrounds as a whole: a fantasyland with little grounding in actuality or future potential. The figure crashing through the gate revealed the emptiness of the sign. In contrast, his proposed design for the fairground complex was grounded not only in the new realities, such as urbanization, but in his hope for what all architecture could be—international and industrialized and, perhaps most of all, modern.

Aalto first encountered the increasingly international and dynamic modern world while in Riga, the capital of Lithuania, on a 1922 trip sponsored by the Finnish government as part of a cultural-exchange program between the two countries. Riga was the second-largest city in the Baltic region, after St. Petersburg, with more than half a million people. An old Hansa town, it was more cosmopolitan than Stockholm. The visit seems to have convinced Aalto, at least for the moment, that Finland's future lay in fostering ties to the so-called border states south of the Gulf of Finland—Estonia, Latvia, Lithuania, and Poland— rather than to Scandinavia. Writing to his fellow students, travelogue-style, in a text later published in a student magazine, he described an emblematic experience, a drink in a bar: "This glass of madeira is a well-timed reminder that bridges the gap from the old, historical Hansa town to the modern transit hub on the

48. Aalto, "The Finnish National Fair," thesis project, 1921

PAN-EUROPEAN ASPIRATIONS

Dvina. I will not speak of the stock exchange and the business world, but prefer to dive into the enchanted Riga of midnight, where German and American business-men take time off from their contract problems."[10]

Aalto develops his text into an extended meditation on increased mobility and the fate of modern nation-states. He focuses on the presence of multiple nation-alities on the city's streets, and the tone is slightly mysterious and daring, a sign that Aalto still considered cosmopolitan culture as something slightly exotic. Aalto demonstrates once again the power of hyperbole, with ecstatic fluvial references—from drinks to rivers to diving—that capture the geopolitical and cul-tural differences between Scandinavia and the eastern Baltic states. Elsewhere he refers to the flow of people and to the city's openness to external influences—Fenno-Ugric, Slavic, German. The presence of American businessmen located the city in an even more expansive territory and was thus an ultimate measure of its modern political and economic power. He saw Riga as a node in an emerging dynamic network of interconnected major financial and economic centers, while Scandinavia was still fairly homogeneous and isolated and perhaps, thus, an abode of order and stability. The present tense of his prose indicated that Riga lived in the present; whereas Stockholm had led him to muse on the glorious past and dream about an equally glorious future, Riga made him feel the pulsing economic and political forces of modernity. The article demonstrates that by 1922 Aalto was beginning to accept and conceptualize Finland's geographic

49. Carolus Lindberg, First National Fair, Helsinki, general view with gate by Aalto, 1920. National Board of Antiquities.

location between East and West—hence the fascination with Riga. He writes: "Copenhagen is Copenhagen, and all our other favorite towns have a charm of their own," he wrote, "but here in Riga the contrast is strongest. Here we find Occident and Orient in one single web."[11] While Scandinavia's stable ethos found its analogy in the idea of the organic whole, the dynamism of the border states was captured with other, different organic metaphors that knew no boundaries: flowing water and webs.

As a consequence, Riga, unlike Stockholm, could not be reduced to a single symbolic center or building to be contemplated, but had to be understood as a complex, intoxicating matrix that overwhelmed the visitor. A gouache done by Aalto in the city depicts how a traveler is enticed to turn yet another corner in the city's endless maze of streets and squares (fig. 50). In fact, Aalto never men-

50. Aalto, view of Riga's medieval town, 1922. Gouache.

tioned a single building that would stand out as unique or of particular merit. He viewed the city as a kind of sublime monster that could be experienced only in its overwhelming totality. Aalto seems to have come to the realization that modern culture, especially capitalist culture, consisted of a complex web of interfaces, overlaps, and connections that would make everybody a producer and a participant in this fluid stream of life. One could experience modernity only by thrusting oneself into the world. As the subject became part of the dynamic flow, it too would undergo change. Aalto describes a joyous night spent drinking and dancing with Russians, Germans, ballerinas, and waitresses at a bar called Bi-Ba-Bo. Amid the revelry, national and class boundaries evaporated. Aalto took particular pleasure in being called a baron—travel, the ultimate modern experience, even allowed one to adopt new identities.[12]

Aalto's fascination with Riga coincided with a period in Finland's foreign relations when the country was seeking alliances with eastern Baltic countries that resembled it—Estonia, Latvia, and Lithuania—small nations with minority languages living in the shadow of immense Russia, newly enlarged into the USSR. The political agreement signed between Finland, Estonia, Latvia, and Poland in March 1922 affirmed the "mutual political and economic interests" of these countries, all of which shared their eastern border with Russia.[13]

This explains, at least in part, why Aalto, who came from a newly independent nation-state, did not look to find in Riga signs of strong national culture or patriotic sentiment. He found, instead, a new Europe emerging from the ashes of the First World War, bringing to mind Nietzsche's exclamation in *Beyond Good and Evil* that "Europe wants to become one."[14] Aalto's celebration of Riga's multinational and multiethnic identity indeed echoes Nietzsche's idea of "Europe in the state of becoming" put forward some half a century earlier: "Behind all the moral and political foregrounds that are indicated by formulas [to describe elevated ideas about Europe, such as democracy and humanism], an immense *physiological* process is taking place and constantly gaining ground—the process of increasing similarity between Europeans, their growing detachment from the conditions under which climate- or class-bound races originate, their increasing independence from that *determinate* milieu where for centuries the same demands would be inscribed on the soul and the body—and so that slow approach of an essentially supra-national and nomadic type of person who, physiologically speaking, is typified by a maximal degree of the art and force of adaptation."[15] The idea of a transnational person was attractive also for political reasons: instead of war, the "Will to Power," as Nietzsche called it, could be channeled into constructive cultural exchange. Just as Nietzsche was motivated by the bloody battles of the 1870s, the Franco-Prussian Wars, and the Paris Commune, the civil war was fresh in Aalto's mind. The idea of world peace achieved by elimination and acceptance of difference was a tempting vision. Nietzsche was undoubtedly a pervasively influential author for Aalto's generation, not least because of his radical pacifistic and global vision.

While en route to Italy for his honeymoon, in search of the stable foundations of Western civilization as well as a national cultural revival, Aalto acquired a copy of *Pan-Europa* (1924). The book was by the Austrian count Richard N. Coudenhove-Kalergi (1894–1972), who, like Nietzsche before him, viewed the idea of a unified Europe from the historical vantage point of the wartime generation. Coudenhove-Kalergi's picture of the politically and economically declining Europe was pessimistic, to say the least. A comparison to the United States was inevitable: while the European nations had been fighting one another, America had become the "wealthiest, the most powerful, and the most advanced country in the world" precisely because of its political structure.[16] Similarly, the newly founded Soviet Union, also a federation of states, was emerging as a world power.

His version of ideal Europe did not consist of independent countries, Coudenhove-Kalergi maintained. His criticism of "European separatism" was triggered by the birth of many new nation-states borne out of World War I, among them Finland. In *Pan-Europa,* he wrote: "The striving for freedom exceeds the striving for order; here even the smallest nation claims its full sovereignty, regardless of whether it can maintain itself in competition with others. While in the big world the process of integration goes steadily on, Europe is regressing further and further towards atomization."[17] The observation that the individual states had become too small was particularly true for Finland, which at that point had only some three million inhabitants; it would have indeed made sense to supplement it with other small European states and develop them into a federation from the start, as suggested by Coudenhove-Kalergi.

Under the influence of such writers (however disparate) as Coudenhove-Kalergi and Nietzsche, Aalto began to consider how architecture could promote a more cosmopolitan, pan-European culture. Aalto, by the mid-1920s a frequent traveler, must have sympathized with Coudenhove-Kalergi's observation that the political structure of Europe lagged in the development of transportation and communications technologies (such as railways and telephone service), which had since the nineteenth century reduced distances between people in other countries: "The spatio-temporal rapprochement of neighboring peoples must be followed by a political rapprochement if conflicts are to be avoided."[18] He called on European youth to build a new, unified Pan-Europa, comprising all the democratic European states, erected on the ashes of the old.

Coudenhove-Kalergi proposed an equally porous understanding of the nation-state. He criticized the League of Nations for failing to effectively eliminate the boundaries between nations: "Instead of grouping the peoples and states of the world according to their economic, cultural, and geographic affinities, [the League of Nations] joins together mechanically, like bricks, large and small states, Asiatic and European, neighboring and distant, without regard to geography, history, culture, or economics."[19] Such a mechanistic organization was not suited to the modern world, which was more "organic"—more dynamic and interconnected—than the prewar world. In addition to being based on actual "economic, cultural, and economic affinities," an organic pan-European community of countries would foster emotional synergy among nations and peoples. Coudenhove-Kalergi warned that the "abstract structure" of the League of Nations failed to produce a "response in the sentimental life of mankind, which, starting from the family, passes by degrees through nations and groups of nations, and culminates in the ideal of world-embracing humanity." [20]

Scandinavian modernism sprang directly from this political climate of competing visions of cosmopolitanism and increased pan-European collaboration. Many of Aalto's Swedish friends were members of Clarté, an organization established in 1919 by the French author Henri Barbusse to promote peace and pan-European culture in the wake of World War I. (The organization was named after a novel that he had published the same year, in which he gave a firsthand account of his experiences on the Western Front.[21]) The Swedish chapter of Clarté was founded in 1921 and included all the leading intellectuals and writers in the country, as well as such prominent members of the Swedish Social Democratic Party as Alva and Gunnar Myrdal, promoters of disarmament and social welfare (and later Nobel Peace and Economic Prize laureates, respectively); Selma Lagerlöf, the Nobel Prize–winning novelist; and Aalto's friend Sven Markelius (1889–1972), a member of the Acceptera group. Clarté did not take root in Finland, mainly because the Finnish intelligentsia was skeptical of its leftist leanings. There were a few exceptions: the playwright Hagar Olsson (1893–1978), a leading figure in the Finnish chapter of Clarté, shared Aalto's interest in pan-European ideals.[22]

Aalto's Clartéan friends taught him that in the same manner that a modern nation was modern only when it opened itself to transnational influence and exchange, transcending the limitations posed by an individual psyche was a prerequisite for an individual to be modern. A truly modern subject was seen as porous and adaptable to new conditions. This, in turn, called for architecture to facilitate this feeling of being part of the world at large in all its multitude and dynamism, even chaos. Aalto's ambition was to find an appropriate architectural strategy, both organizational and semantic, to evoke and embody this new condition.

Aalto designed a stage set for Olsson's antiwar play S.O.S. that offered an inkling of his new architectural strategy, fitting for this new task (figs. 51, 52). The play, performed in 1929 at Aalto's Turku Theater, captured the sentiments of the generation that had come of age during the Great War. Aalto communicated the horrors of the war by using modern media and representational techniques: front pages of newspapers were projected onto the stage flats and fragmentary walls, depicting the destruction of a war based on national and social hatred. He inscribed the word PANEUROPA on the floor in a call for unity among nations. The message was clear: in order to avoid another war, a new political system and a new social paradigm—solidarity—were needed. The design makes the point that art and architecture should connect viewers with reality rather than separate them from it. Art can achieve this by providing a sensory experience in which fragments of reality—in this case newspaper clippings—break down

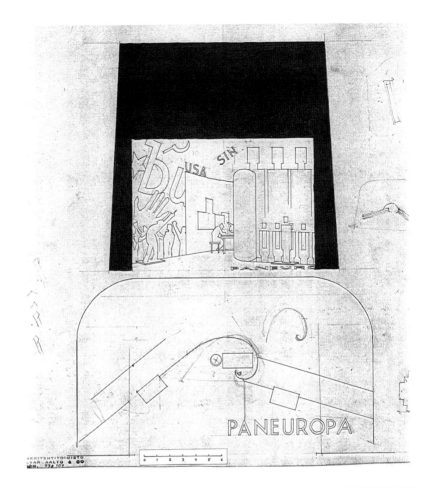

51. Aalto, stage set for Hagar Olsson's play *S.O.S.* at the Turku Finnish Theater, 1929
52. Aalto, stage set for *S.O.S.*

the idea of a pure aesthetic object. In Aalto's vision it was also important to let the world enter the work in all its unmediated complexity, rather than organize the fragments into a neat composition. In this instance, the strategy meant bombarding the viewer with images from all over the world: fragmentary architectural installations and projected newspaper texts. The message was that artists and architects had to address present political events, and that even in a remote country like Finland one could not merely observe the world at a distance.

Aalto's representational techniques for the *S.O.S.* stage set can be traced to the idea of "pan-geometry," developed by the Russian constructivist artist El Lissitzky, whose goal was to promote a new type of identity formation by shattering unified objects into pieces.[23] Lissitzky used the word *irrational* to describe instances when what we see at first glance gets revised through later observations.[24] His 1922 *Self-Portrait* adorns the cover of a special issue of the Swedish magazine *Spektrum,* entitled "Arkitektur och Samhälle" (Architecture and Society), guest-edited by Markelius—a sign that the Scandinavian members of Clarté were looking to Russian constructivism for ways to politicize art and architecture (fig. 53). The main goal was to stipulate a political change. Although it is unclear what firsthand exposure Aalto had to contemporary Russian artists, the design

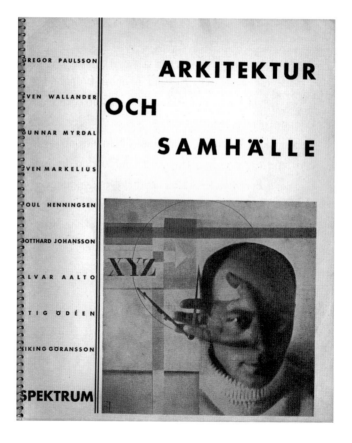

53. Cover of *Spektrum* magazine, Stockholm, 1932, with El Lissitzky, *Self-Portrait,* 1924

for *S.O.S.* demonstrates certain familiarity with their formal and representational techniques (such as collage and photomontage), aimed at constructing a dynamic, nonhierarchical political field that would transcend any particular geographic location or ideological framework. Significantly, the "identity politics" embedded in these techniques was based on the idea of a collective body consisting of different classes and peoples throughout a vast region working toward collective goals. The constructivists understood that a modern identity, be it that of an individual or a nation, was considered to be subject to constant flux and change, since both existed on a "plane of immanence" (to use Gilles Deleuze's more recent terminology) where historically specific constellations of forces constantly reshuffled the political field.[25] The principle behind political art implementing techniques of fragmentation and collage was that history itself was a continuous struggle, one in which the fate of an individual or a nation might play out in different ways. If the new world order was to be achieved by challenging the political status quo, the first step was to make all components lose their independent identity.

These political and artistic ideas called for a corresponding architecture that would allow the individual to become immersed in the world, and that would help create a world without boundaries between people of different nations. The use of glass at the Stockholm Exhibition demonstrated how this could be achieved. Glass was hardly a new material in modern architecture, of course. In fact, since the mid-nineteenth century—think of the Crystal Palace (1851), for instance—glass and iron had come to be associated with the technological progress of the new industrial era. Historically, glass was also associated with utopian and revolutionary architecture movements, most notably with German expressionism, whose practitioners dreamed of constructing whole cities of glass, believing that the material would bring about new kinds of peoples and communities. The Stockholm Exhibition demonstrated that perhaps the most important function of glass was to create spaces marked by simultaneity and overlap of events and images—glass revealed to the outdoors what was happening indoors, and reflected on its surface what was happening outdoors (fig. 54).

These associations did not go unnoticed by the Finnish visitors. Nothing captured the effect and meaning that glass had on the young pan-Europeanists better than Hagar Olsson's 1930 article for *Tulenkantajat,* entitled "Greetings from Stockholm," which praised the exhibition's architecture as a perfect emblem for an emergent international mass society: "The magical architectonic effect of glass is best demonstrated in the concert hall and the city library [both buildings on the fairgrounds, designed by Asplund]. When a wall or part of a wall is made of glass from floor to ceiling, being inside one has a dizzying feeling that the *world is pouring in.* I noticed this when I was standing in the large entrance area of the concert hall. What a modern feeling! *A human being cannot escape the world; one cannot isolate oneself from the buzz of the collective, even when inside.* The world is gliding by as rhythmic shadows—and it calls, it calls!" [26]

Olsson's tone reflects the pacifist ideal of universal love among all human beings of all nations. She establishes links among aesthetic, social, and political formulations: the glass architecture eliminated boundaries between inside and outside, facilitated the union among people, and implicitly endorsed the idea of a dynamic world where such boundaries had lost their meaning. Glass architecture embodied the processes associated with modernity: the emergence of mass society, and increased internationalization.

Olsson exercised considerable influence in Swedish and Finnish cultural circles, and on Aalto personally. In a 1930 interview Aalto concluded that the main task of modern architecture was to carry out a comprehensive union between man and the world. In expressing this idea, he adopted Olsson's hyperbolic rhetoric: "The deliberate social message that the Stockholm Exhibition is intended to convey is expressed in the architectural language of pure, spontaneous joy. There is a festive elegance, but also a childlike lack of inhibition about it all. Asplund's architecture breaks free of all limitations; the purpose is to have a feast, without deciding in advance whether it should be attained architecturally or by any other means that might offer itself."[27] It is telling that Aalto used the word *joy,* a key word drawn from the Romantic tradition, as in Schiller's *Ode to Joy,* composed by Beethoven into the famous choral movement in the 1824 Ninth Symphony. Here joy becomes the unifying force that makes us love the world and our fellow human beings:

Joy, beautiful spark of divinity . . .

Your magic power reunites
All that custom has harshly divided,
All men become brothers
Under the shelter of your gentle wings . . .

You millions, I embrace you.
This kiss is for all the world!

Not without reason was Beethoven's chorale chosen in 1972 as the anthem of the European Economic Community. The idealistic concept of internationalism embraced by progressive thinkers in the Europe of the 1920s and early 1930s as well as the expansionist goals of what is now known as the European Union owe thus a good deal to the theories promoted by the German Romantics of the early nineteenth century.

Aalto used the word *joy* to describe the indiscriminate and intense Dionysian participation in life that connected an individual to the surrounding world and furthermore to the world at large; in so doing he alluded to a new socioaesthetic paradigm. In Aalto's mind, it captured the correspondence between an aesthetic experience and the experience of being part of a social whole. Fireworks over the

Stockholm Exhibition grounds summed up the ambiance and goal of the exhibition, a joyous collective experience: "This is not a composition of glass, stone, and steel, as a visitor who despises functionalism might imagine; it is a composition of houses, flags, floodlights, flowers, fireworks, happy people, and clean tablecloths."[28] The essence of modern architecture for Aalto, particularly Swedish modern architecture, was not to be found solely in its technical or formal qualities, but rather in its ability to foster collective urban experience as the constantly changing "composition" that flickered on the glass surfaces entered human consciousness unnoticed. "I do not wish simply to claim that the Stockholm Exhibition is good," Aalto concluded, "but that it is effective. Many proclaimed enemies of functionalism now carry the virus without knowing it."[29]

Aalto's mixed metaphors—euphoria and illness—turned out to be omens. Certainly, as implied at the end Part 1, the historical realities surrounding the 1930 Stockholm Exhibition made it look, in retrospect, like the last gasp of innocence. In the worldwide economic recession following the 1929 crash of the U.S. stock market, Europe receded into extreme nationalism and economic protectionism. At the same time, two of history's most notorious dictators were emerging: Adolf Hitler and Josef Stalin, who gave the idea of a united Europe a sinister totalitarian and imperialist twist. Both would overcome national and ethnic differences by force rather than by organic processes; Stalin by forced mass migrations and deportations, Hitler by conducting systematic extinctions of ethnic groups, such as Gypsies and Jews, whose nomadic and cosmopolitan mobility he saw as a danger to the idea of an ethnically pure nation-state. And with these events would die the dream of open cities built of glass, welcoming to all.

54. Gunnar Asplund, restaurant building at the Stockholm Exhibition, 1930. Swedish Architecture Museum, Stockholm.

Despite all the talk about internationalization in the 1920s, the truth of the matter was that before the Second World War, Finland was still a remote and little-known corner of Europe. The country belonged to what the French sociologist Francis Delaisi called "B-Europe," a group of agrarian and economically isolated countries, mostly in southern and eastern Europe, lacking modern infrastructural networks that would connect them to other European countries.[1]

Change was on the way when, in 1928, Aalto took the newly established air route from Turku to Paris via Stockholm, Copenhagen, and Amsterdam. This firsthand exposure to other countries had a profound effect on his thinking; rather than referring to large-scale economic, political, and cultural processes in the abstract, he now understood internationalism as meaning an individual traveling, reading foreign magazines and books, and being able to call a foreign friend by phone.

To be sure, Aalto traveled more than most Finns: he took at least one trip to the continent and several to Stockholm each year from the late 1920s on. By constantly seeking out new places and people—and, in the process appropriating new ideas and images—he was living proof that internationalization depended, especially in a small country like Finland, on individuals who wished to be international. For Aalto, traveling was perhaps the most essential part of being modern. He was drawn to metropolises—Stockholm, Riga, Paris, Amsterdam, Berlin, Zurich, and New York—which allowed him to transform himself from a small-town boy into an aspiring cosmopolite and subsequently into an active member of the international network of architects, artists, and critics who formed the modern movement. Thus, Aalto's extended travels to continental Europe not only exposed him to the people and ideas of the international modern movement; they were, in and of themselves, acts of modernism.[2]

Aalto belonged to a group of Finnish artists and intellectuals who, from the late 1920s, sought international contacts, and in so doing fostered the idea of an open and interconnected Europe. The Torch Bearers championed this change with the motto "open doors to Europe." Olavi Paavolainen (1903–1964), the editor in chief of the group's magazine, *Tulenkantajat,* triggered a travel boom among Finland's aspiring modernists with a 1927 essay in which he criticized Finnish poetry as provincial, exhorting: "Young writers: travel to Europe!"[3] A cover of *Tulenkantajat* from 1930 depicts an airplane and declares the group's first goal: "Bring Pan-European Organization into Finland!" (fig. 55). Aalto was among those who eagerly responded to Paavolainen's call, and the two men met in Paris in August 1928.[4]

This was Aalto's first trip to Paris, and his main objective was to meet Le Corbusier, the best-known representative of the modern movement. He had encountered Le Corbusier's work and ideas around 1926, when Uno Åhren, writing in the Swedish magazine *Byggmästaren,* discussed Le Corbusier in vitalist terms: modern architecture embodied the shift from a static to a dynamic worldview. Aalto had also by then read Le Corbusier's book *Towards a New Architecture* in German. The key questions was: How should architects represent this new world order?

Although at that time he was not able to meet the famed architect, he did encounter a number of younger architects who were critical of the master's formalism and politics. In Holland, Aalto met Cornelius van Eesteren, Mart Stam, J. J. P. Oud, and J. A. Brinkman. Each had distanced himself from the utopian aspirations and formal practices of the early 1920s avant-garde, emphasizing instead the more pragmatic problems—functional, structural, and economic ones—faced by architects.[5] In Paris, he spent time with André Lurçat (1894–1970), known for his criticism of Le Corbusier's alliance with the French industrial elite. From the Swiss architect Alfred Roth (1903–1998), who was working in Le Corbusier's office, he learned about the upcoming CIAM meeting, which was to take place in La Sarraz castle in Switzerland the following month.

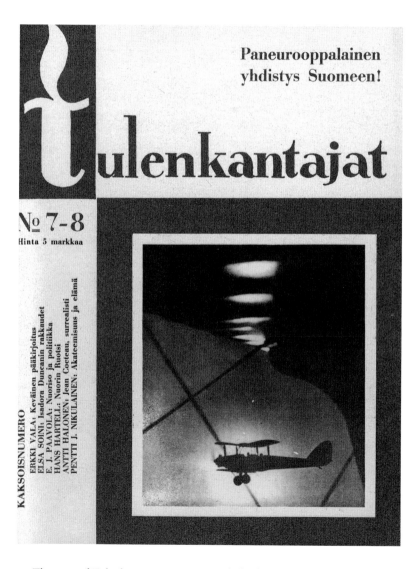

55. The cover of *Tulenkantajat* 7–8 (1930) with the slogan "Bring Pan-European Organization into Finland!"

During this trip he saw a diverse collection of recently completed modernist buildings. In Holland, he saw Bernar Bijvoet and Johannes Duiker's Zonnestraal Sanatorium in Hilversum (1926–28), consisting of light-filled pavilions arrayed in order to optimize the healing effects of sunshine. And on the outskirts of Paris, Aalto visited Le Corbusier's Villa Stein (1927), a more formal exercise in proportions and the art of the free plan. A stop in Copenhagen to visit architect–lighting designer–magazine editor Poul Henningsen, a sharp critic of modernism, further convinced Aalto that the modern movement had its internal debates and disagreements.

Returning to Finland, Aalto highlighted the liaisons between modernist architects in various countries, including his own membership in that collegial network. In an interview in *Tulenkantajat* in spring 1929 Aalto proclaimed, "Modern architects are international!" [6] Indeed, rather than describing modern architecture itself as international, Aalto focused on the individual contacts with foreign architects that constituted his experience of being international. "I visited my Danish colleagues; in Rotterdam I got to know several Dutch architects and saw their work, and in a St. Germain café in Paris I made several pleasant acquaintances with an international group of realist-minded architects." [7] The very casualness of Aalto's tone implies that Paris is just next door, accessible to all Finns.

As Aalto was establishing his contacts with the modernist architects in Europe, the first histories of international architecture had just been published, among them Gropius' *Internationale Architektur* (International Architecture, 1925) and Walter Curt Behrendt's *Der Sieg des neuen Baustil* (The Victory of the New Building Style, 1927). Aalto's library also included a copy of Ludwig Hilberseimer's *Neue internationale Baukunst* (1929). Internationalism meant different things to each of these authors, although they all agreed that the formal outcome was a departure from traditional architecture. For Gropius it represented an all-encompassing synthesizing force among nations, hence his famous dictum: "Architecture is always national as well as individualistic, but the largest of the three concentric circles—individuality, nationality, humanity—encompasses the first two." [8] According to him the world developed in a Hegelian manner toward a new unity in which individual and national boundaries were overcome. "Humanity," referring to humankind at large, works as a kind of supranational and supra-individual spirit that transcends geographic specificity.

Behrendt was not much more specific about how internationalism translated into architectural form. He talked about "the powerful spiritual forces . . . the mighty drama of a sweeping transformation taking place before our eyes. It is the birth of the *form of our time*." [9] "Everything shaped at a given time," writes Behrendt, "is born out of one and the same instinct, one and the same sense of form." [10] The architect's role was to "shape these new realities spiritually and to master them creatively through design [durch Gestaltung]." [11] Hilberseimer acknowledged geographic differences but concluded that they were overruled by economic and social forces: "While [the international new building art] differs depending on the place and national specificity and the personality of the form-giver [designer], it is on the whole a product of the same conditions. Hence the similarity of appearances in these buildings. They are spiritually linked across boundaries."[12]

In contrast to these historians, who focused on the question of form, Aalto, after this first trip to the continent, started to use the words *international* and *universal* in a manner that drew on Clartéan thinking. The new style was an outcome of the merging of national identities, and the individual played a central role: "The new style is international [*kansainvälinen*]. The climate does not require any considerable adjustments. National characteristics don't play much of a role in this, because everybody who dares to be great dares to be universal [*yleismaailmallinen*]; the distinct personality of an individual architect is able to carry through despite all."[13]

The opportunity to participate directly in a fully international dialogue with architects from different countries and to open his thinking to external influence was, to him, more compelling than the idea of an abstract unifying force. Personal and national identities shifted, morphing into something new: "The French almost provoke with their Germanness and the other way round," he wrote.[14] This observation challenged the notion of stable national essence, and by extension a stable international identity.

Significantly, Aalto does not talk about unified international architectural language. He acknowledged that internationalism could acquire different modes of expression in different countries and that a strong national culture offered the best potential for further development. He also acknowledged that there were bound to be local and national modalities despite unifying forces, and he emphasized the role played by national cultures in overcoming local limitations: "Scandinavian architecture, based in part on tradition and in part on 'national' architecture, has perhaps the most potential for further development and has contributed to the development of an international and generally valid standard. Germany, France, Holland, and Scandinavia have already reached a high level of quality."[15]

Aalto's interest in establishing contacts with artists and thinkers in other continental European countries and his reflections on international influence, as well as the status of national culture, mirrored the Finnish government's attempt to establish the country as a member of western Europe. This goal was eventually achieved by Finland's second president, Lauri Relander, who represented a much more active and pragmatic approach to foreign policy than did his predecessor, P. E. Svinhufvud, known for his nationalist sympathies. Soon after being elected in 1925, Relander made a state visit to Sweden, acknowledging, along with the socialist leader Väinö Tanner, that Finland's successful integration into Europe depended on its forging close ties to Scandinavia, despite all the disagreements and distrust. In 1924, somewhat belatedly, Finland joined the so-called Nordic Association (Norden Föreningen), which promoted economic, political, and cultural collaboration among the Nordic countries—Denmark, Finland, Iceland,

Norway, and Sweden. Its political goal was to foster the idea of a politically neutral, economically strong, and socially advanced region.[16]

Relander's efforts were rewarded when Finland became, in autumn 1927, a member of the League of Nations, intended as an intergovernmental forum to deal with international disputes. The goal of the league was to avoid the shifting national alliances and secret deal-making that had governed European affairs throughout the nineteenth century. In early 1921 the league had adjudicated the dispute between Sweden and Finland over the Swedish-speaking Åland Islands in favor of Finland. The appointment of the Finnish foreign minister Hjalmar Procopé as the chairman of the General Assembly in 1928 was another landmark in Finland's ascendancy from a little-known Russian province to an independent member of the international community.

International collaboration, at both the level of the government and the individual, was, as we have seen, not devoid of national and personal sympathies and antipathies. Connections with certain countries and individuals were always more desirable than others. While Aalto's and Paavolainen's desire to travel to the continent aligned with Finnish foreign policy seeking stronger international ties, it also meant leaving old alliances behind. In fact, in departing from the official government policy that fostered strong ties to Sweden, some nationalist-minded members of the Torch Bearers supported the new connection to the continent as a means of distancing Finland from Sweden. Elsa Enäjärvi's article "Finnish—European?" in the first issue of *Tulenkantajat* went as far as to call Sweden an unnecessary "middle man" between Finland and the continent. She suggested that English and French should replace Swedish in Finnish schools, where instruction was still in Swedish and Finnish, and where German was considered the primary foreign language.[17]

Owing to his own bilingual background, Aalto never held such an extremely negative opinion of Sweden. Nevertheless, the trip to the continent was a sign that he was ready to broaden his circle of friends beyond Finland's immediate western neighbor. If the trip to Paris had been motivated by the dream to be modern and to model himself after his cosmopolitan friends, his participation at CIAM made him an official member of the international modernist movement. Yet this transition was possible only through his Swedish friend Sven Markelius, who had recommended Aalto when approached by the organization's president, Karl Moser, about potential candidates. As the only Finn, Aalto was automatically chosen as a member of CIRPAC, the planning committee of the organization, composed of delegates from each country.

Aalto's attempt to manage his personal connections with foreign architects can be linked to the broader question of how to organize international collaboration and exchange at this time. CIAM was modeled on the League of Nations. Each country had a representative (or representatives, depending on its size), and these representatives assembled annually in a different country to discuss the future of architecture and its role in the development of the modern world.

It is worth noting that the initiative for founding CIAM came from Hélène de Mandrot, a Swiss millionaire who had donated land for the League of the Nations headquarters in Geneva. CIAM too had its headquarters in Switzerland, a presumably neutral country that had managed to stay out of the First World War.

This did not mean that CIAM was free of internal disputes or personal and national antipathies. During its early years the organization was dominated by competition between the French faction, led by Le Corbusier, who had pioneered and codified the new style, and a technocratically minded and left-leaning younger group consisting mainly of Swiss and Dutch delegates. The latter group, which included Hans Schmidt, Rudolf Steiger, and Ernst May, was more interested in architecture's social function, and it organized the Frankfurt CIAM meeting, which addressed the theme "The Minimum Subsistence Dwelling" (Die Wohnung für das Existenzminimum), along those lines. Aalto had his own priorities and preferences, both personal and professional. At the Frankfurt meeting he socialized primarily with CIAM's key figures, most of them German-speakers, including president Karl Moser and secretary Sigfried Giedion, as well as Walter Gropius, the former head of the Bauhaus and the president of the National Association of German Architects. Thus he moved directly into the inner circle of the organization. Many more trips to the continent followed, both to attend various CIAM-related meetings and to visit his new friends.[18]

As Aalto grew closer to his new foreign friends he moved farther from his friends and colleagues at home. After a trip to Berlin to visit Walter and Ilse Gropius and attend the exhibition *The Dwelling of Our Times* (Die Wohnung unserer Zeit, deutsche Bauausstellung), Aalto wrote to his host fervently, "We know with astronomical certainty that the only fixed point of our collegial life is in international work. Our private statistics indicate that it isn't possible to find companions among the three million who surround us. Three million is too few."[19] During his second trip to Berlin, in June 1931, to attend a CIRPAC meeting, Aalto found a new friend, László Moholy-Nagy, who visited Finland later that summer. In a subsequent letter to Moholy, Aalto wondered whether, after the riches of the continent, his home country was even worth a visit. "We want to thank you for bringing us so much joy by having the courage to visit our poor Finland, which can offer nothing but mud roads and fly-infested forests."[20]

One can only speculate whether Aalto was drawn to these particular individuals because of their personalities or the positions they represented. Nevertheless, these international contacts surely started to influence his thinking. The Frankfurt meeting gave Aalto firsthand exposure to Gropius' ideas about the social changes behind modern architecture and culture. Gropius' opening lecture, "The Sociological Foundations of the Minimum Dwelling," set the tone: the new architecture was reflective of a major social change and challenged the conventions of the nuclear family. Influenced by the work of the sociologist Franz Carl Muller-Lyer, Gropius argued that society was tending toward collectivization in part because of the radical change in women's social roles.[21] Hence the need for multifamily apartment buildings, ideally with collective facilities, like those planned in the Soviet Union.

In Frankfurt Aalto also saw the exhibition *The Minimum Dwelling Unit,* which presented a survey of apartment plans from different cities based on minimum functional requirements for families of different sizes. Different functions—sleeping, eating, social gathering—were each allotted their own rooms. The manner in which they were clustered was analogous to CIAM's own organizational structure: the whole was an aggregate of discrete units. The subject matter of the exhibition—the individual apartment—convinced Aalto that the road to a truly modern world started with the coordination of everyday life in response to social transformations.

The CIAM conference surely radicalized Aalto; in that milieu architecture was understood as a vehicle for social liberation from the somewhat petit-bourgeois world he was part of back in Finland. The large-scale planning policies put forth to meet massive demographic and economic needs and ambitions challenged him to move beyond viewing the city as a predominantly aesthetic ensemble. Upon his return to Finland, Aalto dedicated himself to exploring the themes of housing and urbanism that occupied CIAM by merging the lessons learned in Frankfurt with the idea of the dynamic and transnational existence of a modern man envisioned by Nietzsche. Aalto's goal was to overcome the fragmented and isolated existence of individuals, families, and countries, and to strive for integration and coordination. Aalto also insisted that housing and planning endorse political and social change rather than preserve the status quo. Echoing his personal taste for travel and moving around, he emphasized mobility as the key paradigm of modernity and modern life.

The first opportunity for this came in November 1930, when Aino and Alvar Aalto coordinated the show *Minimum Apartment Exhibition* at Helsinki's annual Arts and Crafts Exhibition. The couple also designed one of the units on display, which consisted of two bedrooms and a large open area containing living, dining, and cooking areas (figs. 56, 57). Alvar designed the furnishings for the bedroom and living room, while Aino furnished the kitchen, which included details like a garbage bin on wheels and extendable tables.[22] The architectural paradigm included many pieces of mass-produced, transformable furniture, such as stackable chairs and a couch that could be used as living-room furniture in the daytime and as a bed at night. The kitchen, which in bourgeois dwellings was placed out of view and was often the domain of servants, was open to the dining and living areas.

The Aaltos continued to explore the social foundation of their design in an article in the Finnish magazine *Domus* (1930–33) entitled "Our Apartments as Problems." In it they put forward the idea that ideal apartments should accommodate the increased mobility of modern individuals. Whereas the Frankfurt exhibition had addressed mobility by attending to programmatic needs, Aalto focused on the evolving daily routines of a modern individual during a twenty-four-hour cycle. As a consequence, instead of separating functions into rooms, he designed

a sixty-square-meter dwelling in which functions overlapped. The emphasis shifted from providing standard housing functions and calculating floor areas and volumes to allowing a fluid occupation of space. The article introduced the concept of *biodynamism* to describe his planning principle: "An apartment is an area that forms a sheltered space for eating, sleeping, working, and playing. These biodynamic forms must serve as the basis for the internal divisions of a home, not obsolete symmetrical axes and standard rooms dictated by façade architecture."[23]

In order to illustrate his dynamic and flexible approach to function, Aalto distinguished between *huone,* a regular room with a single function (kitchen, bedroom, and so forth) and *tupa,* a large, multifunctional room found in traditional Carelian farmhouses. Since both were rectangular, the difference was not formal but structural. While rooms compartmentalized functions into separate spatial units, the vernacular tupa allowed different daily activities—cooking, working, and sleeping—to unfold organically in a large, nonprogrammed space. Logistical coordination allowed different functions to take place at different times. This had both economic and ritual benefits. For example, a living room could double as a bedroom. At the same time, biodynamism allowed the structural and logistical coordination of various functional scenarios within a single space: "One might say that an apartment in which moving about, the transition from one task to another, etc., can take place organically—without difficulty or disturbance—and which has advanced insulation, internal acoustics, correct distribution of light, etc., already confers a high degree of comfort."[24] Space was not simply considered a container of functions but rather an extension of the dynamic movements of the human body. The key notion behind Aalto's insistence on movement and dynamism was the idea that architecture should help human beings participate in the dynamism of modern life. In a dwelling, the furnishings and the space

56. General view of *Minimum Apartment Exhibition*, Helsinki, 1930, with unit designed by Aino and Alvar Aalto in front

itself should therefore be designed to facilitate this dynamic spatial flow through movement. The apartment was conceived as part of a larger territory occupied by the modern "nomad."

Aalto's notion of biodynamism can be traced to the vitalistic and biocentric worldview central to Bauhaus thought throughout Gropius' tenure, from 1919 to 1928, and shared by Moholy-Nagy and others. The goal was to enhance the idea of an organic society in which every individual and every thing was part of the unifying field of life-energy. The ethical and moral principle underpinning biocentrism was captured by the concept "life," which mingled vitalism's belief in a mysterious, all-encompassing life essence, and Nietzsche's celebration of lived experience and human will. The vitalist philosopher Henri Bergson, writing at the turn of the century, provided the dictum: "Life in general is mobility itself."[25] Bergson makes no distinction between an organism and its exterior, be it a form or a space the organism occupies. The main premise is that the world does not simply exist but must be discovered by the perceiving and experiencing subject. Vitalism influenced modern art from art nouveau to Alois Riegl's theory of *Kunstwollen,* both of which were based on the idea that an individual can capture the energy and movement of life in form. In turn, such forms had the ability to intensify life.

57. Aino and Alvar Aalto, Minimum Dwelling at *Minimum Apartment Exhibition*, view from the living area toward the dining area. Museum of Finnish Architecture, Helsinki.

A dynamic conception of space becomes a key element in Aalto's architecture at this point. His thinking about space encompassed two scales. As the installation at the *Mininum Apartment Exhibition* demonstrated, space operated on the human scale, dealing with the question of how people occupy space as a tangible reality through daily activities, and it also operated on the expansive scale of modernity, whereby processes of modernization—increased internationalization and mobility—radically altered people's understanding and experience of space.

Although Aalto never set foot in the Bauhaus, two people who might have contributed to Aalto's new understanding of space were Moholy-Nagy, who taught preliminary design there, and the artist and performer Oskar Schlemmer (1888–1942), who taught sculpture and stage design from 1920 to 1929. Schlemmer, whose chief artistic problem was to define the relationship between the human figure and space, provides perhaps the most succinct definition of the "biodynamic" and "organic" occupation of space in his article "Mensch und Kunstfigur" in *Die Bühne im Bauhaus*. According to him, the interaction between human beings and space is not based on visual experience alone; people interweave with space as complete physiological entities. A space is therefore not conceived as an empty container or volume, but as something that comes into being only through bodily movements and functions. "An organic body is regulated by the invisible functions of internal organs: heartbeat, breathing, brain functions, and nervous system. These functions comprise the center of the human being, whose movements and extremities comprise an imaginary room. Cubic-abstract space is therefore only a horizontal-vertical support system for this fluid condition. These movements are organic and based on tactile sensations."[26]

The pictures accompanying Schlemmer's article defined the relationship between the human body and space in three stages. The first illustration depicted a figure in an abstract cube-shaped space, mapped with horizontal, vertical, and diagonal lines marking the greatest physical extent of arms and legs in motion (fig. 58). In the second image, lines described the curvilinear movement of arms

58. Oskar Schlemmer, illustration from "Mensch und Kunstfigur," in László Moholy-Nagy, Oskar Schlemmer, and Farkas Molnár, *Die Bühne im Bauhaus* (Stages at the Bauhaus) *Bauhausbücher 4* (Munich: Albert Langen, 1924), 13

and legs, radiating outward in concentric gestures, depicting the space being carved by the moving body. In the third diagram, the two networks form an interlaced system, suggesting a continuum of spatial organization and the human body's nervous and circulatory systems (fig. 59).[27] These images implied that the human subject is part of the vital forces of the universe. Architecture's function was to make the dynamic cosmic forces palpable. The occupant of a room was conceived as being interwoven with space and its dynamic flow. Schlemmer's understanding of how a figure occupies space comes close to Bergson's definition of what it means to occupy space: the world resolves "into numberless vibrations, all linked together in uninterrupted continuity, all bound up with each other, and traveling in every direction like shivers through an immense body."[28]

Aalto invented the word *biodynamism* by employing various biocentric and vitalist concepts in common use among German, Dutch, and Russian modernists in the 1920s (for example, the Bauhaus critic Ernst Kallai's term *Bioromanticism;* the *Biotechnik* of the biologist Raoul Francé, a friend of Moholy-Nagy; and the painter Jean Arp's biomorphic art) and the key word of modernity, *dynamism.* Dynamism, in part generated by a mysterious force embedded in all life, was what distinguished the modern condition, and what differentiated the modern aesthetic from the classical—old art forms and aesthetics were static, modern art forms and aesthetics dynamic. The question became how to capture dynamism through

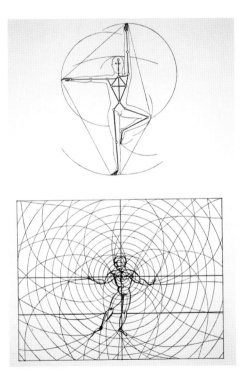

59. Oskar Schlemmer, above: notation of human movements and nervous system; below: dancing figure meshed with space. From *Bühne im Bauhaus*, 14.

art—how to represent it and how to experience it. Moholy-Nagy used the word *dynamic* repeatedly in *Die Bühne im Bauhaus* (1924) and *Malerei, Fotographie, Film* (1925) when stressing the camera's ability—both in still photography and film—to capture the dynamism and tempo of modern life.[29]

Moholy-Nagy and Schlemmer, working in the late 1920s, were building their ideas about space and dynamism on the legacy of Russian constructivism, whose goal, as summarized by two of its key practitioners, the artists Naum Gabo and Antoine Pevsner, was "to deny volume as a spatial form of expression . . . to eliminate (physical) mass as a plastic element. . . . [and] to incorporate our experience of the world in the forms of space and time: this is the single goal of our creative art."[30] In other words, artists and architects should stop designing objects and concentrate on providing spatial and temporal experiences. The key words are *creation* and *experience,* the idea being that true creativity is able to bring new experiential realities into being, not just mere objects. In practice this meant shifting the emphasis from objects to space. Moholy-Nagy had grappled with these ideas as early as 1922, when, while living in Vienna, he and his countryman Alfred Kemeny wrote an article for the expressionist magazine *Der Sturm,* in which they declared that their art was founded on what they called a Dynamic-Constructive Energy System: "We must therefore replace the *static* principle of *classical art* with the *dynamic* principle of universal *life*. In practice: instead of static *material*-construction (relationships of material and form), we have to organize dynamic construction (vital constructivity, *energy relationships*), in which the material functions solely as a *conveyor of energy."*[31]

The key concept for artists and architects thinking in spatial terms was *life.* Despite its quasi-mystical overtones, the concept introduced a pragmatic, everyday dimension to art and architecture. This idea—that art was born out of life and should therefore enhance all aspects of life—was central to Russian constructivism. Gabo and Pevsner wrote in their "Realist Manifesto" of 1920 that "arts should attend us everywhere that life flows and acts . . . at the bench, at the table, at work, at rest, at play; on working days and holidays . . . at home and on the road . . . in order that the flame to live should not extinguish in mankind."[32]

Aino and Alvar Aalto paid particular attention to the coordination of everyday activities when designing the unit at the *Minimum Apartment Exhibition.* Aino Aalto's kitchen diagrams are particularly interesting because they take into account the movement of the body; for instance, the woman reaching into the kitchen cabinets and pulling out a cutting board (fig. 60). The body responded to the environment and vice versa—a perfect synthesis. It is interesting to compare the Aaltos' approach to body and movement in space with Ernst Neufert's (1900–1986) diagrams in his hugely influential book *Bauentwurslehre: Handbuch für den Baufachmann, Bauherren, Lehrenden und Lernenden* (Architect's Data) from 1936, the first attempts to codify and systematize the relationship between the human body and everyday architectural space. Again the Aaltos' contribution was to emphasize mobility over the static cataloguing of postures and programmatic tasks.

Aalto developed his thinking about space and dynamism sometime in 1931 when he read Moholy-Nagy's *Von Material zu Architektur,* which introduced him to the notion of the dynamic and expansive space of modernity. Moholy-Nagy identifies the complex relationships and forces that constitute life as it is experienced. Architecture is no longer to be understood as a mathematical construction but as a set of relationships that allow a variety of sensory experiences to occur. Moholy-Nagy conceived architecture not as a collection of isolated objects but as an organic entity existing within a larger spatial field of dynamic forces, in which near and far, foreground and background, above and below endlessly fluctuate and merge. His definition of space was simple: "Space is reality." [33] Architecture was understood as a "dynamic structure for mastering life as it constitutes an organic part of life itself." [34]

Von Material zu Architektur led Aalto to expand his thinking about architectural geography beyond particular locales, to encompass the expansive space of modernity, and to represent this new spatial concept that was beyond the eye to

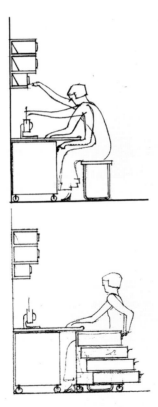

63. *Housewife working, seated in front of sliding units in the minimum apartment kitchen.*

60. Aino Aalto, kitchen sections, "Minimum Dwelling"

see. Here the still young medium of photography began to play an important role. Moholy-Nagy's trademark photographic techniques—oblique angles, spatial layering, and aerial views, which Aalto soon adopted—captured the key qualities of the space of modernity: expansiveness, dynamism, and simultaneity. Moholy contended that "through photography we can participate in a new experience of space. . . . With photographers' help, and with that of the new school of architects, we have an enlargement and sublimation of our appreciation of space, the comprehension of a new spatial culture."[35]

The new spatial culture promoted by Moholy-Nagy countered the homogeneous abstraction of Cartesian space. Modern space was based on an interlacing of actual forces in different scales and registers—psychological, physiological, biological, economical, and even political—which formed a large, integrated force field. A now lesser-known Bauhaus member, Siegfried Ebeling (1894–1963), defined the task of the new century as "cultivating a new human type where *constructeur* and artist meet, a person who is discerning and striving to a new evaluation of himself and of his connections to the mystery of the world which he radiates outwards." He put forward an idea of "biological architecture" and talked about an "integrated existence that relates all parts with one another and adjusts automatically to exterior space." The "geo-political" and "geo-social" dimension of collective human life on earth was based on the notion that everything and everybody was interconnected through mysterious ether. As a result he saw "nations' most immediate natural obligations as part of a complex system of the earth organism."[36]

It is unlikely that Aalto ever read Ebeling, but traces of the German's thinking are present when Aalto starts to make connections between human habitation, nature, and geopolitics in the article "The Geography of the Housing Question," published in *Architecture and Society* (1932; fig. 61). In it he continued to examine the idea of an organic and dynamic approach to design through large-scale planning, making a case for how Finland could become part of "A-Europe."[37] *Acceptera* had defined the criteria on the same lines as Delaisi: "A-Europe is like a big 'organism,' where all functions are at once specialized and centralized, and where all cells from small gardens to the big factories and banks are dependent on one another."[38] A-Europe thus participated in the processes of modernization, being connected by infrastructural networks such as railroads, whereas B-Europe was isolated, and, hence, inorganic, and therefore did not participate in economic progress (figs. 62, 63). The authors distinguished between the city as a "living organism" and the city as a "work of art": "A city as a work of art is a dangerous concept. [A city] is not something permanently static like a sculpture or a painting. It is a result of real needs, whose changing nature should be taken into consideration. A city is an expression of movement, work, life of a thousand different kinds; it is a living organism. . . . The environment is and must be a changing entity."[39]

Aalto's chosen illustrations—images of fields with crops organized in quiltlike patterns—demonstrate what he learned from Moholy-Nagy: the aerial view was

ALVAR AALTO

BOSTADSFRÅGANS GEOGRAFI

Storstaden i sin reala form eller som embryot i allt vad befolkningsanhopning och produktionskoncentrering innebär är en direkt produkt av industrialismen. Dess nära nog absoluta kontrastförhållande till landet — landsorten och dess individualism — är allom bekant, ehuru få göra sig mödan att undersöka vad kontrasten i verkligheten innebär. — I korthet: vi ha två livsformer (stad och land) — A- och B-Europa ha de kallats — där ett flertal livsfunktioner ha olika praktisk lösning. Av den summariska tillväxt som kommit A till del uppstår ett för vår planlösa kultur typiskt kontrastförhållande med desorganiserande verkan för utvecklingen.

Följande påståenden ha ofta gjorts: den industriella utvecklingen, de tillämpade vetenskaperna, uppfinningar etc. innebära icke enbart koncentreringstendenser, man kan alltid hos dem finna även en motsatt tendens — uppfinningar som underlätta decentraliserade bostadsformer, organiseringsmöjligheter för trafik och samfärdsel, distansernas minskning genom snabbare fortskaffningsmedel, förbättring av personlig kontakt — trots distanser — genom telefon och radio etc.

[top] 61. Aalto, "The Geography of the Housing Question," *Arkitektur och Samhälle* (Architecture and Society) (Stockholm, 1932), 87

[bottom left] 62. "Industry: A-Europe," ca. 1930, *Acceptera* (Stockholm: Tiden, 1980), 16

[bottom right] 63. "Agriculture: B-Europe," *Acceptera*, 18

the best way to represent the expansive and interconnected notion of modernity, as the images of landscapes formed by settlements, agriculture, and infrastructure gave a graphic imprint of the dynamic processes of modernization. These images start also to address what Ebeling called the "geo-political" or "geo-social" dimension of human life—even if politics separate us, our coexistence is shaped by and shapes the earth we share (figs. 64, 65).

The vitalist notion of "life" framed the key artistic problem that unites all the strands of modern art: how to study and represent something that is constantly in flux. Aalto's chosen images capture some key formal tropes. The landscapes are depicted as patterns that can go on forever, infinitely multiplying themselves in different scales (for example, individual plants form rows of crops, which in turn form fields, and so on). Diagonals offset the balance and introduce a sense of depth to the images. The layering of elements emphasizes simultaneity of information and events.

Indeed, Aalto's article might seem like a mere copy of the chapter "The New Cultural Situation: A- and B-Europe" in *Acceptera* if not for the photographs that accompanied it, which pick up on the theme of life. While the images in *Acceptera* merely catalogued and illustrated the differences between A- and B-Europe (depicting farmers with modern machinery contrasted with horses pulling plows,

64. Aerial views. From Aalto, "The Geography of the Housing Question," 91.

and so on), Aalto's photographs made the new space of modernity manifest. Moholy's description of aerial photography can further help us conceptualize the new spatial order marked by surprising relationships, juxtapositions, and overlaps happening around us: "The photograph . . . produces space without existing spatial structure only by articulation on the plane. . . . So it seems that the most abstract experiment of space-time articulation carries a sensible reality. . . . Such experiments may signalize a spatial order in which not single structural parts . . . will play the important part, but the relationships of neighbor units, buildings and free areas, shelter and leisure, production and recreation, leading towards a biologically right mode of living, most probably through a right regional planning; towards a unity of city and land."[40]

Aalto's article and the images that accompanied it supported the idea that in the modern, increasingly international and industrialized world, conventional distinctions between city and country could not hold. The new view of nature was that it was the outcome of the interplay of multiple forces—natural, social, and economic. Indeed, an aerial view of the earth's crust (still something of a novelty in the 1930s) revealed that it was imprinted by mechanical processes and overlaid by manufactured constructions: one could no longer speak of "pure nature." In "The Geography of the Housing Question" Aalto called this hybrid *land urbanization,* a combination of land forms, habitations, and modern infrastructure, and made the case that it followed the organizational principles of nature: "The telephone, with its trunk lines, local exchanges, and branch lines, is organizationally the closest thing possible to *the biological order of nature, the communication between locally clustered cells.* . . . The economy of the telephone, however, leads to an organic ramification of housing areas, *permitting geographic decentralization, but calling for local clusters.*"[41]

This emphasis on the ordering of territory by natural and organic means was antithetical to the static, conventional way that political boundaries ordered space. As Aalto saw it, all spatial boundaries were multifaceted and could be overcome. The new approach to organizing territory, in his view, should be through large-scale infrastructural interventions.

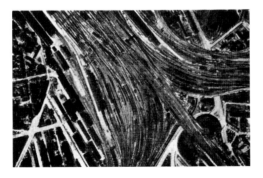

65. Aerial views. From Aalto, "The Geography of the Housing Question," 88.

In another article from the same year, "The Housing System in the USSR," Aalto offered an even more encompassing approach to the planning of large territories. In this case natural resources work as the main organizing strategy (fig. 66). Aalto discussed Ernst May's design proposal for the agricultural city of Tirgan, whose site plan was reproduced. The design was based on a continuous checkerboard matrix, consisting of so-called *mikrorayons,* high-density residential quarters each containing housing and all communal functions, such as day-care centers, schools, laundry facilities, and dining halls. The splitting of the urban fabric into such units allowed the "organic shifting of city boundaries and close calibration to topography" and other natural registers.[42] Here, too, Aalto used the term *land urbanization* to describe a "geographical 'urban plan' for the whole country [where] all towns are mere details of a larger plan."[43]

As the two articles—"The Geography of the Housing Question" and "Housing System in the USSR"—show, in the early 1930s Aalto and many of his continental colleagues were beginning to see the Soviet Union as the only place where radical experiments in modern architecture were possible, and perhaps the only hope for the future of the modern movement.

Indeed, there were many reasons to look east, not the least of which were economic. The opening of the Frankfurt CIAM meeting in 1929 coincided with the stock market crash on Wall Street, but the crisis had not deeply struck Russia because of its low industrial output and strong government control of currency markets. The USSR had just launched a five-year plan in 1928, and the goal was to turn its predominantly agrarian economy into a powerful urbanized, industrial one. The scale of the building operation this provoked was unprecedented: fifty million people were relocated into new industrial areas built around the country. The Russians were thinking and operating at a scale that Western architects had only dreamed about. The country, which spans half the globe, might have held a particular appeal for those who were endorsing pan-European and internationalist themes, at least until they learned of Stalin's brutal treatment of minority populations and of his forced mass migrations.

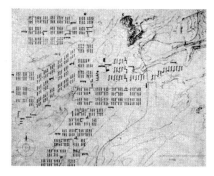

66. Ernst May, plan for the city of Tirgan. From Aalto, "The Housing System in the USSR," *Granskaren* (July–August 1932), 104.

Aalto got firsthand information about the developments in Russia from several western European colleagues who had taken jobs in the Soviet government. These included, most significantly, Hans Schmidt, Mart Stam, and Ernst May. During a visit to Berlin in the fall of 1931, Aalto heard Stam lecture on the industrial towns he was helping to plan in the Soviet Union. In 1932 Hans Schmidt and his wife visited Aalto in Turku on their way back to Germany after a two-year stay in the Soviet Union. Stam and May led teams of architects and urban planners from western Europe in charge of planning new industrial towns, predominantly in Siberia, which was rich in natural resources. The city of Magnitogorsk in southern Siberia was one of the largest of the coal-producing planned urban centers on which the two collaborated. By that time Finland's relationship to Russia had improved. Whereas in the 1920s it was marked by suspicion and hostility, by the end of the decade Finns realized that the Soviet Union was there to stay. The turning point came in early 1932, when Finland and the Soviet Union signed a treaty on "non-aggression and the peaceful settlement of disputes."

The immense Soviet plans offered a radically new approach to spatial planning and governance and stimulated great interest among western modernists. Instead of political or ethnic considerations, it was the distribution of natural and human resources and geographic formations like rivers and mountains that drove the planning. This approach averted hierarchies of center and periphery, city and countryside, and the endless quarrels between different national constituencies. In a similar vein, these plans were not limited to individual republics but rather applied to the vast empire in its entirety, as the new planned cities formed an urban and agricultural network that spanned the Soviet Union from western Europe to the Sea of Japan. The new cities were strategically near mines and rivers so that efficient use could be made of raw materials, energy sources, and transportation routes. New housing quarters could be added as the need for workers grew. The Soviet model of urbanization truly reflected the processes of modernization—industrialization and internationalization—and embraced an elastic and expansive notion of space that met the constant demand for change. Perhaps most importantly, the Soviet experiments were a dream come true for modernist urban planners: for the first time they were able to put their ideas into practice on a large scale.

These Soviet planning principles made sense from the Finnish perspective. Some 70 percent of the country's population still lived in rural areas, mostly on small farms. The production facilities of the country's large paper and lumber industry were distributed in small towns along the main water routes.[44] "The Geography of the Housing Question" applies lessons learned from Soviet plans by bridging the gap between country and city with a series of smaller semi-urban cluster settlements, organized around the country's major infrastructures, both natural and manufactured (rivers, highways, and railways). At times, Aalto's model reads as a critique of centralized urbanization and the very cities he had come to love, notably Stockholm, Paris, and Berlin: "Industrialism has given rise in its infancy to an uncritical centralization of population; in the future, counter-balancing forces will come into play. Every new invention facilitates communication between people in some way, and distances are becoming irrelevant to them. Anything that is unsound and exaggerated in the town-country relationship will fall away naturally and be replaced by equilibrium."[45]

Although Aalto had never been too keen on the Finnish countryside, he at this point came to terms not only with Finns' traditional attachment to the land but also with the economic realities and internal geographic dynamics within the country. Even the Torch Bearers, known as promoters of urban culture, came to realize by the late 1920s that it was not enough to establish a network of cos-mopolitan centers and likeminded people throughout Europe. It is interesting to compare Aalto's call for decentralization with the views of *Tulenkantajat*'s new editor in chief, Erkki Vala, who wrote in a 1929 editorial:

UNTIL NOW Helsinki was considered the nerve center of Finnish intellectual life. WE CLAIM that the country's intellectual life does not have any single nerve center. It has multiple nerve centers.
UNTIL NOW only the intellectual life of the capital has triggered interest.
WE ARE GOING also to follow the intellectual movements of the countryside.[46]

Vala's words are emblematic of the fact that by 1929 the group originally known for its celebration of the cosmopolitan lifestyle had matured into thinking that a broader and more nuanced territorial dynamic lay at the heart of modernity. They began to consider Finland a kind of subnetwork spanning the whole country nested within the international network of locales. The two scales supported each other: international collaboration and commerce required strong national economy, and a strong national economy required resource management across the country. The interest in restructuring the countryside was also response to the resistance to internationalization. The American stock market crash had demonstrated the vulnerability of worldwide markets. In the West, the world eco-nomic downturn made the internationalist ambitions of both communism and capitalism suspect, threats to national cultural and economic integrity. Conspiracy theories about various worldwide plots for economic dominance were rampant. In Finland, as elsewhere, this led to the emergence of ultra-right-wing nationalist groups, like the Lapua Movement, which was growing in some small western towns.[47] The countryside needed this restructuring.

Since modern architecture had by that time become synonymous with inter-nationalization, it too suffered its first setbacks in early 1930s. The backlash against modernism was shared by different political systems. The Soviet Union's commitment to international modern architecture lasted only until about 1933.[48] André Lurçat, traveling from Moscow back to Paris via Helsinki in spring 1934, surely brought Aalto the news about the change in the intellectual, political, and artistic climate. Around the same time, modern architecture also started to come under attack in the West. Hitler associated it with communism and preferred a neoclassical foundation for the *Heimatstil* he was developing for both monumental and domestic architecture.

The story of the Artek furniture company, Aalto's venture into commercial design and manufacturing, can be told within the economic and political context of the early 1930s, which tried to reconcile national interests with increasing internationalism. The saga began when Aalto started collaborating with the Turku-based furniture maker Otto Korhonen on the furnishings for the 1930 *Minimum Apartment Exhibition*.[49] The ensemble encompassed a cantilevered living-room chair with tubular steel frame and bent plywood-seat, designed by Aalto, and a set of wooden dining room chairs, codesigned with Korhonen. Aalto presented his next lineage of furniture in summer 1932 at the Standard Furnishings exhibition at the Nordic Building Fair in Helsinki. Among the items was what later became known as the Paimio chair, fabricated by Korhonen's Huonekalu-ja Rakennustyötehdas. The chair consisted of two components, both made of wood: a seat formed by a single plywood surface bent into an L-shape and rolled into a circle at both ends, and a supporting leg and arm rest made by "gluing together specially molded layers of solid wood" by hand (fig. 67).[50] Korhonen's pioneering contribution was to develop seriality aimed toward greater variability; the seat was produced in a special mold that allowed production of numerous variants. New models soon followed: the L-shaped furniture—a leg is screwed from beneath onto a horizontal surface—came out in 1933 and was first used at the Viipuri Library.

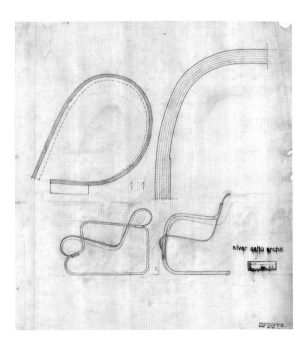

67. Aalto, Paimio chair, details and elevations, 1931

The impetus for using wood did not come out of the blue but originated from the protectionist policies introduced in Finland, as elsewhere, during economic recession. At that time, the Finnish government began taking a more active role in the coordination of trade agreements, including assigning special quotas for both exports and imports. Bentwood as a material had in this context the virtue of being both economical and thoroughly Finnish—it was made in its entirety of Finnish birch, not least because the importation of steel, the preferred material of modern furniture, became restricted. The fact that as soon as Aalto's furniture became more "Finnish" its appeal rose overseas further underscores the complex convergence of internationalism and nationalism at this point in history. A year after Aalto exhibited the Paimio chair at the Nordic Building Congress, Aalto-designed wooden furniture won the gold medal at the Milan Triennale and was displayed in the Fortnum and Mason Department Store in London.[51] Although Aalto's wooden furniture had been exported through exclusive contacts with firms in Zurich, London, and Stockholm since 1932, the volume increased. In 1935, responding to the growing demand, Nils-Gustav Hahl (1904–1941), an art historian and friend of the Aaltos, suggested founding a company to coordinate the business of manufacturing and export.[52] The international distribution network grew soon after that to include Amsterdam and New York. By the late 1930s, 50 percent of production went to London and 25 percent to other countries.

Calibrating nationalist sentiments with internationalism became Artek's ethos. "For Increased Global Activity" ("*For ökad mondial aktivitet*") became the company motto. Importantly, the three main partners in the enterprise—Aalto, Hahl, and Maire Gullichsen (1907–1990), a patron of the arts and an heiress of Finland's largest forestry company, A. Ahlström—used the concept "mondial" in their shared mother tongue, Swedish, instead of the concept "international." It fit their emphasis on global reach beyond the limited zone of mostly western European countries that had participated in international organizations in the 1920s—a bold idea considering that the product was made in a single factory and mostly by hand.[53] At the same time, Artek's advertising slogan for the domestic market, "Made at home—known all over the world," reflected the economic policy of protectionism, whose goal was to guard the Finnishness of products and capital. A visiting card from the early years depicted the roster of Artek's distribution centers abroad using internationalism as a marketing tool (fig. 68). Patriotic sentiments were thus channeled into pride over Finnish products and exports, an attitude that still drives Finnish industry. Internationalism also meant openness to foreign artistic influence: to be internationally competitive required products that were both exotic as well as in tune with international trends. To keep these lines of influence open, the Artek gallery—a not-for-profit arm of the company dedicated to promoting modern art to the Finnish public—exhibited the work of such artists as Fernand Léger and Alexander Calder, as well as older craft items and archaeological objects.

To be sure, Artek's brand of international design was very different from the notion of international architecture conceived some ten years earlier. By the mid-1930s the League of Nations proved incapable of handling the political and financial problems caused by the economic recession. In the vacuum left by its failure, most nations, including Finland, did what they had done in the past, developing bilateral agreements one at a time. The ever more international world was thus not as harmonious as internationalists had hoped. However, Aalto—never fond of the administrated internationalism practiced by groups like CIAM in the first place—and his fellow founders of Artek were quick to adjust to this new international landscape, seeing internationalism and nationalism no longer as ideals but as pragmatic constraints on a business plan. Like the Finnish government, the company promptly sought strategic partners. Its business abroad was often initiated and bolstered by a network of loyal friends: Sigfried Giedion in Zurich, James Johnson Sweeney (curator of architecture at the Museum of Modern Art) in New York, and Philip Morton Shand (critic for *Architectural Review*) in London. Rather than seeing internationalism as a homogenizing force, Artek's leaders were well aware that operating internationally in the 1930s required responsiveness to the increasingly volatile geopolitical and economic conditions. They were, for example, swift to recognize America's emerging economic power while realizing that the European continent, particularly Germany, was becoming less welcoming for modern architecture and design. Therefore, fifteen years after getting his first taste of the world beyond Finland during his trip to Riga, where he had celebrated the vitalist merging of cultures within the ever-expansive space of modernity, Aalto could see that internationalism was increasingly bound up with harsh and sometimes inflexible geopolitical and economic realities.

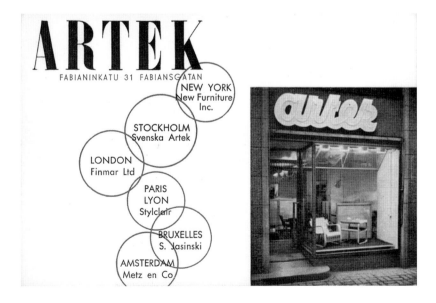

68. Artek business card, late 1930s

When Alvar Aalto started to engage in the discussion about urban and national planning in the early 1930s, the combination of the economic recession and the rise of the extreme right had diminished the prospects for architects, particularly modern architects, in western Europe. The situation in Finland was different, however. Except for a brief downturn in the early 1930s, the interwar years there were marked by economic growth as the country developed from a supplier of raw materials to a producer of advanced industrial products.[1] During this period many single-unit factories started to develop into multiregional, export-oriented companies.

Industry has historically played a significant social and political role in Finland. During the 1940s industry joined forces with the public sector to help reconstruct the country, which was hard hit by the Second World War. Economic interest merged with nationalist sentiments, and the era gave birth to a "patriotic manager" type of leader, who understood industry's role in ensuring the economic and social well-being of the nation.[2] Artturi Ilmari Virtanen's 1945 Nobel Prize in chemistry for his work in animal nutrition contributed to making industrial and technological prowess, along with the country's natural setting and cultural achievements, integral to Finland's national identity.[3]

As Aalto's connections to Finnish industry and local governments grew closer during this period, his thinking about architecture's social and geopolitical function started to include economic, social, and even security concerns. His professional activities grew to encompass roles as a businessman (1935–), a wartime public relations figure (1939–), the head of the Finnish reconstruction office (1942–47) established by the Association of Finnish Architects (SAFA), and the chairman of SAFA (1943–58). Starting around 1940, his commissions started to include regional plans, a subject which will be elaborated in this chapter. Extended stays in the United States, with its ethnically heterogeneous population and expansive territory, led him to think differently about the development, power structures, and spatial governance of his homeland. Exchanges with leading American architects, critics, and business leaders provided him with a new framework for thinking about the relationships between individuals, communities, private entities, and the public sector.

The year 1935 marks, in many ways, a turning point for Aalto, not least because in that year he moved his family and office to Helsinki. In addition to meeting Maire Gullichsen, the daughter of Finland's leading industrial families, the Ahlströms, who became a founding partner and a shareowner of Artek that year, he developed a productive professional relationship with her husband, Harry Gullichsen (1902–1954), an economist and a managing director of her family's business, A. Ahlström Company, a manufacturer of forestry products and Finland's largest industrial conglomerate at the time. Harry Gullichsen became Aalto's most important repeat client and an access point to the nation's political and economic elite. In addition to completing the family's residence, Villa Mairea, in 1938–39, they worked together on many large-scale planning and building projects for the growing company.

Aalto gained a new outlook on Finland, its future, and how it should be run after Gullichsen invited him to join a think tank of politicians, industrialists, and cultural leaders charged with shaping a vision for Finnish society based on American-style economic pragmatism and left-leaning social ideals. Gullichsen aligned himself with the American technocracy movement of the 1920s and 1930s, advocating the view that engineers and other professionals were more analytical and therefore could do a better job of governance than could politicians, who were too caught up in ideological disputes. At the same time, following the Swedish model, he believed firmly that a market economy provided the best foundation for building a modern welfare state and promoted social reforms and programs. Both the husband and wife believed that with privilege came social responsibility, such as providing quality housing for workers. The first assignments that Aalto's office received from the company entailed refurbishing canteens, playgrounds, nurseries, and clubs for workers and their families in existing factory towns. It must be noted that the economic power of the country was at that time still in the hands of a few Swedish-speaking families, who owned most of the country's factories. As a Swedish-speaker himself, Aalto fit right in.

The biggest commission came in 1936, when A. Ahlström, along with four other paper-producing companies, selected Aalto to design a new industrial community around a new sulfate pulp mill in Sunila located some 100 kilometers west of Helsinki. The project was planned and executed in three phases: the General Plan of the Town of Sunila (1936), the Pulp Mill (1936–37), and a Residential Area (1936–52). When completed, the project encompassed almost sixty buildings. The industrial buildings were on two neighboring islands, not far from a major port in Kotka, a town at the mouth of the Kymijoki River, which offers access to the country's inland water network and vast reserves of wood. The housing area was located on the mainland and was conceived as Finland's first forest town. The factory proper was located atop a rocky hill, which the company originally suggested leveling. The industrial complex, puffing away smoke and spitting out pulp, and juxtaposed with dramatic rock formations and pine forests, provided an ideal synthesis of nature and technology (fig. 69). The siting recalls the sports stadium project from 1927, only this time industry was being celebrated as the highest level of cultural achievement. The massive infrastructural undertaking required construction of new rail lines and a new harbor jetty (fig. 70). The scale of the Sunila project and the fact that it took just two years to build—the factory began production in May 1938—speaks to the economic and political power of the Finnish paper industry at the time.[4]

Upon completion of the main part of the plant and the housing area in 1938, Aalto had this to say: "The Sunila Sulphate Pulp Mill came about as a result of co-operation between some of the leading names in big industry and did not derive from a single group or consortium—an occurrence with few parallels anywhere else. Through it, the mill has attained a kind of national rationale status,

69. Aalto, Sunila Pulp Mill (1936–38)

70. Aerial view nr. 3560 of Sunila Pulp Mill from 1930s showing logs being floated to the factory

for both organization and the scale of production. As such, it can be linked to the results of a variation of free co-operation which, without theoretical 'planned economy' arrangements and political coercion, originated primarily in the Nordic countries and, in its own way, has left us with a solid reputation internationally."[5] The statement suggests that at the time of worldwide economic recession and rise of totalitarian regimes all over Europe, Aalto believed that Finland would be best served when industry would be allowed to follow its own rationale, mostly free of government regulation and oversight.

Although Aalto cited the Nordic countries as a model for large-scale industrial cooperation, one needs to go beyond Europe to find a contemporary example of the integration of community planning, industrial production, and nature that characterized Sunila's executed plan. Those that come closest are the American government programs and projects implemented between 1933 and 1937 under President Franklin D. Roosevelt's New Deal, which were intended to improve industrial and agricultural production and employent, coordinate the use of natural resources, and make social assistance widely available in the areas hit hardest by the Great Depression of the 1930s. The most ambitious of these, the Tennessee Valley Authority (TVA), was in charge of developing a large area of the Tennessee River Valley, consisting of Tennessee and parts of Alabama, Mississippi, Kentucky, Georgia, North Carolina, and Virginia, with the goals of providing navigation, electrical power, and flood control for the region.

The notion of a region was significant as American regionalist planners, such as Benton MacKaye, managed to convince politicians that working for the benefit of a larger region required overriding the interests and responsibilities of individual states.[6] American regionalist planning ideas challenged Europeans, including Aalto, to privilege the logic of industry and natural resources over state and national politics and boundaries. Furthermore, the word *region* is in itself, as the political scientist Perry Anderson has pointed out, ambiguous many ways. One can talk about a natural region, an "ecologically bounded zone, demarcated by climate, fauna, soil, rivers, and mountains," or a political region containing several states.[7] As the TVA experiment indicated, region could also refer to an economically depressed zone as a means of acknowledging the effects of the unequal economic development of capitalism. Finland, which was mostly agrarian, certainly fit this description well into the 1930s.

The term was introduced into mainstream architectural discourse—and probably also to Aalto's architectural lexicon—by Lewis Mumford (1895–1990), a prolific and influential writer and, along with MacKaye, one of the founders of the Regional Planning Association of America (RPAA) in the 1920s. In his 1924 book *Sticks and Stones: A Study of American Architecture and Civilization* he used the term to counter architects' obsession with cosmetic styles, which overlooked local material resources and conditions, an idea central to regionalist planning. Writing in *Technics and Civilization,* published 1934, Mumford clarified that regionalism was not a reaction against technology and modernization but a higher form of thinking about the possibilities of new technologies. He distinguished between the "paleotechnic" and "neotechnic" periods to describe society's transition to light, transportable technology and energy. Paleotechnic industry was fueled by coal and emblematized by the grim working and living conditions of industrial unskilled labor. The neotechnic era began with the discovery of how to produce, store, and distribute electrical power, which allowed decentralization to occur. In Mumford's vision, producing clean energy and living closer to nature were among the benefits of new technologies, while proliferation of scientific knowledge and skilled labor would lead to wider distribution of wealth.

All in all, Mumford's regionalism was a broad cultural theory, progressive and idealistic, with economic, demographic, political, and territorial implications. At times he explained his thinking along Marxist lines: capitalism had led to an unhealthy accumulation of wealth, populations, and industry, and this in turn had led to the crisis of urban living conditions and would eventually cause the demise of the countryside as well. Instead of monoculture, he promoted economic and ecological diversity, with everybody and everything existing in complex causal relationships to one another. It was thus important "to see the interdependence of the city and country, to realize that the growth and concentration of one is associated with the depletion and impoverishment of the other."[8]

Seeking alternatives to both capitalist creeds and modes of governance, Mumford drew from the Russian anarchist and naturalist Petr Kropotkin, whose work Aalto also had read as a young man. Kropotkin promoted the decentralization of power and saw in centralized industry the source of all the evils associated with the Industrial Revolution: unhealthy living conditions, pollution, class struggle, and specialization at the expense of economic diversity. In *Fields, Factories, and Workshops; or, Industry Combined with Agriculture and Brain Work with Manual Work* (1901), Kropotkin argued for an alternative: small, self-sufficient communities distributed along waterways, combining industrial and agricultural production, which would take into account the significance of natural resources in determining settlement patterns and economic well-being.

Kropotkin's planetary model comes close to many of the ideas we associate today with globalization. He saw the world as a dynamic entity where individual locales were increasingly interdependent on one another. He predicted many of globalization's evils and planned for them—urging, for example, self-sufficiency over dependency on imported goods. Mumford saw that Kropotkin's new world order was already becoming a reality in the 1930s: "The basis of the material elements in the new industry is neither national nor continental but planetary: this is equally true, of course, of its technological and scientific heritage. A laboratory in Tokio or Calcutta may produce a theory or an invention which will entirely alter the possibilities of life for a fishing community in Norway. Under these conditions, no country and no continent can surround itself with a wall without wrecking the essential, international basis of its technology: so if the neotechnic economy is to survive, it has no alternative other than to organize industry and its polity on a worldwide scale."[9] According to him, in a world restructured by new types of industry and technological know-how, national boundaries were becoming increasingly insignificant. If there was one hindrance to worldwide industrialization and subsequent economic prosperity, it was nationalism, which was on the rise at the time. Mumford ended with a warning note: "Isolation and national hostilities are forms of deliberate technological suicide. The geographical distribution of the rare earths and metals by itself almost establishes that fact."[10]

There are many reasons why American regionalism was a fitting model for Finland. The country's forest industry was by nature decentralized, with its roots in small communities dispersed throughout the country. The industry was already export-oriented—by the mid-1930s, exports accounted for 80 percent of its output. Because of its connection to nature and natural processes and cycles, the industry also exemplified the ideal future technology as defined by Mumford—it benefited from managing natural resources in beneficial ways, at least in theory. The technology transfer and dissemination of technological and scientific know-how that characterized the neotechnic period had already allowed even a remote country like Finland to start developing an equal footing with the traditional industrial and population centers. Industry's adaptation of sulfite pulping technology in the 1890s, some twenty years after the first commercial pulp mill using the method had opened in Sweden, marks the beginning of Finland's transformation into a producer of advanced industrial products.

For a small, newly independent country, the rise in industrial production and technological know-how fulfilled its long-lasting dream of economic self-sufficiency and equal membership in the international community. In many ways Finland could be considered Mumford's model country. Its development from an agrarian to an industrialized nation, in fact, proved Mumford's thesis that in a neotechnical age the center-periphery hierarchy no longer held. Yet there was one aspect of Finnish industrialization that neither Mumford nor Kropotkin accounted for: its great motivation, brought on by national pride and nationalist sentiments triggered by events surrounding the Second World War. I will discuss how regionalism was invested with a complex geopolitical scenario when translated into the Finnish context, but first I will trace Aalto's firsthand exposure to America and the regionalist debates.

Aalto's first trip to the United States took place in fall 1938. There he came into contact with a group of architects, historians, and critics at the Museum of Modern Art (MoMA) interested in finding an approach to architecture and urbanism that would counter the stylistic confines of international modernism. As evidence of the changing interests at the museum, just three years after the exhibition *Modern Architecture Since 1922: International Exhibition* in 1932, which celebrated the International Style, visitors were presented with *Architecture in California, 1935,* which celebrated architecture founded on local conditions and ways of living. Patriotic sentiments certainly played a part in this shift of focus; the motivation was to find an American answer to European modernism.

The second trip, in the spring of 1939, to supervise the construction of the Finnish Pavilion for the New York World's Fair and to attend its opening on April 30, broadened his circle of friends and deepened his knowledge of regionalism. During his stay he attended a conference in Phoenixville, Pennsylvania, where he met Mumford and the Austrian-born architect Richard Neutra (1892–1970), who had helped to introduce modern architecture to southern California. Later he made a cross-country trip to visit Neutra in Los Angeles and William Wurster (1895–1973) in San Francisco. The latter was a leading representative of the Bay Region style of architecture, a local version of modernism characterized by the elimination of the style's most iconic formal tropes—white walls, flat roofs, and strip windows—in favor of the logic of wood construction. The link between the two men had been established the year before when Wurster had traveled to Finland to see Aalto's buildings.

Although at first glance there seems to be nothing inherently Californian in Neutra's buildings—they had clean, crisp lines, flat roofs, and large windows, just like their European counterparts—his ideas about American building technology and the relationship between building and site offered a new way of thinking about architecture's relationship to place and available resources, including labor. Also, while Neutra did not explicitly use the word "regional," his ideas were similar to Mumford's. Neutra, like Mumford after him, distinguished between the paleotechnic period (the first industrial age, dominated by iron and coal) and the neotechnic era (the second industrial age, dominated by alloys and electricity). And Mumford's claim that "instead of bigness and heaviness being a happy distinction, these qualities are now recognized as a handicap: lightness and compactness are the emergent qualities of the neotechnic era," could very well have been written with Neutra's architecture in mind.[11]

Neutra's 1927 book *Wie Baut Amerika?* which Aalto owned, and his 1930 book *Amerika,* published in the series *Neues Bauen in der Welt,* suggest what the two might have talked about. The former focused on the organizational and technical skills of the engineer-architect. Neutra celebrated the industry bible Sweet's building catalogue as a link between the architect, industry, and builders, and praised the standardization of the products it represented as an alternative to the technological determinism and excesses of European machine-age architecture.[12] Neutra believed that "modern technology did not develop randomly, but is a result of numerous steps from the massive, curious wall construction to skeleton construction."[13]

In his second book Neutra explored the geography of new building technologies, arguing that standardization allowed a wider distribution and availability of building products and know-how throughout the country. For this reason he praised lightweight steel construction, a technology easily applicable to disparate geographic conditions. To make his case he cited the change from the paleotechnic to the neotechnic. The former had forced habitation and production to center on material and energy sources, whereas the latter phase allowed the free spread of production and know-how. According to his thesis, the new technologies facilitated a spatial order that dissolved traditional center-periphery hierarchies. California, Neutra's adopted home, was a product of these opportunities.

Wurster, whose work drew on the vernacular tradition, was interested in building technology and was developing prefabricated housing typologies.[14] Judging by his work on a prefabricated house project on his return to Finland, Aalto might have seen Wurster's design for the Unit Steel House of 1937, a one-bedroom dwelling unit based on a four-foot module, a goal of which was to coordinate architecture and newly available standardized building parts, like windows, in order to produce the most economical building. The system paid particular attention to variability within prefabricated design, in which a basic house type, "Scheme A," could be expanded to produce a two-bedroom version, "Scheme B." These ideas found their way to Aalto's prefabrication experiments.[15]

We have no direct records of what Aalto and Wurster discussed during the several days they spent together in the early summer of 1939. But the meeting made a great impression on Aalto—the two men seem to have made plans to establish a research institute with branch offices in different parts of the world. In a letter to Wurster written upon his return to New York, Aalto defines the study of the "technological," "social," and "regional" aspects of architecture as the imagined institute's goals. The value of architectural research became apparent to Aalto: instead of an outcome of a creative individual genius or group, architecture would rely on the global sharing of information—one of the key principles of regionalism as defined by Mumford.

The institute was conceived as small research labs distributed across the globe. Unlike the bureaucratically rigid and top-down CIAM, Aalto and Wurster's organization would be nimble and would work in reverse. With its tentacles reaching far and wide, the institute would gather and spread information around the world, questioning the conventional idea that innovations always disseminate from the center to the periphery: "But research in architecture cannot be carried on in a single laboratory, such as is suitable for research in some technical product. Architecture covers the whole wide field of human activity and human life in its various social and climatic settings. To provide an institute for architectural research is a major world problem today requiring [an] international solution. It can only be solved by various units of a large organization working in different parts of the world."[16] According to Aalto, "some places in the world are more suitable for experimentation in some special field than others. It might be advantageous to localize research in small wooden buildings, for instance, in California and in Finland."[17]

The trip to California made Aalto aware also of fundamental differences between European and American culture and society. He returned to Finland in midsummer 1939 celebrating the state's "mixture of races and cultural impulses."[18] America gave Aalto his first exposure to a country that was truly diverse and international. America's cultural pluralism helped him to acknowledge the nationalist subtext that fueled European architecture and culture, and which would play a role in yet another continentwide war.

Aalto addressed the desire to challenge the very foundation of European nationalism—that is, the idea of the insular, culturally and ethnically homogenous nation—in a lecture in Gothenburg, given a month after World War II started. "Everything good in Finnish culture is the result of the stimulating effect of having two competing languages. . . . Nordic collaboration has had an equally positive effect on Finnish culture. The unity is richer, giving [us] an opportunity to see more clearly both from within and without," he announced.[19] At this point the celebration of transnational collaboration within the Nordic region had gained new urgency. Undoubtedly its aim was also to guarantee Swedish solidarity in the wake of Soviet territorial demands on Finland advanced in the autumn of 1939. Russia's subsequent attack on Finland on November 30 led to worldwide uproar and Russia being expelled from the League of Nations. Mumford was among the first of the American liberal intelligentsia to condemn the Soviet attack.[20]

In that same year Aalto joined forces with his old friend from Stockholm, art historian and critic Gregor Paulsson, and decided to begin a magazine, *The Human Side,* to address the burning cultural, moral, and geopolitical issues of the time. Aalto and Paulsson asked Mumford to contribute. The outline for his article—"Is Collectivization of the Social Organism the Only Alternative to Bourgeois Liberalism and to the Forms of Organization and Culture Inherited from It?"[21] which still survives in the Aalto Archives in Helsinki—reveals that at a time when the world was being divided between East and West, Mumford was seeking a "third way," combining aspects of the two political systems. Aalto endorsed these ideas in a memorandum regarding the magazine as follows: "In the construction of the industrial and productive infrastructure in the country a large amount of socialist ideas have in all peace been integrated with those of capitalism. This has led to an all-embracing, generally accepted social mode of thinking."[22] An essay by the Swedish economist and politician Gunnar Myrdal, entitled "Cultural Race and Blood Race," captured the topical political message of the magazine: how to overcome the national hatred that had dominated European thinking for centuries.

Soon after Russian attack on Finland, which led to the so-called Winter War (1939–40), Aalto was required to work under the control of Ministry of Social Affairs. Besides running his own architectural office—now called "Office A"—as best as he could, Aalto's activities included sending letters and cables to his powerful American friends for assistance. In them he made the claim that Finns represented the Western "free" world, presumably free of any political or racial bias. In his equation, western Europe embodied values of democracy and freedom, the Soviet Union those of tyranny. A letter to Frank Lloyd Wright, written in early January 1940, demonstrates Aalto's mastery of tailoring an argument with this new geopolitical position in mind. It is worth quoting the letter at length to show how Aalto persuaded Finland to align itself with the United States and the West:

As you know, the first real, open fighting of the world war has begun in Finland. It is the Russian terror-system which now shows its will to expand all over the world. Western social thinking—constructive activity—has shown itself more of a success than the Russian collective system can stand. All of us who have worked for a real socially positive future now have the same battle to fight, the battle that has begun here.[23]

The letter also demonstrates that Aalto was particularly aware of the importance of deemphasizing national Finland's motivations, even when writing to gain support for a patriotic cause:

I hope that this will confirm to you the idea that the battle is "our common" —in a way a religious battle—not for a nation, that is an obsolete idea, nor a schematic conception of inherited Western culture, but a battle for the constructive will and the constructive knowledge, which exists in all of us and everywhere in the West. It is a fight of the balanced social progress against modes and systems, which have shown themselves incapable of constructing a development and where blind theory is combined with destructive and profoundly conservative methods.[24]

In an attachment sent to dozens of other friends across the world, Aalto focused on his critique of the Soviet system, which had in its twenty years of existence proved less successful than northern European social democracies in providing a better standard of living to the working class. He described the social model of the Nordic countries as a hybrid between capitalism and socialism, and individualism and collectivism, in Mumfordian terms:

Within the constitution of their states the Northern democratic countries have shown innumerable cases and methods whereby social progress has given permanent results. At the same time as their standard of living has shown an uninterrupted rise they have been able to gain an elastic social system where new and old methods—state socialism side by side with private initiative and co-operative activity—have formed an elastic basis for civic life.[25]

Aalto further shows his political savvy by arguing that the war Finland was fighting was not a territorial dispute but a war over values. He knew well that since the U.S. and Soviet Union were military allies at this point, Americans would support only humanitarian causes. He continues:

The Russian attack on Finland was more directed against a social development which proved superior to the practically untried doctrines of [the] Soviets than by geographical or territorial motives. Because of that the front in Finland is not a national front nor a front of socialism against bourgeoisie but the front no. 1 of the west—the front where the unsuccessful theory overpowered by tsaristic methods stands on one side and a balanced Western social development with a bright future stands on the other side.

After successfully soliciting a check for $1 million from the personal funds of Laurance S. Rockefeller to aid the Finnish war effort (Aalto's cable to Rockefeller had read: SEND LAFAYETTE FIGHTER PLANE CORPS TO HELP US. AALTO), he convinced his superiors that the country would benefit from sending him to America as a sort of one-man propaganda unit in search of additional American sympathy and aid for his beleaguered little nation.[26]

His commission was to last six weeks, but Aalto extended it intentionally as he was certainly interested in getting himself and his family out of harm's way—his patriotism did not extend to a willingness for self-sacrifice. He spent March to October 1940 visiting his American friends, giving lectures, and writing articles to gather assistance for the Finnish war effort. Results of his further fundraising efforts were meager—the Hoover Foundation managed to contribute only $2 million—probably because the United States was still maintaining isolationist policies and hoping to avoid involvement in the European war.[27]

Although Aalto's efforts failed to yield more assistance for the Finnish government, the time spent in America helped Aalto to develop his thinking on architecture's geographic and increasingly political dimension, going beyond the simplistic dichotomy between national and international architectures that had dominated European architectural debates in the early part of twentieth century. His article "Finland" for the July 1940 issue of *Architectural Forum* outlines the alternative: regionalist principles (fig. 71). Aalto starts by situating Finnish architecture in the context of the international modern movement: "In Finland the revolution in architecture is naturally part of the whole international movement, but, at the same time it is not an isolated phenomenon in the country's internal life. As in other countries with a more or less provincial culture, modern architecture did not appear in Finland as a superficial style trend in imitation of the great European centers."[28] Aalto continues: "Even though there is today in Finland, as in all countries, a good deal of superficial modernism, the country itself, its climate, resources, topography and ways of living afford a mass of material which forms a good base for the solution of problems of contemporary architecture."[29]

While Aalto participated in the wider intellectual debates over what constitutes architecture's relationship to a particular geographic location, in the end, "Finland" was aimed at convincing his American audience that the Finns had nothing to do with the (putatively) communist-infested international modern movement. The best of Finnish modern architecture, by which he probably meant his own work,

bore witness to this distance: it had presumably developed independently of International Style, similar to the way Mumford had described the sources of American regionalism. As in the letter to Wright, Aalto avoided using words like *national* or expressions that might suggest that Finland was motivated by a nationalist agenda. He drew attention to Finland's "absence of fortification buildings in the country" not only to emphasize that Finland had throughout history been a victim, not an aggressor, but also to underscore that Finland was committed to the technologically supple architecture outlined by Neutra and Mumford as being characteristic of a neotechnic society: "In the wide open areas in Finland, where great forests, numerous lakes and rapids always have been the country's 'fortifications,' the single house and the embryos of city building have grown without the heavy characteristics which fortification buildings lent to architecture."[30]

Hardly taking into account his earlier infatuation with cities and urban lifestyle, Aalto emphasized decentralization, another touchstone of regionalist thinking. He pointed out that out of a population of three million, only 15 percent of Finns lived in cities. "This is no new phenomenon in Finnish life, but one which goes back centuries. Obviously we have here an excellent basis for the development of architecture and large-scale planning." Because of this, Finland could naturally advance to the neotechnic stage without having faced the ills of industrialization and unhealthy urbanization. He also seemed to imply that, without decentralized power, Finland was free of totalitarianism of any kind; Finns, in other words, minded their own business. Aalto's new Finland was thus naturally inclined to develop its architecture on regionalist lines. He concludes, "A native tradition of frame construction, special ways of living, peculiar climatic conditions—these form a sound beginning for new architecture."[31]

In the same article Aalto put forth his plan for reconstructing and repairing the destruction caused by the Winter War. Basing his proposal on regionalist principles of decentralization and lessons learned from American mass production,

71. Aalto, "Finland," *Architectural Forum*, June 1940, 399

he called for rebuilding in "complete harmony with nature" using "standard types of building."[32] The use of wood formed a further link between American and Finnish building traditions. He cites the planning ideals outlined during the first Russian Five Year Plan as a model, and warns against the "barrack" mentality that followed. He also calls for the creation of new cultural centers, since Finland's second-largest city, Viipuri, had been lost to the Soviet Union.

After the end of the Winter War, Aalto focused his attention on reconstruction. His initial plan was to get American money to fund actual projects. A brochure entitled *Post-War Reconstruction: Rehousing Research in Finland,* published through the Finnish consulate in New York for American distribution, made a case for one of them, an experimental new town entitled "An American Town in Finland." Aalto hoped that the project would raise the interest of the Rockefeller Foundation, which funded humanitarian causes, making the argument that the project yielded information about standardized mass housing beyond Finland. His key words were *flexibility* and *adjustability:* "Standardization here does not mean a formal one with all houses built alike. Standardization will be used mainly as a method of producing a flexible system by which the single house can be made adjustable for families of different sizes, various topographical locations, different exposures, views, etc."[33] The distinction Aalto makes between absolute (the need for standardization) and real conditions (the need for variability) was, perhaps not accidentally, emphasized also by military strategists. Indeed, the chart of variable types in *Post-War Reconstruction* resembles uncannily a troop deployment plan (fig. 72).

Although the funding never came through, Aalto was offered a research position at the Massachusetts Institute of Technology to pursue the project. He joined the MIT faculty as a visiting professor in the fall of 1940. At the beginning of October his students began to work on developing the project laid out in the brochure: to design the first of many prospective "American Towns" in Finland. The first task was to design a wooden single-family home based on the idea of flexible standardization. As further proof that Aalto sought to avoid any semantic or stylistic references to Finnish national culture, the diagrams produced by the students rejected the idea that design should be based on a single overruling formal or organizational idea. Instead, the architecture emerged from a "design field" that took various factors into consideration: "nature, orientation, seclusion," followed by "plan experiments" and "size experiments" (fig. 73). The method yielded various types of dwellings that were organized in a matrix that showed twenty to thirty variations of each standard house type, according to differing site conditions. The studies cited positive and negative factors of a generic site (fig. 74). Other factors that influenced the planning and siting of the house included size, family requirements, and natural conditions.[34] In designing a house that could be repeated, Aalto created units that could be endlessly enhanced and varied—a prototype deployable to different sites. Unfortunately, Aalto's involvement in the studio was cut short just ten days into the semester when the approaching Continuation War sent him hastening back to Finland in October 1940.

By that time, the peace treaty signed in March 1940 had forced Finland to cede the eastern part of Carelia to Russia. The loss of the province, which had been considered the heartland of Finnish culture, led to a second wave of what might be called Carelianism. The first wave had taken place at the turn of the century, when National Romantic scholars, artists, and architects made pilgrimages to the province to document its buildings, folklore, and way of life, reading them as expressions of a hidden national ethos. The second wave was a kind of quiet expression of protest and mourning: countless exhibitions were mounted and magazine articles and books published, of which the best known, *Carelia: Land of Memories* (1940), was by Olavi Paavolainen, the pioneer of Finnish literary modernism.[35] The book catalogued buildings, people, and landscapes in every town and village in the lost territory. The Carelian coats of arms on the cover reframed the significance of the province in light of the war: rather than the heartland of Finland, it was the locus of the great battle between East and West (fig. 75).

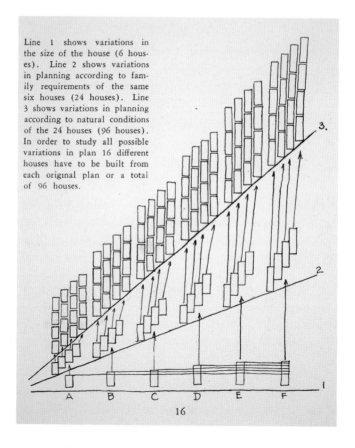

Line 1 shows variations in the size of the house (6 houses). Line 2 shows variations in planning according to family requirements of the same six houses (24 houses). Line 3 shows variations in planning according to natural conditions of the 24 houses (96 houses). In order to study all possible variations in plan 16 different houses have to be built from each original plan or a total of 96 houses.

72. Aalto, diagram showing the process of creating variations of a single-family house, based on "size of house" (line 1), "family requirements" (line 2), and "natural conditions" (line 3), from *Post-War Reconstruction: Rehousing Research in Finland,* 16

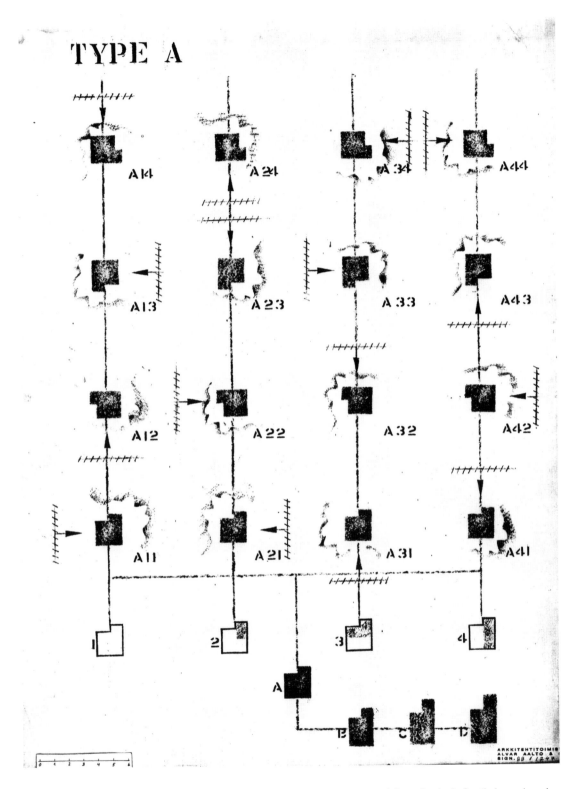

73. Aalto with MIT students, chart showing variability of a single-family house based on site conditions

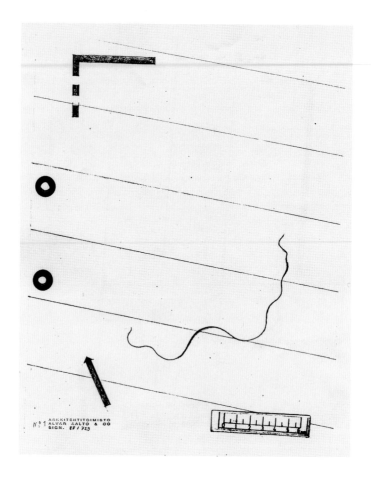

The loss of a beloved region might at least in part explain why the new AA-system of houses designed during the interim peace combined strategic planning with nationalist sentiments. The first series, commissioned before the war in 1937, had ended up bearing Gullichsen's pragmatist stamp: the goal was to produce large quantities of modern, practical, inexpensive worker houses.[36] In the late 1930s, hundreds of units were built in company towns, where the factory acted as developer, planner, builder, landlord or real-estate agent, mortgage-holder, and bank. Regrettably, these were not always architecturally exciting. Photographs of housing estates built before the war to Aalto's designs in Inkeroinen, Sunila, Valkeakoski, and Varkaus by Tampella OY, a manufacturer of paper products, make manifest the bleakness that results from too much uniformity (fig. 76).

The second series paid particular attention to the landscape and topography. Variability became the key (fig. 77). Aalto started with two new versions of a basic plan for a standardized housing unit: a V-shaped plan, in which a bedroom

74. Aalto with MIT students, chart showing how a single "Type A" home responds to site conditions

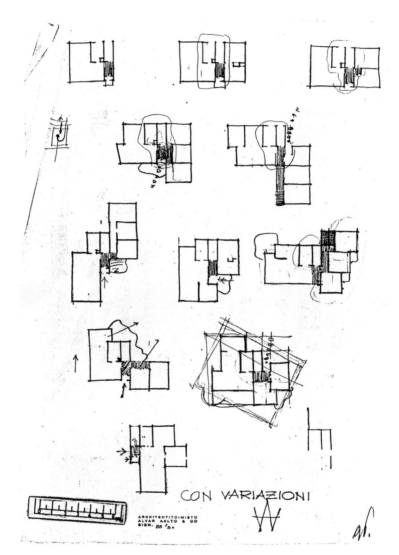

75. Cover of Olavi Paavolainen, *Karjala Muistojen Maa* (Carelia: Land of Memories) (Helsinki: Otava, 1940)

76. Tampella House catalogue, 1941, showing the first completed phase of the worker housing for Sunila Pulp Mill, 1936–38

77. Aalto, Con Variazioni, c. 1940, pencil on paper

wing fans out from a core building, and a so-called growing house, in which additional spaces can be added to a core unit consisting of a living room, kitchen, and bathroom (fig. 78). The designs demonstrate an acceptance of the existing conditions, both in terms of program and site. Regionalist mutualism with the site gains a picturesque twist in a 1941 study for a prefabricated summer cottage, also conceived for mass production although never built (fig. 79). The plan shows how the massing of the building negotiates details of different landscape features, such as rocks and trees, and creates outdoor living areas through massing and paving. The building consisted of a bedroom wing, a living area, and a semi-open kitchen and dining area, loosely configured around landscape features.

Aalto's 1941 article "On Carelian Architecture" synthesizes many of the architect's ideas about flexibility, site, and vernacular typology into a theory of regionalist architecture with a patriotic subtext. He starts by provocatively proclaiming that "it is difficult, even unnecessary to draw national borders when it comes to material culture."[37] The Carelian vernacular should therefore be appreciated not as either Russian or Finnish, but as possessing a "culture" able to integrate architectural form, way of life, and physical site. By considering Carelian vernacular architecture as regional rather than national, Aalto denied the new rulers of the province any right of authority over its culture, restating the thesis that cultures are always multifaceted because they are born from varied local conditions. Aalto used the analogy of organic growth to explain how the traditional Carelian farmhouse had evolved from an "embryo" into a large unit based on wealth and need; new units were simply added to the core. Aalto's conceptualizations of an ideal prefabricated house merged the generic and the symbolic aspects of the Carelian vernacular (fig. 80).

Aalto wrote this article during the brief period of peace in 1941 between the Winter War and the Continuation War. Nevertheless, a war of national and racial hatred was consuming most of Europe. From the text we can surmise that he was well aware that the terms *vernacular* and *national* could easily be interpreted as indicating a pro-Nazi aesthetic or ideology. By emphasizing regionalist principles he was distancing the Carelian vernacular from the *Heimatstil*—a coded quasi-vernacular style preferred by Hitler, especially for buildings for the Hitler Youth. For the same reason, perhaps, the nationalist sentiments fueled by the loss of Carelia became invested mostly in the landscape rather than in the architecture. The Ahlström Company's catalogue for its AA House line of 1941 exemplifies this new paradigm. On the cover, a single-family house is overlaid on a photograph of a forest landscape (fig. 81).[38]

Considering the nuanced resurgence of nationalist statements during the Second World War, it comes as no surprise that an aerial view of a Finnish lake landscape should accompany Aalto's article. Scholars have cited this photograph repeatedly to draw a link between Aalto's architecture and his Finnishness. Aalto himself used the same image in several projects, articles, and lectures: it appeared as a huge enlargement on the exterior wall of the Finnish Pavilion at

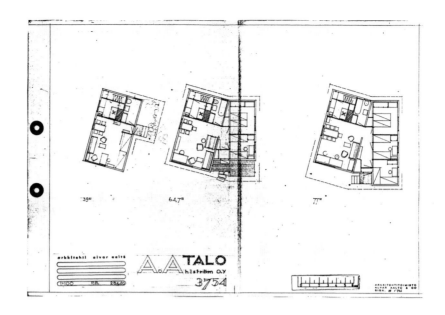

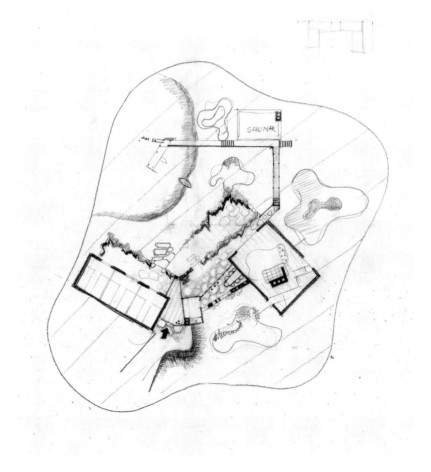

78. Aalto, V-shaped variant of the AA-House, 1940
79. Aalto, sketch for a summer house, 1941

the Paris and New York World's Fairs in 1937 and 1939, respectively. It turned up again in his "Finland" article and accompanied his 1941 lectures on reconstruction.

While photographs of lake landscapes have been widely used since the late nineteenth century to convey an essentialist representation of an ideal, pastoral Finland,[39] the "Finland" article makes the slightly changed ideological agenda behind Aalto's choice explicit: the image made Finland appear as an innocent, politically neutral nation in the eyes of the foreigners while continuing to trigger nationalist sentiments in the Finnish audience.[40] For the former audience, Finland, Europe's easternmost corner, was presented as a politically and culturally neutral region, as pure nature. The emphasis on the undulating form as an outcome of geological processes naturalized and thus depoliticized Aalto's own forms. Emphasis on geological time and processes pointed to an era well before the formation of nation-states, a time when the world consisted simply of differing natural regions.

For a Finn, the image gained a new political meaning after the Winter War, when the serene and malleable forms of the lake landscape revealed that Finland's situation was in peril, in part because the country lacked any natural defensive border to the Soviet Union. The Continuation War, fought between 1941 and 1944, bore this out. After some initial successes in stopping the Russian advance, and even a counter-advance beyond the 1939 border, the Finnish Army, now backed by Germans, had to yield to the Russians, who began a massive ground and air attack on the Carelian Isthmus in June 1944, with a thousand tanks and hundreds of bombers. The offensive front was extended north of Lake Ladoga in late June. Setbacks faced by the German Army on the continent limited its ability to aid its allies, including Finland. A truce was called in early September. In the subsequent peace treaty most of Carelia was lost for good, and it remains a part of the Russian Federation today.

80. A house in Kiestinki, Carelia, 1894. National Board of Antiquities, Helsinki.

In the end, World War II forced Aalto to revisit some lessons of regionalism, according to which states were supposed to be static and outmoded entities. But in reality, political boundaries are on occasion subject to sudden and violent change. Therefore the elastic term *region* proved to be not only the most pragmatic way of approaching architecture's relationship to a particular geographic location, but also the most appropriate concept for understanding Finland's multiple cultural and political affinities from the Declaration of Independence onwards. The challenge became not so much how to define the country in regionalist terms but how any country could survive such challenging situations in the first place.

To further express his indebtedness to American regionalism, Aalto helped to bring to Helsinki the exhibition *America Builds,* based on MoMA's 1944 exhibition *Built in U.S.A.: 1932–44.* As Schildt has noted, holding an American exhibition in the capital sent a strong political message about Finland's political affinities at a time when it seemed uncertain whether Finland would remain outside the Eastern Bloc.[41] In an article for *Arkkitehti* he endorses the "democracy of American architecture," more "vital" and "flexible and better adapted to the practical demands of everyday life," as well as more open to influence than that of European countries. Aalto ends his article by celebrating the TVA's initiatives and postwar planning of the "overall social fabric."[42]

81. Cover of the AA-House catalogue of the A. Ahlström Company

Regionalist planning ideas were put into practice on a large scale when Aalto and Gullichsen joined forces in 1940 to conceive the Kokemäki River Valley Regional Plan for the town of Pori and its surroundings. The plan was to encompass new settlements, infrastructure, production, and recreational facilities, as well as to regulate the spatial relationships between these functions (fig. 82). The plan demonstrates how Aalto ended up applying regionalist ideas in the

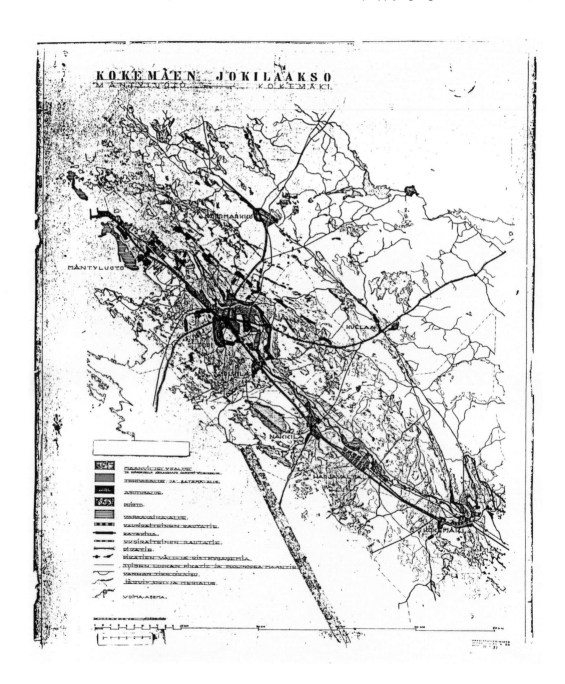

82. Aalto, Kokemäki Joki Valley Plan, 1941

Finnish context: by balancing the interests of the state and the individual and by paying particular attention to local conditions and politics. It was the first instance of small municipalities becoming active subjects in the national planning discussion. Equally significantly, it was neither funded nor initiated by the Finnish state, but it did have national consequences.

Aalto outlined his goals for the plan in his 1949 article "Stateplanning and Our Cultural Goals," first delivered as a lecture. In it he replaced the concept of regional planning with the term *stateplanning,* defining it as a tool for cultural development and making the case that it is a collaborative enterprise: "Stateplanning belongs to the realm in between art and labor. It is so far-reaching in scale that it is impossible to execute it in any conventional means solely by drawing and creating visions. Words outline the plan and only fifty to sixty percent is based on design.... Since [stateplanning] projects way into the future, it encompasses a lot of social and economic factors and becomes by necessity a hybrid between a legal document and a design document. Furthermore, a stateplan needs supporters who are willing to execute the plan."[43] A stateplan should have equally far-reaching impact on all aspects of human life. Stateplans, declared Aalto, "*can be considered as a tool for ethical development, which hold back centralization, steer away from the ills of blind development and foster ethics and human freedom.*"[44] The plan was, in other words, conceived as a comprehensive social, economic, and territorial strategy, whose goal was to guarantee that the common (read: national) good would prevail even in a framework for individual and local development. Aalto's Kokemäki plan gained wide interest and led to further commissions for Kymijoki River Area, the main industrial river route in Finland, and the Imatra Master Plan (1947).

The Second World War offers a backdrop, even an answer, to the question of why it became desirable to regulate and coordinate these functions. The Kokemäki River Valley Plan was, for example, initiated soon after the signing of the Moscow Peace Treaty between the Soviet Union and Finland in the spring of 1940, which led to the evacuation of more than 400,000 Finns from Carelia to the western part of the country. Its goal was to meet official, regional, and national needs. The Imatra plan was commissioned by another paper giant, Enzo-Gunzeit, after changes in the country's eastern border caused its largest production facilities in Kaukopää and Enso to be ceded to Soviet Union.[45] Aalto's regional plans were based on national policies that understood that economic activity and foreign trade were crucial for national prosperity, and by extension, national security.

Since the 1950s local governments across the country have executed regional plans, or *seutukaava,* modeled after Aalto's. Even though regional planning has become a normative practice, it is important to remember the original political and territorial dimension of Aalto's regionalism: to guarantee the country's long-term economic well-being and security. The fact that Finns associate national identity with cultural and social development rather than with nationalist ideology is perhaps the most important legacy of regionalism today.

Formal Registers

A postcard from Aalto to Walter Gropius (1883–1969) in October 1930 contained a curious reference to his countrymen: "We are eagerly looking forward to our 'next visit with the Gropiuses,' while trying in the meanwhile to make buildings for people into whose heads the 'organic line' will not fit for another 100 years."[1]

Why would Aalto find Gropius, presumably an advocate of geometric *Sachlichkeit,* more sympathetic to the "organic line" than his own countrymen, living amid the bountiful Nordic forests? The idea that Finns don't understand organic forms is baffling, because curvilinearity is considered the very hallmark of Aalto's architecture and a sign of his unique Finnish sensibility. In this chapter I will reassess that reading by reconsidering the sources of Aalto's quasi-natural forms and their geographic origins, their genesis, and their meaning.

Curvilinear forms first emerged in his furniture designs in the early 1930s. The forms reappeared in various materials and scales throughout the 1930s, from a small decorative object, the glass Savoy vase (1936), to a complete building, the Forest Pavilion (1938), made of vertical wooden boards (fig. 83). Although serving completely different functions and made of different materials, both are based on the same form: a sinuous line closing on itself, extruded into the third dimension. The idea that forms follow a material and functional logic (for example, lamination allows wood to bend, curvilinear forms are more ergonomic) falls short when we consider how the forms migrate to new uses and materials.

The prevailing assumption is that the emergence of the curvilinear form in Aalto's work around 1931 signaled that he was distancing himself from international modernism, with its passion for the rectilinear box and the grid. Furthermore, the organic line is considered in some way a true expression of his national origins and is often linked to an essentialized notion of Finland as a place of flowing rivers, rolling hills, and leafy rural scenery, a notion that dominated the country's image abroad.

83. Aalto, Lapua Forest Pavilion, 1938

These readings are easy to counter: organic ideas and forms were hardly alien to the key figures of early modernism. The writings of Moholy-Nagy, Giedion, Gropius, and Mies, among others, contain many indications that biocentrism was a prevalent worldview among modern architects, artists, and critics, and that in adopting organicist ideas and curvilinear and biomorphic forms Aalto was moving closer to the German branch of the modern movement.

Aalto's wood reliefs from the early 1930s to the late 1940s reveal some generative ideas behind the undulating form. These studies depict wood in different stages of formal and functional articulation, from raw material to finished product. One explored the energy inherent in the material as the fibers cluster and overlap (fig. 84), while in another, structure was imposed on wood by human and mechanical processes—bending, lamination, and mass production. When combined, the inherent qualities and imposed techniques gave birth to a curvilinear formal language devoid of any particular functional signification.

Two structural variations and functional applications emerged from this set of studies. In the first case, laminated wood gained striated structure, which allowed it to be bent in a single direction; Aalto used this technique to make L-shaped legs for chairs and tables from 1931 onward (figs. 85, 86). The second version highlighted wood's fiberlike structure, which allowed it to be bent in multiple directions. This principle later led to the fanned table and chair legs in the early 1950s. These studies suggest how Aalto viewed the genesis of form: the human hand and industrial processes simply aided nature in what he celebrated as form's triumph over chaotic raw materiality. The memory of the process remained visible in the final product.

In *Alvar Aalto: The Decisive Years,* Göran Schildt has rightly traced the impetus for material experimentation to Aalto's friendship with Moholy-Nagy. During his visit to Finland in 1931, he gave Aalto a copy of his 1929 book *Von Material zu Architektur,* volume fourteen in the *Bauhausbücher* series, which introduced his Finnish colleague to the material studies conducted in his introductory course at Bauhaus. In a thank-you note Aalto praised the book as "excellent, clear and beautiful, perhaps your best book," indicating that he was already familiar with the other two, *Die Bühne im Bauhaus* (1924) and *Malerei, Fotographie, Film* (Painting, Photography, Film [1925]).[2]

Moholy-Nagy's book was a pedagogical treatise with wide-ranging cultural and social implications. Its underlying premise was based in cultural criticism: nineteenth-century technological and economic changes had led to the atomization of societies, to alienation, and to the degradation of nature. The critique harked back to the idea of the organic whole. The reintegration of the world should start with the creation of the "whole man," whose intellectual and emotional powers would be in balance. This, argued Moholy-Nagy, could be achieved by sensory education, which would unleash the creative energies inherent in

84. Aalto, material study with wood, showing a twisted tree trunk, 1930

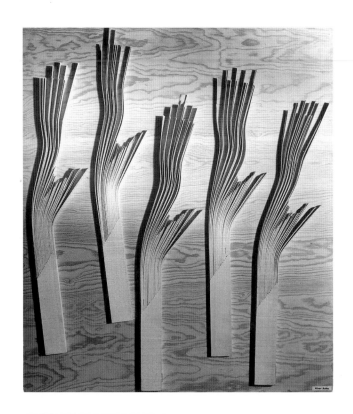

85. Aalto, material study showing lamination, 1933
86. Aalto, material study showing a laminated chair leg in the making, 1929–35

each individual. The first task was to break through inhibitions and social conventions; he gave the spontaneous creativity of children and of "primitive" peoples as examples. Moholy-Nagy based his pedagogy on various school-reform programs then in vogue—"Montessori, Daltonsystem, Gyneken-Wickenhof, Wendekreis, etc." —which pioneered the idea of individual creativity as a means to achieve collective well-being.[3]

Moholy-Nagy's pedagogical ideas fit comfortably into the goals set by Gropius' 1919 inaugural manifesto, which called for the unification of the arts through hands-on training. The goal of the Bauhaus education, as envisioned by Gropius, was to overcome the divisions of labor that had reduced the architect and artist to mere designers, and art to a mere profession. "Architects, sculptors, painters, we all must return to the crafts! For art is not a profession," he exclaimed, continuing in a neo-vitalist mode that came to characterize much Bauhaus literature: "In rare moments of inspirations, transcending the consciousness of his will, the grace of heaven may cause his work to blossom into art. But proficiency in a craft is essential to every artist. Therein lies the prime source of creative imagination."[4]

While art was understood as an outcome of spontaneous self-creation analogous to the way nature created forms, architecture had the task of following nature's organizational and functional principles. "Architects, painters, and sculptors must recognize anew and learn to grasp the composite character of a building both as an entity and in its separate parts," wrote Gropius. "Only then will their work be imbued with the architectonic spirit, which it has lost as 'salon art.'"[5] The link drawn between nature and art fostered reintegration over fragmentation, as attention was drawn to relationships between things and, further, to dynamic processes, such as flows, growth, and metamorphosis, which allowed organisms to adopt and respond to surrounding conditions. Ultimately art would unite with life and its processes.

Writing to Gropius some ten years after the founding of the Bauhaus in 1919, Aalto lamented that his countrymen had failed to grasp this synthetic essence of modernity. It is exactly this fascination with the dynamic and organic ideal that distinguishes Aalto from many of the other Finnish modernist architects, such as Erik Bryggman, Martti Välikangas (1893–1973), Hilding Ekelund (1893–1984), and Aulis Blomstedt (1906–1979), who each failed to understand the larger social and cultural underpinnings of the modern movement. Välikangas, the editor in chief of *Finnish Architecture Review* from 1928–30, was slow to recognize the value of the emerging modern movement in the first place. Ekelung, who followed Välikangas at the *Review* from 1931–34, settled into a domesticated version of international modernism. And Blomstedt, also an editor in chief from 1941–45, became a promoter of universal architecture based on modular systems.

Aalto was, however, not the only critic of the narrow understanding of modernism in Finland. In his 1932 book *Clean-Up; or, Notes from the Literary Nursery* (1932) Olavi Paavolainen criticized his fellow modernist writers, many of them members of the Torch Bearers, for trivializing modernism and turning it into an anti-intellectual celebration of bohemian lifestyles without psychological perspective or social conviction. Paavolainen too founded his criticism on biocentric and neo-vitalist theories, exclaiming, "'Life' is in the human being, not around him. DESCRIPTION OF BEHAVIOR HAS TO BE REPLACED BY DESCRIPTION OF THE SOUL ."[6] The message had a Bergsonian tone: "soul" referred to the oneness of the world, which did not isolate the human being from its surroundings.

In the visual arts, the idea that the artist's task was to tap into this synthetic life force was a central notion of the early avant-garde. Early in their careers, Moholy, Hans (Jean) Arp, Raoul Haussmann, and Ivan Puni had discussed how forms came into being in their 1921 article "Call to Elemental Art": "To surrender to the elements of form-giving is to be an artist. The elements of art can only be discovered by an artist. They do not come about as a result of his individual choice; the individual is not an entity broken off from the whole and an artist is but an exponent of the forces that give shape to the elements of the world."[7] The idea of elementalism was based on the epistemological principle that people did not observe the world from outside but experienced it from within. Therefore, an elemental artist did not represent or abstract the visible world but tried to capture and make visible its constitutive processes and relationships. In other words, forms were the concretization of dynamic forces inherent in the real. El Lissitzky wrote in 1921, "Every form is a frozen instantaneous picture of a process. Thus a work is a stopping-place on the road of becoming and not the fixed goal."[8]

Moholy's book *Von Material zu Architektur* defined these forces clearly. In it he establishes three categories of form creation: structure, texture, and index (*Faktur*). The first highlighted the internal structure of the material; the second, external forces imposed on it; and the third, the effect of mechanical processes. A cut through a tree trunk was given as an example of structure, wrinkles on the face of an aging man illustrated the meaning of texture, and a study by a student demonstrated patterns made by different tools (figs. 87–89).

Aalto's material studies followed Moholy's three-part hierarchy: The process started (presumably) with raw wood, with its inherent material structure visible. The next step introduced bending as external force. The final products bore the mark of mechanical processes, such as lamination and pressing; technology existed in a reciprocal relationship with materials and nature. According to Moholy, technology had been misappropriated and misunderstood. We must, he said, reassess technology's essence in order to maximize our own and nature's resources to the fullest. This could be achieved by learning from nature. "Technology is an organically evolving life force. It stands in a reciprocal relationship with humanity. . . . The real reason for a conflict between life and technology [*Teknik*] can be located in [the] lack thereof. Therefore, today's production systems and processes have to be rethought from the ground up. . . . The solution is therefore not to be against technology but to work with it."[9]

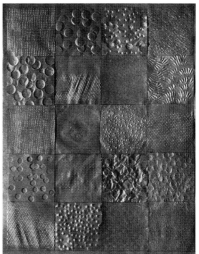

[above, top] 87. Moholy-Nagy, *Holzstruktur.* From *Von Material zu Architektur*
(From Material to Architecture), *Bauhausbücher 14* (Munich: Albert Langen, 1929), 39.
[above left] 88. Moholy-Nagy, "*Textur:* A 130-Year-Old American Man from
Minnesota." From *Von Material zu Architektur,* 41.
[above right] 89. Gerda Marx, *Papier-fakturen (ein Material, verschiedene Werkzeuge)*
(Paper *Fakturs* [one material, different tools]). From Moholy-Nagy, *Von Material zu*
Architektur, 57.

Aalto's Paimio chair from 1931 can be understood as a product of multiple forces originating in nature, technology, and human labor, as theorized by Moholy. The movement of the body was added to the list of factors that needed to be registered in form. Moholy used the word *biotechnik,* borrowed from the German biologist Raoul Francé, widely read at the Bauhaus, to describe the interdependence of form, process, and function. *Biotechnik,* he wrote, means that "every process has a necessary technical form, which fulfills a particular functional process."[10] Yet, as a photocollage made for the 1938 MoMA exhibition of a woman hovering over the Paimio chair suggests, in Aalto's mind the form of the chair and that of the body did not completely align (fig. 90). The form was not, in other words, completely dictated by material, techniques, and function, but had its own raison d'être.

In this context it is hard to ignore the fact that Aalto's forms greatly resembled Jean Arp's wood reliefs, which he had probably seen for the first time when visiting Sigfried Giedion and his wife, the important art historian and critic Carola Giedion-Welcker (1893–1979), in Zurich in the fall of 1930. Giedion might have taken him to see a show he had curated, *Produktion Paris 1930,* which featured works by Arp and Piet Mondrian.

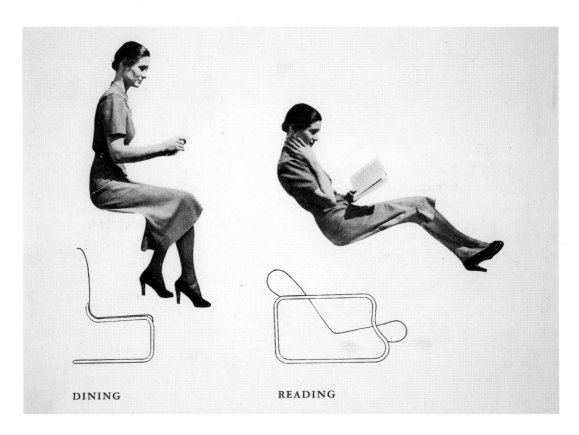

DINING   READING

90. Aalto, reclining woman and the Paimio chair, from *Architecture and Furniture: Aalto* (New York: Museum of Modern Art, 1938), 18

Born Hans Arp in Alsace, Arp (1887–1966) was a truly European artist in the Nietzschean sense, living in many countries and bridging many artistic movements. Arp was educated in Strasbourg, Weimar, and Paris. He came into his own during the 1910s in Zurich, where he became one of the founding members of the dada movement, along with Tristan Tzara. In the 1920s he exhibited with the French surrealists and then joined the group Abstraction-Création, formed to counter the surrealist movement in 1931, which brought together various representatives of nonobjective art, among them Naum Gabo and Piet Mondrian.

At this point Arp's art went through a major transformation. If the earlier work had been preoccupied with techniques of automatic writing and collage, where the outcome was often left to chance, after 1930 it sought equilibrium among parts. Series of reliefs with titles like *Configuration, Constellation,* or *Construction* emphasize the gathering together of disparate elements to form a whole. Arp described his interests around 1930: "Concretion signifies the natural process of condensation, hardening, coagulating, thickening, growing together. Concretion designates the solidification of a mass."[11] The reliefs depict fluid shapes that seem to float in space, like drops of water in the process of coming together. The neutral backgrounds give the images a cosmic, universal dimension. These forms can be considered "emblem[s] of all natural growth and change."[12] These works, which Arp called "fluid ovals," seemed to be in a constant state of reconfiguration.[13] One of Aalto's material studies features two curving laminated strips of wood that descend diagonally across a rectangular background, first next to each other then splitting apart to form a kidney shape in the middle (fig. 91). The image resembles Arp's *Amphora* (1931) from Giedion-Welcker's extensive art collection, which depicts a white figure on a black background (fig. 92).

91. Aalto, material study with laminated wood, 1929–35
92. Jean Arp, *Amphora,* 1931. Kunstsammlung Nordrhein-Westfalen, Düsseldorf.

Giedion-Welcker was one of the leading theorists of biomorphic abstraction and among the first to discuss the interest in nature of artists like Arp and Constantin Brancusi. Her contribution lay in developing the concept of "organic elementarism," based on the constructivist principle that instead of depicting visible nature, an artist should seek to represent the fundamental underlying principles of nature.[14] Sharing the biocentrist worldview, she viewed humanity as part of nature, rather than outside it. In a mystical vein she referred to the unity between humanity and nature as the "mysterious participation of man with nature and the world of creatures" that "blurs all biological and psychological frontiers."[15]

Giedion-Welcker located Arp's form-giving somewhere between surrealist psychological automatism and active *Kunstwollen.* Therefore, on the one hand, she saw Arp's forms as seismographic notations of the fluctuation of his psychological state in an ever-evolving psychophysical environment: "A 'pure poetry' allows everything anecdotal and specific as well as psychological and individual to flow into one large reservoir of unexpected and bizarre everyday human incidents."[16] On the other hand, she later contradicted this reading, noting that around 1930 Arp rejected surrealist automatism by focusing on form-giving: "More and more in the reliefs of his later years, Arp discarded the mocking methods by which he had once interrogated the disordered world while, at the same time, giving them through his imagery a fresh compositional unity."[17]

So conceived, the design process gained a new moral and epistemological implication: the world was not an a priori entity observed from without, but was created by and for the experiencing and perceiving subject.[18] Artistic form, rather than expressing the world and its processes, was a version or interpretation of the world—past, present, and future. In this scenario an artist, rather than reflecting on his or her own psychic processes, was responsible for nothing less than the psychophysical well-being of humankind.

As Aalto moved closer to the Giedions in the early 1930s after the National Socialists came to power, he started to speak of architecture and design on these lines. Architecture was a complex part of humanity's total psychophysical environment, which had an impact on the way people lived and how they felt. He wrote in a 1935 lecture "Rationalism and Man" about how to access the mystery of life: "A whole series of questions that can be asked of virtually every object, but have hitherto been very seldom considered, surely relates to another science altogether, psychology. As soon as we include psychological requirements, or, rather, as soon as we are able to include them, we will have extended the rationalist working method enough to make it easier to prevent inhuman results."[19]

These words suggest that by the mid-1930s Aalto had become familiar with current psychoanalytical and psychological theories, which saw the mind as a dynamic entity existing in a reciprocal relationship with the surrounding world. The mind did not thus simply view the world as an empirical fact, as rationalism would have it, but rather as a series of complex interacting relationships.

Finland's preeminent philosopher of the first half of the twentieth century, Eino

Kaila, can be credited with introducing Sigmund Freud's theories into Finland. His 1934 book *Personality* was a landmark text on the subject.[20] Aalto was not the only Finnish modernist interested in the connection between artistic practices and the human psyche. His expanded notion of rationalism came close to Paavolainen's call for "deep, modern, non-dogmatic, scientifically rigorous and at the same time emotionally apt psychological understanding of human beings."[21] Like Paavolainen's, Aalto's scientism was accompanied by a belief in a mysterious essence of life that could be grasped only through an intuitive artistic process. By the same token, the artist and architect could manipulate and reconfigure relationships and processes that might have been previously taken for granted.

The formal and material experiments that Aalto started to explore in the early 1930s led ultimately to a break from the traditional functional and representational strategies of modern architecture. If the model that had dominated modernist architectural discourse was based on establishing unambiguous relationships between form, function, and structure, Aalto's abstract forms were laden with open-ended functional, representational, and experiential ramifications. They in fact reversed the process of form-giving altogether. Rather than indexing function or structure, for example, the curvilinear forms that he made a centerpiece of his investigations in the 1930s seem to have begun as formal explorations, gaining functional applications only later. This allowed the same basic forms and processes to acquire various functional and formal applications: furniture, vases, acoustic ceilings, door handles, whole buildings.

A series of works in which the curvilinear form plays a significant role reveals a key aspect of Aalto's new formal strategy: investing form with multiple meanings. In the case of the Savoy vase this had to do with the play of figuration and abstraction. The original competition sketch was titled "The Eskimo Girl's Leather Breeches" (*Eskimåerindens skinnbyxa*), which suggested, sportively, that the purely abstract, undulating form was derived from this distant reference, which bore no relevance whatever to the task of designing a vase (fig. 93). It playfully questions the origin of architectural form. Rather than based on functional or structural logic, the form plays with figuration, teasing out various readings without ever settling into one particular reading. The message is clear: by the mid-1930s, Aalto had come to the conclusion that forms migrate from culture to culture and get appropriated in different ways. As the French art historian Henri Focillon pointed out around the same time, forms have a life of their own; their relevance and meaning had only to do with the moment of their appearance in a temporal sequence. The same form could gain different meaning and significance depending on the context and time of appearance.[22]

Another sketch featured a cross-section of the vase rendered in overlapping lines suggestive of the automatic drawing processes used by artists like Arp, who worked in the orbit of surrealism (fig. 94). The surrealist technique of automatic drawing had grown out of the influence of Freud and other theorists of the unconscious. The pencil was allowed to wander as the artist's mind relaxed

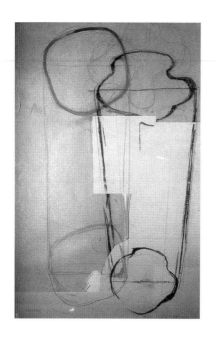

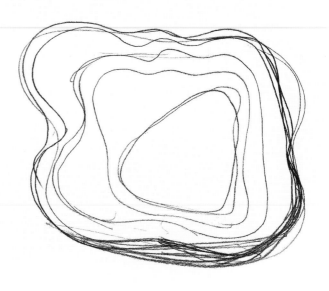

93. Aalto, "Eskimåerindens skinnbyxa," entry for a glass-design competition organized in 1936

94. Aalto, sketch of the Savoy vase, late 1930s

95. Aalto, Viipuri Library, 1927–35, auditorium with undulating wood ceiling

and ceased to direct the hand, so that it responded to the unconscious, creating loose, fluid images. Aalto transferred this gestural, spontaneous creative mode from drawing to the shaping of three-dimensional objects in which abstract, symbolic, and functional significations were combined within one form, without it ever settling into any single reading. This flexibility was analogous to the synthetic drifting of the mind, in which one idea gave way to another without conflict.

The process produces a surprising effect: while the vase and its form did not derive directly from material qualities or the requirements of its function, it did not deny them either. In fact, the undulating form amplified glass's amorphous origins and allowed a completely new way of displaying flowers. By suspending traditional ways of producing forms, Aalto let new functional and material meanings emerge.

In the wooden acoustic ceiling in the auditorium of the Viipuri Library (1927–35, fig. 95) this tension between formal experimentation and functional requirement led to the creation of an experientially rich and multilayered environment. One can interpret its genesis in two ways. On one hand, the forms appear to be the result of pure play. On the other hand, the sectional drawing depicting the distribution of sound waves in the auditorium suggests that the forms are the outcome of particular functional and material considerations (fig. 96). This tension can be traced to two previously discussed aspects of the biocentric worldview: psycho-vitalist perceptual theories and the idea of *Biotechnik.* According to the first, form facilitates an experience of being part of the dynamic processes inherent in the world; according to the second, form is the outcome of efficient functional processes.

The way the ceiling fluctuates between these two readings demonstrated that biocentric architects could never reduce function to a mere fulfillment of a particular task—function had to translate into sensation and feeling. The goal was to let life in all its complexity evolve in space. The relationship between form

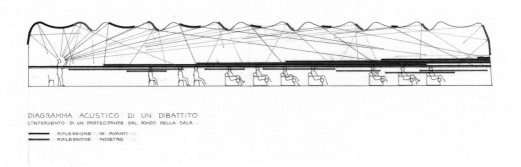

96. Aalto, Viipuri Library, section of the auditorium

and life was therefore noncausal: one took life in all its dynamism and fixed its energies in pure form. Life was then reinserted, as it were, into form through function. This "mediation between formal experimentation and its use in daily life," as Yve-Alain Bois has called it, was based on the critique of a priori ideas, such as functionality, that were forced upon life from outside.[23] Functional, technical, and formal solutions presumably arose from life's inherent patterns and forces.

In Viipuri, Aalto succeeded in maximizing the emotional impact of functional form on the body. Therefore, rather than being just a mere reflector of sound, the pulsating ceiling—Aalto's first use of undulating form as a spatial element—combined sound with visual and spatial effects to produce multifaceted sensory stimuli. Aalto realized—and herein lies the brilliance of Viipuri—that acoustic experience has a visual and spatial, and thus bodily, dimension. A link can be drawn to the quasi-mystical theory of "synesthesia," a presumed union or coupling of the senses, explored by symbolist and abstract painters and poets in the early twentieth century. It indirectly informed the widely applied ray theory, which assumes that both light and sound travel in straight lines and reflect when they meet a surface.[24] What is now often considered a scientific way to create functional form was conceived as mysterious ether that would stimulate the mind and the body.

Further analogy could be drawn to eurythmic dance, which rejected the old notion of the body as an anatomical-physiological entity occupying space in favor of a more holistic biological-psychological understanding according to which the body mediated between external stimuli and internal psychophysical states.[25] Aiming at reconciliation between "necessities of individual and collective existence," its origins can be drawn to the turn-of-the-century French philosopher Jean-Marie Guyau, a contemporary of Henri Bergson's, who can be credited with introducing vitalism into aesthetic theory by establishing links between beauty and functionality.[26] Not only did Guyau suggest that beauty equals activity and energy—we experience something as beautiful when we act it out and feel it in our bodies—he also expanded the idea of private aesthetic experience toward the notion of a collective aesthetic effect. Guyau based his theory on the dual ideas of the "expansion" and "contagion" of form,[27] which themselves are based on the "absolute homology between aesthetic experience and the sociopolitical doctrine of 'solidarism.'"[28] The goal of art—and by extension architecture—was to grab the onlooker and break through his or her existential solitude. Guyau's thinking had roots in the nineteenth-century pseudoscientific fascination with the occult and with collective spiritual experience, which included a popular interest in séances and other forms of paranormal experimentation.

These vitalist ideas about the merging of art, life, and humanity were more central to the modern movement than previously acknowledged. Guyau's ideas were introduced to the architectural mainstream by the German architectural critic Adolf Behne, who, in his 1926 book *The Modern Functional Building,* cites

Guyau's phrase "Art in tenderness" ("L'Art c'est de la tendresse").[29] Unlike his contemporaries, Behne does not talk about international or national architecture but sees only one type of truly modern architecture, born out of life's energy and characterized by flowing, organic forces. Behne considered these forms functional, not because they fulfilled some particular functional task, but because they were born out of the source that united all humanity. "The flow of organic life knows no right angles and no straight lines. And as the functionalist always appeals to the flow of organic life as the finest example of pure functionalism, his fondness for the curve is entirely understandable. Straight lines will always resist the ultimate adaptation to functional mobility and fluidity. They allow only a general, approximate adaptation, nothing absolute. Thus the consistent functionalist has to take curves rather than straight lines as his starting point."[30]

He then continues to claim that, "Functionalists are concerned with solving a program of general significance to our culture. . . . Their attitude inclines toward philosophy and has a metaphysical basis. . . . [The functionalists] could more readily be classified as romantics than as rationalists."[31] As Behne points out, functionalism should not be confused with utilitarianism's means-to-an-end approach. Its basis was found in these pseudo-scientific organicist theories, which invested everything with lifelike qualities.

Understood in this context, the undulating ceiling at Viipuri did not simply provide good acoustics so that every individual in the hall simply could hear well, but amplified the listeners' feeling of being part of the general life force that connects man to the world and people to each other within communities and across boundaries. The curvilinear form thus connected a complex set of ideas about visuality and identity. It depended on the anti-anthropocentrism of several modernist theories—biocentrism, eurythmic dance, and vitalism—all of which shared the idea of the "individual's lack of autonomous subjecthood within the unitary system of nature."[32] Loss of individuality was both necessary and desirable also from a geographic standpoint: it celebrated humanity at large beyond national boundaries. The organic line can thus be understood as an emblem of the push and pull between the self and the world that formed the basis of the truly human—that is, truly modern, intersubjective, and, by extension, transnational.

Foreign critics discovered Aalto in about 1930, when the Stockholm Exhibition drew attention to Scandinavia's nascent modernist movement. Aalto attended the opening and used it as an opportunity to freshen old contacts and acquire new ones. He reconnected with Sigfried Giedion and met the writer and critic Philip Morton Shand (1888–1960), who became his main champion in England. And although the two did not meet at the time, he was brought to the attention of Philip Johnson, who included Aalto's Turun Sanomat Building in the groundbreaking exhibition *Modern Architecture: International Exhibition* at MoMA in 1932.[1]

Giedion's essay "On Finnish Architecture," published in the German magazine *Bauwelt* in 1931, was the first international review of Aalto's work, issued in conjunction with the completion of the Turun Sanomat Building (1928–30). Although the building had all the formal and material tropes of Le Corbusier's version of international modernism—white stucco walls, roof terrace, strip windows, and window walls—Giedion paid special attention to Aalto's country of origin, giving an overview of its history, geography, and forest industry. He undoubtedly did so primarily because he had been educated to read architecture through geographic and cultural lenses, but also because Finland was little known outside its borders and needed to be explained.

Giedion's reading of Aalto was also informed by his own cultural and political agenda. He called Finland a *Randstaat,* a border state, implying that because of its remote location it occupied a geographically and historically distinct position, and was still in a state of becoming—politically, economically, and culturally. An image of logs being transported by river to feed the lumber trade, reproduced in the article, was an emblem of an industry close to nature and thus distinct from that of the old industrial countries. Reading between the lines, for Giedion economic infancy paralleled cultural infancy: Finland had not yet formed a strong national identity, an issue that, in the 1930s, was beginning to become a problem in some of the more culturally and politically established European countries. The image's emphasis on movement and dynamism suggested at the same time that the country's culture promised to be equally distinct and even more vital than that of the more industrialized nations.

A reversal of the traditional center-periphery hierarchy followed. Rather than considering Aalto's Turun Sanomat Building as a mere copy of continental precedents, Giedion saw it as an indicator of "independent development." "It is a sign of the advanced state of today's architecture that the border states of culture don't always merely accept the result of the previous development, which dominates production. Instead they have demonstrated a capability for independent development, which in turn reinforces and invigorates the origins. Although these border states lack developed industry, they often possess an immediate ability to create form [*Gestaltungskraft*], which helps to overcome this limitation."[2] In a prose that borders on the mystical, Giedion used the word *Gestaltungskraft,* or form-giving power, to explain this reversal. Aalto "possessed a rare talent to approach the building task organically, to grasp and give form to function in an unmediated manner."[3] His talent was presumably innate, raw, and powerful, and Giedion implied that he was the only architect who had the power to bestow the kind of vital form called for by the original avant-garde.

Giedion had proposed a similar geographic reversal in "The Contemporary Role of Painting," an essay in the catalogue *Produktion Paris, 1930: Werke der Malerei und Plastik,* written for an exhibition of contemporary painters he curated that year. Here, using a more overtly political tone, he claimed that the most promising new art came from small countries like Switzerland, which, "due to its location between German and French culture, is able to take a relatively free approach. Here the clear, neutral atmosphere is untouched by local considerations of a different kind."[4] With extreme nationalism on the rise all over Europe, Giedion considered the ability to transcend national disputes, and even national traits, a prerequisite for art's pure, nonideological essence to come forth. He thus preferred artists who were products of in-between regions with multiple cultural influences. For example, he featured the work of the surrealist Jean Arp prominently in the exhibition. Arp, an Alsatian, was arguably both French and German, and he used both versions of his first name, Jean and Hans, moving between two linguistic groups and cultural identities. The idea of an individual artist in an in-between region offered an alternative to both extreme nationalism and homogeneous internationalism. Aalto's case was slightly different because his was a young country whose national identity was less fixed and more innocent than the French or German.

While Giedion put forward the idea of the ambiguous Randstaat, Shand, writing at about the same time, argued that Nordic architecture provided a nationalist alternative to the internationalist tendencies within the modern movement. His response to emerging Scandinavian modernism was even more overtly political than Giedion's, but from the opposite perspective. In an issue of *Architectural Review* devoted to the Stockholm Exhibition he celebrated nationalist tendencies in modernism, using a pro-Germanic, aggressive, even proto-Nazi rhetoric and proclaiming that a "fresh artistic *Volkswanderung* is being unleashed upon Christendom. Le Corbusier's blood will soon be quaffed out of his own massy skull, just to show there is no ill-feeling; Gropius' Communist Bauhaus will be razed to the ground so that a new Valhalla may arise at Dessau."[5]

Aalto's international reception after 1930 was necessarily colored by the political situation in Europe, marked by geopolitical dynamics and accompanied by varying intensities of national and racial passion. For Shand, whose rhetoric suggests clear nationalist sympathies, Scandinavia represented liberation from the internationalist (read: leftist) tendencies within the modern movement: "May our own Viking blood, the only blood in us that matters, rouse itself to join in the massacre of those traitors of our age." Those like Shand who blamed the increasing internationalization and modernization of Western societies for the world's political and economic troubles, the relatively isolated and racially homogenous

Nordic countries represented an alternative. "If we refuse to follow the lead of Germany or the States, . . . why not cast an eye on the Swede, a quiet, amusing fellow, closely connected by birth, who is not quite such a heavy friend as the German, nor such a loud one as the Yankee. Sweden could teach us quite a lot." Therefore it was understandable that Swedish architecture was "destined to be imbued with wholesome Nordic sanity and that very Swedish 'sweetness and light.'"[6]

Shand's prejudices and affinity for Scandinavian functionalism imbued his view of Aalto, who, he wrote, is a "'functionalist' in the sense that he moulds form in the semblance of basic construction and purpose, working outwards from plan instead of inwards from elevation. His work, though renouncing ornament per se, evinces an almost tender regard for the design and arrangement of incidental practical details."[7] Following the early German proto-functionalist theories of Mebes and Schultze-Naumburg, who rejected the nineteenth century's stylistic imitations in favor of a simple, practical German architectural tradition, Shand considered Aalto's functionalism anti-internationalist because it was firmly rooted in the practical needs of his country's people.

Giedion's and Shand's early reviews are indicative of a pattern: Aalto was accepted and celebrated by people who represented different, even conflicting political and ideological positions. The geopolitical status of his homeland shifted accordingly. Finland could be considered part of multiple geographic, cultural, and political alliances within Europe, depending on the viewer's outlook. It could be an extension of Scandinavia, a member of the eastern Baltic States, or an extension of the territory occupied by the Germanic race.

MoMA's 1932 exhibition *Modern Architecture: International Exhibition* ignored the political subtext that fueled the international modern movement. The exhibition and catalogue were organized around individuals rather than countries. The goal of its curators, Philip Johnson and Henry-Russell Hitchcock, was to portray an image of a coherent modern style. An exterior image of the Turun Sanomat Building neatly conformed to the main stylistic principles: volume instead of mass, fine proportions instead of ornament. Their book, *International Style: Architecture Since 1922,* included an interior shot of the Sanomat Building's printing hall, dominated by massive sculptural columns. While avoiding making national distinctions, the caption emphasized Aalto's form-giving prowess: "Industrial building raised to the level of architecture by fine proportions, smooth surfaces and carefully studied forms. The shape of the concrete supports expresses frankly the structural stresses."[8] In his foreword to the catalogue, Alfred H. Barr, Jr., the director of MoMA, seemed less deterministic about the formal outcome, noting "the wide personal variations possible within what may seem at first glance a restricted range of possibilities."[9] In fact, more than Hitchcock and Johnson's, Barr's historical vision allowed for distinct geographic developments. Tellingly, the museum presented *Early American Architecture: Chicago, 1870–1910* in 1933, only a year after the *Modern Architecture: International Style* exhibition.[10]

The coherence of the international modern movement was shattered when Germany, and to a certain extent France, became unsympathetic to modern art and architecture. The Athens CIAM meeting of 1933 was the swan song of the movement as a unified body of European architects working in their national settings. In a travelogue in *Hufvudstadsbladet,* Nils-Gustav Hahl, who acted as Aalto's representative on the trip from Marseilles to Greece, described boarding the ship for Greece: "Early in the morning of July 29, a bus draws up alongside a steamer in the port of Marseilles. A dozen people crawl out and enter negotiations to get their luggage off the roof. They speak French with many different accents and degrees of perfection, since they are Frenchmen, Englishmen, Hungarians, Swiss—and one Finn. Finally up on deck, they melt into an even greater confusion of nationalities: one can hear all of Europe's known languages and some of the unknown."[11] Hahl's observations gain significance in the context of the emerging nationalist extremism of the time; they challenged the idea of the purity of nation-states by highlighting the in-between zone of cultures (the boat) and languages (broken French as a lingua franca).[12] Subsequently, Hahl celebrated the "fringe" figure Moholy as "a man, who does not play a role in the official program, but who belongs to the central figures of the congress, [although] his importance is understood only in a small circle ... [yet] he has had more influence on the breakthrough of a modern feeling for form [*formkänslan*] than any one else."[13] His account of the discussion, followed by Legér's lecture "Discourse to Architects," gives a sense how CIAM's focus had by 1933 shifted to include architecture's psychological role, a theme that Aalto had engaged through his material studies.[14] "[The lecture] gave rise to an interesting debate, in which Le Corbusier and Alvar Aalto took part enthusiastically. In discussing the suitability of various colors, both of them typically considered only the physiological effect colors have on people, and almost wholly disregarded their aesthetic qualities."

By 1933 the question regarding the experience of architecture, which had preoccupied Aalto for some time, had arrived at center stage. Aalto's status rose in tandem. Hahl proudly assured Finnish readers of Aalto's exalted role on the continent: "Aalto is highly esteemed everywhere, as the participants of the congress assured me. Many foreign architects have already visited his newly completed sanatorium in Paimio, and their comments have been uniformly full of praise."[15]

Legér's talk set an upbeat and optimistic tone for the meeting. The architects and artists enjoyed each other's company as well as the beauty of the Greek archipelago and its architecture. The Athens trip seems to have been a particularly happy and relaxed one for Aalto. Aalto's time in Athens was spent visiting monuments with the Giedions and Moholy. Hahl's report mentions Aalto sleeping on a deck chair on the return trip while being captured on film by Moholy-Nagy. After the official meeting Aalto, Moholy, and Hahl joined the Giedions on a car ride from Marseille to Zurich, paying a visit to Madame Hélène Mandrot at La Sarraz castle along the way.

It is therefore hardly a coincidence that Giedion started to pay increasing attention to Aalto's work in about 1933, the year Hitler came to power. Giedion's concern for the future of the movement is evident in a postcard he sent to Aalto from Milan: "In the Milan Triennale your wooden [bentwood] chairs represent one of the few cheering prospects [*Lichtblicke*] in the international section."[16] Another card, written later that summer, after Giedion had seen photographs of the newly completed Paimio Sanatorium, underlines Aalto's idiosyncratic formal and material sensibility: "Dear Alto [*sic*], Your sanatorium has arrived. . . . One can sense your (or Aino's?) hand in every [formal] *cliché!* You will one day became the 'Magus of the North!'" (fig. 97).[17]

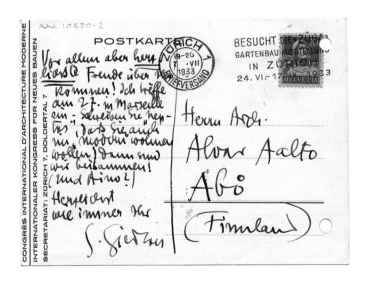

97. Sigfried Giedion, postcard to Alvar Aalto, sent 7 July 1933. Alvar Aalto Archives, Helsinki.

The epithet "magus" means magician—one able to work wonders. In German culture it is often used to refer to the eighteenth-century German philosopher Johann Georg Hamann, best known for his criticism of the Enlightenment notion of pure reason, and celebrated, somewhat reductively, as an irrational individualist, though more subtle readings credit him with introducing historicity and a certain earthiness to the intellectual enterprise. In comparing Aalto to Hamann, Giedion revealed his new value-laden geopolitical agenda: the North represented an abode of fierce, semiprimitive peoples who were more bound to sensuous experience and myths than those in the South. Giedion located this imagined North, home of a benevolent regional ethos that represented common sense in politically convulsed times, on both sides of the Baltic. The conservative nationalist theorist Julius Langbehn had done the same in his influential 1890 book *Rembrandt als Erzieher* (Rembrandt as Educator), widely read and republished in the 1920s: the true German spirit was to be found along the shores of the Baltic.[18]

Giedion did not include Aalto in the first edition of *Space, Time and Architecture: The Birth of a Tradition,* based on the Norton lectures at Harvard, which he delivered during the academic year 1938–39 and published in 1941. He may have felt that the American public hardly knew the core figures, and Aalto was still peripheral, or that the idea of national expression was alien to American architectural debates. The Aalto retrospective held at MoMA in 1938 changed that.

Aalto's relationship with the innovative young museum began at the 1937 Exposition Internationale des Arts et des Techniques Appliqués à la Vie Moderne in Paris, where his Finnish pavilion attracted the attention of its curators and supporters (fig. 98). Among them was Henry-Russell Hitchcock, who singled out Aalto in *Architectural Forum* as the "greatest individual architect represented

98. Aalto, Finnish Pavilion at the Paris Exposition Internationale des Arts et des Techniques Appliqués à la Vie Moderne, 1936–37, south facade with stairs leading to the film booth

in the Exhibition."[19] The rise of nationalist sentiment in Europe turned out to be lucky for Aalto: the fair that year was marked by the absence of most of the pioneers of the modern movement, with the exception of Le Corbusier, who, having worked on several comprehensive urban plans since 1932, was here given only a minor commission, the Pavillon des Temps Nouveaux. The countries central to the development of the international modern movement—France, Germany, Russia, and Italy—now shunned modernism and turned instead to neoclassical monumentalism, so that the exhibition became a showcase of modernism from the smaller countries: Finland, Czechoslovakia, and Sweden, all of which garnered Hitchcock's praise. Ominously, Albert Speer's German pavilion and Boris Iofan's Russian pavilion formed the gateway to the foreign section at Trocadéro (fig. 99). Aalto's tiny Finnish pavilion was nestled just below the Palais de Chaillot. Not that the pavilion was without nationalist bravura: the large photomurals of synchronized gymnasts and workers that adorned its exhibition of Finnish society, designed by Aalto, could very well

99. Paris Exposition Internationale des Arts et des Techniques Appliqués à la Vie Moderne, 1936–37, axonometric plan of the "Foreign Section" on the Trocadéro, reproduced from *Le Journal Hebdomadaire Universel* (29 May 1937). Framing the axis by the Seine are Boris Iofan's Russian Pavilion on the left and Albert Speer's German Pavilion on the right. Aalto's pavilion is the first down from the Palais de Chaillot on the left.

have decorated a German or Russian pavilion (fig. 100). Nevertheless, John McAndrew (1904–1978), the curator of the department of architecture at MoMA, instantly offered Aalto an exhibition at the museum.

Why was Aalto, relatively unknown in America, singled out for such an honor? He was only the second architect—Le Corbusier was the first, in 1936—to gain such recognition by the museum. The exhibition catalogue, *Architecture and Furniture: Aalto* reveals the motivation behind the choice. Aalto was celebrated as an arbiter of post–International Style architecture: "Like the design of other men first active in the '30s, Aalto's work, without ceasing in any way to be mod-

100. Photomurals depicting Finnish society displayed in Aalto's Finnish Pavilion at the Paris Exposition Internationale

ern, does not look like the modern work of the '20s." McAndrew defined the shifts and reengagements of the new generation: "Certain materials and forms once renounced because of their association with non-modern work are now used again, in new ways or even in the old ones. To the heritage of pure geometric shapes, the younger men have added free organic curves; to the stylistic analogies with the painters, Mondrian and Léger, they have added Arp."[20]

Aalto was, however, not an easy fit, and the architecture part of the exhibition sent somewhat mixed signals about his position vis à vis the International Style. With their white stucco walls and flat roofs, the Turun Sanomat Building, Paimio Sanatorium, and Viipuri Library could easily be placed within the legacy of 1920s modernism. In order to highlight a paradigm shift the catalogue published only their completion dates. The extensive use of wood in Aalto's own house (1936–37) and the Finnish Pavilion at the Paris Exposition Internationale (1936–37) made a clearer case for a new version of the style, with a national flavor. The furniture section of the exhibition made the gap between first-generation internationalism and this new, more local variety, more explicit: Aalto's furniture was based on a single formal trope, curvilinearity, and on a single material, wood. Individual pieces were mounted on the wall like art objects in order to celebrate their formal and material qualities (fig. 101).

101. Installation of furniture in the exhibition *Architecture and Furniture: Aalto* at the Museum of Modern Art, New York, with Paimio chairs hung on the wall

McAndrew borrowed the idea that the modern movement was experiencing a shift from the "geometric" to the "organic" from Barr, who, in his 1936 catalogue *Cubism and Abstract Art,* had identified these as the "two main traditions of abstract art" (fig. 102). He called the first tradition "intellectual, structural, architectonic, geometrical, rectilinear and classical in its austerity and dependence upon logic and calculation," and the second its polar opposite, "intuitional and emotional rather than intellectual; organic or biomorphic rather than geometrical in its forms; curvilinear rather than rectilinear, decorative rather than structural, and romantic rather than classical in its exaltation of the mystical, the spontaneous and the irrational."[21] In fact, the Aalto retrospective might not have taken place if not for Barr's artistic and intellectual agenda.[22] This relatively

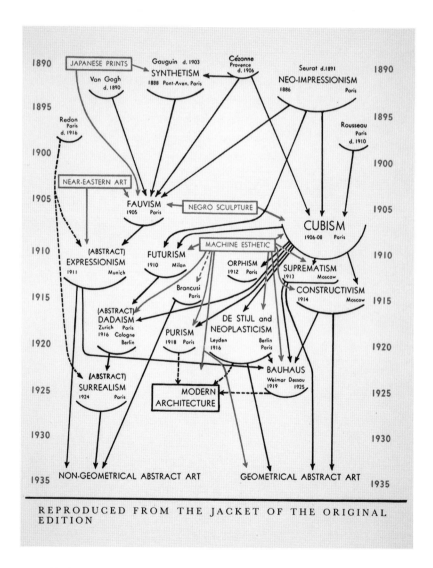

102. Alfred H. Barr, Jr., chart. Reprinted by permission from *Cubism and Abstract Art* © 1936 Museum of Modern Art; Art Resource, New York

unknown Finnish architect supported Barr's claim of a nonlinear and pluralistic evolution of art while at the same time confirming his prediction that the "geometric tradition in abstract art . . . is in decline."[23] McAndrew adapted Barr's formal taxonomies, associating the shift from the geometric to the organic with that from internationalism to an emphasis on national character. Reflecting Barr's sympathy for individual expression, McAndrew labeled Aalto's formal language "personal."

One must add that in Europe, abstract art, including biomorphism, had by the late 1930s lost its political relevance to everyday reality, and that the founders of the historical avant-garde were most out of sync. *Circle: International Survey of Constructive Art,* a catalogue for an exhibition bearing the same name, was edited by the Russian sculptor Naum Gabo, the British painter Ben Nicholson, and the British architect Leslie Martin and published in 1937. Aalto's friends Gropius and Moholy-Nagy contributed to the volume. It called for "universal laws" and "transnational cultural unity" in art. The chosen samples of Aalto's work included in the book seemed by then somewhat dated (fig. 103). And the notion that creating a universal language for art and architecture could play a constructive role in society had a naïve optimism that in retrospect is quite tragic. It is now hard to ignore the fact that the *Circle* exhibition took place at the same time as the Paris Exposition Internationale, whose Soviet and German pavilions embodied the dangers looming on the political horizon.[24]

103. Work by Aalto in J. L. Martin, Ben Nicholson, and Naum Gabo, eds., *Circle: International Survey of Constructive Art* (London: Faber and Faber, 1937)

To be sure, when transposed to a new context and when viewed from a difference vantage point, words and concepts change in meaning. By the late 1930s, American intellectuals had begun to associate internationalism and the International Style with Marxism and other socialist ideologies. Hence, Aalto's presumably "national" style spoke for the need and ability to resist these forces. The shift from uniformity to "personal" expression rides the same political moment. Clement Greenberg's landmark essay "Avant-Garde and Kitsch," written a year after Aalto's MoMA exhibition, juxtaposed kitsch, a product of totalitarianism, with avant-garde, an outcome of the individual artist's fight against authority.[25] By using the conceptual pair of terms *national* and *personal* to describe Aalto's architecture, McAndrew subtly avoided any association with the "debased" totalitarian nationalism of Nazi Germany. The seamless link between formal, psychological, and cultural taxonomies neutralized any ideological meanings. The exhibition, a critical and popular success, was a triumph for MoMA, which had already established itself as a kingmaker and arbiter of trends and styles. McAndrew wrote a jubilant letter to Aalto: "We [have been] pleased to see the great number of architects who visited the show. Wright, Gropius, Breuer, Neutra, Asplund, Lescaze and others have been here." [26]

In singling out Aalto as the European man of the moment and as a representative of a national approach to modernism, MoMA was endorsing the idea of localized, nationally distinctive trends in modernism. The 1932 exhibition *Modern Architecture: International Exhibition* was followed by *America Can't Have Housing* (1934), *Modern Architecture in California* (1935), *Architecture of H. H. Richardson* (1936), and *A New House by Frank Lloyd Wright* (1938).[27]

So when Aalto set to work on the competition for the Finnish Pavilion for the 1939–40 New York World's Fair in the months following the opening of his MoMA exhibition, he was surely cognizant of what Americans might want to see. As if to fulfill MoMA's prediction that architectural culture was shifting from the geometric to the organic, he designed the pavilion with a dominant tilted curvilinear multimedia wall. What the exhibition catalogue called a "vigorous expression of the work and culture of the Finnish people" was celebrated with photographic enlargements of Finns and displays of industrial products (fig. 104).[28] The size of the photomurals—like those made by the constructivists some twenty years earlier—aimed to provoke a strong emotional reaction in viewers. The exhibition continued this tradition of Northern exoticism and the promotion of Finnish identity through architecture. It consisted of an installation in an existing building, and included a large exhibition space dominated by a tall, undulating wooden wall made of narrow vertical strips of wood on which a montage of photos was installed. Whereas the acoustic ceiling of the Viipuri Library built on a tension between form and function, the New York wall played on the multilayered symbolic meanings embedded in form.

The competition entry was entitled "Aurora Borealis" and suggested that the form attempted to mimic the shapes created by the natural phenomenon. The

104. Aino and Alvar Aalto, Finnish Pavilion in the New York World's Fair, main display wall, 1939

large, undulating wall, with its long vertical lines, resembled the patterns of the northern lights in the sky, to be sure. Photo enlargements of a Finnish lake landscape with similar undulating forms gave an alternative narrative about the meaning behind the formal language. A closer look at the installation reveals yet another, more subtle, relationship between the form of the wall and nature in Finland. The photomontage constructs a narrative of how wood, Finland's most celebrated raw material, was transformed into skis, paper, furniture, and other export items, and how these products were in turn transported around the world. It showed how wood could be used as a building material, even replacing other materials, such as tile (fig. 105). Finnish nature is depicted both as something pure and exotic, and as a source of the industrial products that form the foundation of the country's economic and social well-being.

Aalto was careful to avoid any vulgar display of nationalist propaganda when talking about his exhibition strategy. "Large exhibitions suffer from so-called exhibition nausea," he told the *Helsingin Sanomat* in June 1939. "Finland's good reputation in America relies on the sensitive use of advertising."[29] As a conse-

105. Aino and Alvar Aalto, Finnish Pavilion at the New York World's Fair, detail of the film screen

quence, he steered away from infusing his pavilion design with any explicit meaning, wanting rather to create an "impression on the visitor psychologically and instinctively." "A true image of a country cannot be conveyed with individual objects alone; it can be done convincingly only by the atmosphere such objects create together, that is, only by the overall effect perceived by the senses."[30] The creation of a politically innocent and materially allusive "atmosphere" was based on carefully considered representational strategies: displaying objects in a state-of-becoming, endlessly repeating the undulating line in all scales, blurring the hierarchy between objects and their background, and integrating different media—objects, photographs, films. These representational strategies shared with the vernacular what Roland Barthes has called the "reality effect," marked by an "overabundance of details" and images that, rather than forming a coherent narrative, simply claim: "we are real."[31] The frantic overlapping of lines and textures added to their mystique (fig. 106).

The emergence of quasivernacular motifs in Aalto's work in the late 1930s supported similar readings. In this context the vernacular represented a benign

106. Detail of the exhibition installation in the Finnish Pavilion at the New York World's Fair

version of national architecture in a politically charged moment in history.[32] A rustic sauna and fence that he added to the Villa Mairea around the time of the MoMA exhibition allude specifically to the Finnish vernacular building tradition. When cited by modernists in this emblematic way, the vernacular always points to local culture in its innocent state, prior to the birth of nation-states. The sources of this "politically correct" version of national expression in Aalto's work are ambiguous. Sometimes he cited vernacular architectures far removed from the Finnish or even the European tradition, as may be seen in the vaguely Japanese details of the Paris Pavilion (fig. 107). To be sure, in the prevailing political climate he would have hardly gained sympathy in the United States for simply asserting an insular nationalism like the German *Heimatstil,* whose Finnish version would have been Carelianism. Importantly, he pointed to a time before the formation of nation-states, suggesting that all vernacular architectures had once shared the same local origins.

At the same time, there was something ominous in the way the tilting wall loomed over the spectator; it made the visitor's agitation manifest in an instant, and in this sense, the reference to the northern lights was a reference to Finland itself, imperiled in view of the approaching crisis of the war. The combination of all these different references—nature, industrial production, and world politics—signaled that Aalto continued to believe in architecture as a tool for nationalist propaganda. A parallel could be drawn to the Finnish Pavilion at the 1900 Exposition Universelle in Paris, designed by Gesellius-Lindgren-Saarinen, which was a highly speculative attempt to create a uniquely Finnish style in order to promote the country's desire for independence at time of Russian oppression (fig. 108).[33]

107. Aalto, Finnish Pavilion, Paris Exposition Internationale, detail of the entrance canopy

These layers of material, symbolic, and political meanings were aimed at two audiences: Finns and others. To the American audience, the organizers—Finnish business groups and government representatives—wanted to communicate that the Finnish culture and economy were strong. To Finns, the pavilion and its reception were intended to boost self-confidence. The accompanying English-language publications emphasized Finno-American relationships and mutually beneficial economic ties (fig. 109).

Aalto never addressed the charged political message of his installation. So when asked to reflect on his contribution to the New York World's Fair in 1939 by the American Federation of Art, he responded vaguely: "Unfortunately I lack the words to explain what the Finnish pavilion and exhibition were intended to convey. After all, exhibitions are explanations in themselves, although they seek to persuade by force of matter rather than of words." He then shifted the discussion to what he considered a more important function of the exhibition pavilion—as a node in a global information gathering and dissemination network: "If planned wisely, [world's fairs] have a mission today that greatly surpasses their previous influence. They could be used to form permanent, purposeful national pedagogic institutes in each country, and a kind of global school for all,"

108. The cover of *Le Pavillon Finlandais*, the official brochure for the Finnish pavilion for the Exposition Universelle held in Paris, 1900

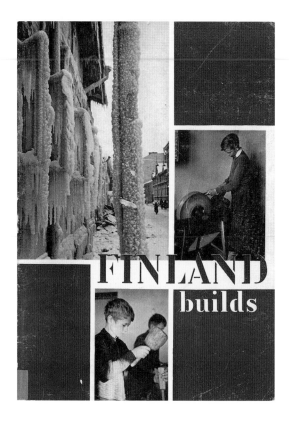

he declared, continuing that their "rightful role [is] as a spur to human progress."
In his view, a "detailed presentation of an average American farm and of farm life
in general, and the way it is organized, was more interesting to the public than
the fair structures, each one larger and more heavily decorated than the last, for
their message is an empty shell, being either too thin or too utopian in content."[34]

The start of the Finno-Russian Winter War in November 1939 gave a new
urgency to the effort to communicate Finland's political interests. When sent by
the Finnish government to the United States in 1940, Aalto found that the
American media were on his side: tiny Finland was depicted as a modern-day
David heroically fighting the Goliath of the Russian army. Giedion, informed of
Finland's hardship as well as of Aalto's American fame, willingly joined the propaganda mission. In 1941, while Aalto embarked on a lecture tour in Switzerland
to solicit financial and humanitarian aid, Giedion wrote a second article on Aalto,
"Irrationality and Standard[ization]," articulating the complex relationship between
his architecture and Finland's political condition. No longer hesitant to offer
historically and culturally specific commentary, Giedion leapt into statements like,
"[Finland] provides [Aalto] with that inner source of energy which always flows
through his work." Whereas in his 1931 article he had celebrated the mystical

109. The cover of *Finland Builds* (New York: Finland's New York World's Fair
Commission, 1940)

nationalist essence flowing from Finland through Aalto into his work, he now considered Aalto's relationship to Finland ambiguous, even tormented. "Aalto is restless. He cannot always stand to stay amidst the Finnish birch forests."[35] He compared Aalto with émigré artists like James Joyce and Pablo Picasso to reinforce the political dimension of their shared existential condition as outsiders. Aalto too, he suggested, was a kind of exile, and that status further removed him from any single national context.

In the immediate aftermath of the Second World War the convergence of nationalism and internationalism in Aalto's architecture and persona appealed greatly to American political and cultural sentiments, which coupled international interests with a growing sense of national pride. In this context Aalto and Finland represented a triumph over Russia, America's former ally and now principle enemy. Finland's heroism surely colored Elizabeth Mock's words, when she wrote in the catalogue for the 1944 exhibition *Built in U.S.A.: 1932–44* that the American audience considered Aalto's forms a visual manifestation of the "will to freedom." Aalto was indeed one of the few European modernists left who exemplified the national origins of the modern movement and thus remained a suitable model. Mock retrospectively credits the 1938 Aalto show at MoMA with affirming the growing dissatisfaction with International Style modernism among American architects.[36] Aalto and Finland represented resistance to all tyranny, be it imposed by totalitarianism or the International Style.

By the mid-1940s, what Mock had labeled as Aalto's "fresh and sympathetic forms" had found their way into American architecture and design to the point that the "free form" became the hallmark of free (American) society. The use of organic, curvilinear forms open to different functional applications, which Aalto had made his signature form in the 1930s, gained a powerful rhetorical symbolism in America, becoming associated with individual and political freedom.

But any political residue in the curvilinear form soon disappeared as the "free form" became an emblem of a new "lifestyle modernism" that MoMA helped to pioneer in the late 1940s. The influential exhibition *Modern Art in Your Life,* curated by Robert Goldwater in collaboration with MoMA's director, René d'Harnoncourt, in 1948, was structured to reflect the formal categories established by Barr in 1936 in *Cubism and Abstract Art:* abstract geometric form, organically stylized form, geometrically stylized representation, and, echoing the *Fantastic Art, Dada and Surrealism* catalogue and show of 1936, one artistic category, "Surrealism and the fantastic." Each category juxtaposed examples of European art, architecture, and design from the 1920s with work by living artists, architects, and designers working in the same formal idiom to prove that abstract forms were able to migrate between mediums, geographic locations, and cultural contexts, and through time. For example, the category "abstract organic form" included two wood reliefs by Arp from the late 1920s juxtaposed with sculptures by Isamu Noguchi and Alexander Calder and furniture by Charles and Ray Eames and George Nelson from the 1940s.

Aalto was curiously absent from this exhibition and catalogue, though he made frequent visits to America through the 1940s. His biomorphic and curvilinear forms had been by that time been appropriated so widely that they had lost their political resonance. The new generation of American architects, among them Eero Saarinen and Charles Eames, who won the Organic Furniture Design competition in 1941, approached the "free form" simply as a technological challenge and as a means of conveying comfort. Curvilinear forms now promised a new modernism that was exuberant, liberated, and fun. Aided by institutions like MoMA, organicism helped modernism enter a new phase of mass consumption.

Those committed to the original socioaesthetic program of modernism were appalled. Among these was the Californian planner Catherine Bauer, who was married to William Wurster. In 1950 she sent Aalto a newspaper clipping of an advertisement for a quasi-biomorphic lampshade and table that drew on the organic shapes that he had pioneered a decade earlier: "Said you were a dangerous man," she wrote. "Here is what Free Form has come to—Even worse than California Ranch Houses."[37]

So swiftly did the once-potent political element vanish from modernist debates on form that in 1946 Edgar Kaufmann, Jr., son of the patron of Frank Lloyd Wright and a curator of industrial design at MoMA, wrote to Aalto, asking him about the origin of the curvilinear form. His question is couched in almost purely aesthetic and practical terms:

You could help me by answering a question, which has been much discussed here in the Museum in the past few days. That is, what do you think was the most important reason or reasons for you developing the curved forms that you have used in your furniture, particularly the pieces where the curves close back upon themselves. It seemed to be a very special expression, quite different from what other modern designers previously tried. I think that some main reasons, such as fitting the chair to the general postures of the human body, were always assumed by us, but perhaps there were other ideas in your mind while these pieces were designed about which we know nothing. The whole problem of the transition from geometrical shapes, which we much used in the early days of modern furniture, to the freer shapes. If you can help us to understand how this development occurred, we would be very grateful.[38]

Kaufmann suspects that there may be more to the shift to "curved forms" than greater concern for ergonomics. A response from Aalto would have been fascinating, but he never replied to Kaufmann's question. Had Aalto tried to answer he would have had to reflect on his own sources of influence (such as Arp) and dwell on what happens when forms are disseminated to different geographic locations, historical moments, and into new mediums. He would have had to discuss the power embedded in an innocent image of Finnish lakes and how it gained an ominous subtext in the context of Finland's desperate political and military conflicts. Aalto's silence may have had to do with the self-censorship that soon afflicted even the most outspoken members of the intellectual and artistic elite in Finland as the defeated country started to adapt to the harsh new reality of its position between the Russian and Western spheres of influence.

The erasure of this tormented period of world history from current Aalto scholarship has led to a distorted understanding of the deepest meanings of the curvilinear form and the organic idea in his work. Too often today the curvilinear form is used as a designation for something represented—that is, Finnish nature—rather than as a reminder of the historical and personal events that went into the making of it.

Chapter Nine **Ambiguity**

With the highly political backdrop of Aalto's career, life, architecture, and reception now forgotten, viewers see his architecture simply as exemplary of a softer, more human version of modernism, one invested with indeterminate qualities that are hard to describe or quantify. In this chapter I trace the origins of this reading both in his writings and his reception, and I argue that the very notion of ambiguity—that is, architecture operating as a "floating signifier"—could be interpreted as Aalto's ultimate geopolitical endgame during the Cold War years.

Aalto's architecture started to be viewed as ambiguous and complex during the 1960s. He is, for example, one of few the modern architects whom Robert Venturi (1926–) endorses in his 1966 book *Complexity and Contradiction in Architecture* for being able to invest his architecture with richness of meaning and formal effects, signs of all good architecture throughout the ages, according to the author. Venturi singles out eight of Aalto's buildings—all but one from the postwar era—for analysis, among them Baker House dormitory at Massachusetts Institute of Technology (1946–49), Vuoksenniska Church (1955–58), and Maison Carré in Bazoches-sur-Guyonne, France (1956–59), buildings that Venturi sees as combining contradictory architectural ordering principles (the duality between the two facades at MIT being one of them). While stopping short of drawing geographic conclusions, Venturi does make a historical argument, claiming that increasing societal complexity makes such architecture more in demand than ever before. Venturi also sees formal ambiguity as being somehow true to the "richness and ambiguity of modern experience."[1] A quote by August Heckscher, an eminent public advocate and President John F. Kennedy's special advisor on the arts —"Rationalism proves inadequate in any period of upheaval. . . . A feeling of paradox allows seemingly dissimilar things to exist side by side, their very incongruity suggesting a kind of truth"—opens a door for multiple cultural interpretations of Aalto's work that Venturi does not pursue.[2]

It is perhaps no surprise that such readings started to emerge in the late 1960s, a period of great worldwide social and political turmoil that called for reassessing architecture's social role. Apart from its formal complexity, architecture started to be viewed as a potent cultural product able to affect people's behavior and social patterns.

Venturi's reading of Aalto thus must be viewed in the larger discursive framework of the 1960s, which brought forth questions about the social role of art and architecture. The genesis and meaning of form was a key aspect of this debate. One of the important books of the era was Umberto Eco's *Opera aperta* (Open Work, 1962), which proposed that, ideally, an artist would leave an artwork "open" to allow plurality and multiplicity of meanings. Such "open work" had the ability to engage the viewer psychologically; the more meanings generated, the better the work. Important for the discussion about architecture's relationship to a particular time and place is the notion that a subject is called to read his or her own existential states and cultural priorities into the work of art. In Eco's words: "As he reacts to the play of stimuli and his own response to their patterning, the individual addressee is bound to supply his own existential credentials, the sense conditioning which is peculiarly his own, a defined culture, a set of tastes, personal inclinations, and prejudices. Thus, his comprehension of the original artifact is always modified by his particular and individual perspective. In fact, the form of the work of art gains its aesthetic validity precisely in proportion to the number of different perspectives from which it can be viewed and understood."[3] The meaning of a work of art was no longer tied to the time and place of its creation but remained open for reinterpretations in different cultural contexts.

In his landmark book *Notes on the Synthesis of Form* (1964), Christopher Alexander considered architectural work as such a nexus of communication, although his focus was on the design process. He reasoned that as the world became more complex, designers needed to take a more diligent approach to analyzing and solving problems. This included gathering all necessary information and data that might influence the design. In addition to programmatic, material, and economic considerations, designers needed to think about the future development of societies.

The Italian architect-critic Leonardo Mosso's (1926–) 1981 book, *alvar aalto: systematic and structural reading,* and the exhibition of the same title, drew from Eco and Alexander by balancing an analysis of Aalto's design method with speculation on how his forms gained social significance and meaning. Mosso's interpretation of Aalto is worth examining in detail because of the way it reverses the relationship between art and reality—he sees Aalto's architecture as a generator of Finnish culture, rather than vice versa. While written from a particular Italian political and cultural perspective, his interpretation also illuminates Finland's and, subsequently, Aalto's new status during the Cold War.

Mosso's exhibition, which opened in the Alvar Aalto Museum in Jyväskylä in July 1979, consisted of dozens of black and white images of Aalto's architecture—mostly from the postwar era, which were laid out in a matrix that covered the walls and part of the floor and ceiling (fig. 110). The reproductions were roughly 30 centimeters square. The six sections of the exhibition—"nature," "work," two sections entitled "aalto's city-house," "aalto's city-culture," and "city given back to the citizen"—refer to the idea that Aalto's architecture and, subsequently, Finnish culture grows, as if naturally, out of its context, be it natural or man-made.[4] The form is characterized as a registration of material, programmatic, and contextual forces, open-ended enough to endorse different readings and associations but ordered enough to support existing societal structures and suggest new ones. In his essay "alvar aalto, architect of social and cultural communication," Mosso asserts that Aalto's goal was nothing less than to "build and together change society." What he calls "social and cultural communication by means of architecture" is based on the idea that, first, Aalto's architecture fosters interaction between people; second, it acts as a hinge between the historical city and its future; and third, it communes with nature.[5] The dialectical model aimed at dissolving the opposition between social formulations and architecture in each instance.

Mosso's reading of Aalto was informed by his own work on what he called "self-generative form" and planning, where architecture was seen as a kind of open structure or lattice that would allow humans to create "their own environments and destinies," as he and his collaborators put it in a 1971 article, "Self Generation of Form and the New Ecology."[6] Mosso paraphrases Ernesto Baroni, the Marxist cultural historian: "Historical process only becomes history if it actualizes the destiny inherent in man: that is, as we should say, if it realizes the self-planning of the community." For Mosso, the word *culture* meant nothing less than "everybody's knowledge and awareness." In the case of architecture, this means that in an ideal society people are not just subjected to built envi-

110. Leonardo Mosso, *alvar aalto: systematic and structural reading*, exhibition installation, 1979

ronments and political systems from without but are in full control in generating those systems. In other words, in an ideal society people are finally able to take their destiny into their own hands. In Mosso's words: "Only the personal and collective generation of form, including not only houses, cities and surroundings, but also political choice and collective aims, in a perennial dynamic equilibrium with the ecological and ecosocial situation, represents true and complete self-consciousness; it is the indispensable premise for self-realization."[7]

These words make Mosso's intellectual project explicit: to apply Marxist ideas to local contexts and to shift focus from the analysis of economic structures to cultural critique. His reading of Aalto was informed by ideas about Finland. By using the main assumption among Italian Marxists about the collective subject's progressive ability to forge its own history, Mosso de facto "re-nationalized" Finland as a country "self-generated" by its people.[8] Mosso believed that in order to foster social and cultural transformation, both the architect and critic rely on the scientific method of analysis. In that vein, Mosso believed that Aalto's "architectural revolution is entirely one of method, and only as a result of this is it also a revolution of form."[9] He also explains why Aalto had by the end of his life given up writing and other social activities: Aalto "believed above all, and perhaps uniquely, in the communicative capacity inherent in the material product of his work and hence in the message derived from the quality of his own extremely high professional specificity."[10] Word and actions did not speak alone; the complex architectural product could trigger social transformation.

Following the structuralist model of Louis Althusser, Mosso believed that cultural transformation does not necessarily require changes in the political or economic system. Finland, as a capitalist country, could still sponsor radically engaged subjects able to take their historical destiny in their own hands. In Mosso's reading of Aalto, this revolutionary end culminated with the empowerment of a new class of "citizens."

The political subtext of Mosso's analysis leads us consider how Aalto himself saw the relationship between architectural forms and reality, and how he understood architecture's historical role. Here Mosso's emphasis on open-endedness and self-generation are not at odds with Aalto's own pronouncements from the 1930s onward, when he started to use the word *complex* to describe the constellation of issues that architecture needed to take into consideration. Aalto becomes, for example, notably sensitive to the instability of meanings when he wrote in a 1930 article how "the same words, used in different situations by different people in different social classes, can mean almost entirely different things; sometimes they may even have diametrically opposed meanings."[11] At times Aalto makes it sound as though ambiguity was both the necessary and only possible solution. I argue that his emphasis on open-endedness and ambiguity became increasingly invested with a geopolitical subtext in the postwar era.

Aalto's first plea for a more complex understanding of form—its creation and social impact—is put forward in "Rationalism and Man," a lecture he delivered in 1935 at the annual meeting for the Swedish Society of Industrial Designers. He came to the same conclusion Mosso did some fifty years later: the main problem of modern architecture was its emphasis on form and style at the expense of a more complex understanding of architecture's impact on human life and culture. At this point he started to talk about a "human" approach to architecture, proclaiming that the "reason why the now predominant trend in applied art, formalism, arouses so little enthusiasm is partly the entirely insufficient role of human objectives as its driving force."[12] According to him, the modernist emphasis on Sachlichkeit and rationality was compromising the complexity of human life by overlooking unobservable aspects of the human psyche, such as feelings and intuition. He uses an organic analogy to make a case for the self-generation of form, and to suggest that all architecture and all human action evolves around everyday human life:

Nature, biology, has rich and luxurious forms. With the same construction, the same tissues, and the same principles of cellular organization, it can create billions of combinations, each of which represents a definitive, highly developed form. Man's life belongs to the same category. The things that surround him are hardly fetishes or allegories with mystical eternal value; more than anything else, they are cells and tissues, living beings like himself, building components that make up human life. They cannot be treated differently from other biological units, lest they run the risk of not fitting into the system and becoming dehumanized.[13]

Even though Aalto, unlike Mosso, does not actually use the term *ecology,* which became a special field of study in the mid-1930s, his thinking is focused on the interaction between organisms and their environment.[14] This model presumed that human beings were embedded in the world rather than observing and acting on it from without. Everything coexists within a complex reciprocal web of relationships and responses.

Another lecture, "The Influence of Structure and Material on Contemporary Architecture," delivered at the Nordic Building Forum conference in Oslo in 1938, continues to call for architecture that "can fulfill its task in supporting broad ranging humane, socio-economic, and psychological decisions."[15] Aalto makes the case that in order to meet these goals architects should focus on the process instead of the results: "On deeper examination, architecture is not merely a set of given structural results, but to a much greater degree a complex process of development, whose inner interaction steadily produces new solutions, new forms, new building materials, and constant changes in structural ideas."[16] Architects should not, in other words, obsess about final results but be ready to engage a "complex" synthetic process, which leads to unpredictable new solutions and forms. An open-ended process would presumably result in an equally rich and complex open-ended product, which would in turn engage the viewer in the production of meaning. Aalto continues to claim that only then can architecture gain social significance: "If architecture is to fulfill its task in supporting broad ranging humane, socio-economic, and psychological decisions, it must be given the widest possible freedom of maneuver, both internally and in external form. All outward formal constraints—whether deep-seated stylistic tradition or superficial standardization arising from a misunderstanding of new architecture—hinder architecture from contributing with its full potential to man's struggle for survival, and therefore diminish its significance and effectiveness."[17] Architecture's social value is for him directly proportional to the level of freedom and openness in the design process.

In an article from the same year, "The Humanizing of Architecture," Aalto continues to praise gentler values. "Architecture is not a science. It is still the same great synthetic process of combining thousands of definite human functions, and remains architecture. Its purpose is still to bring the material world into harmony with human life. To make architecture more human means better architecture."[18] Implicit in this argument is that architecture does not only reflect life and its processes but is an integral part of life.

As mentioned earlier, these ideas resonated with a certain generation of Italians who had experienced fascism and believed that the country's future relied on social programs and the creation of livable environments akin to those that had been built in Scandinavia—Tapiola Garden City, constructed in the 1950s near Helsinki, for instance. Tellingly, Mosso's first book, an exhibition catalogue for the 1965 Aalto retrospective in Florence, *L'Opera di Alvar Aalto,* was published by the Edizioni di Comunità, funded by the industrialist Adriano Olivetti and devoted to social causes and urbanism.[19]

Before Mosso, Aalto was endorsed by the eminent architectural historian Bruno Zevi (1918–2000) and his Association for Organic Architecture (APAO).[20] His 1949 book *Towards an Organic Architecture* celebrates Aalto's ability to combine functional rigor with "artistic intuition."[21] His architecture proposed an alternative both to ultrarationalism and megalomaniacal formal expressions by infusing architecture with subtle psychological and programmatic nuances. As common to representatives of organic architecture, he placed "psychological and social interests"[22] over aesthetics, and focused on the potentials of three-dimensional space. Zevi sums up the shared goals of what he labels as the school of "organic architecture" as follows: "A freedom from the T-square and from geometric composition has opened up the road to the most imaginative developments in the organization of living space. . . . Man's happiness is the aim of architecture to-day."[23]

Zevi called for architecture that would revolutionize consciousness by creating forms and spaces able to liberate human imagination and energy in the service of a better future. However, Zevi's prose made it difficult—if not impossible—to adapt these powerful architectural ideas into wider use. While stimulating, Zevi's mantra—"Organic architecture equals architecture of democracy"—was, as

Manfredo Tafuri has noted, too vague to become widely applicable to real-life problems faced by postwar reconstruction.[24] Perhaps in part because of Zevi's endorsement, in the survey *Modern Architecture* (1976) Tafuri and his coauthor, Francesco Dal Co, went as far as to claim that Aalto's "historical significance has perhaps been rather exaggerated; with Aalto we are outside of the great themes that have made the course of contemporary architecture so dramatic. The qualities of his works have meaning only as masterful distractions, not subject to reproductions outside the remote reality in which they have their roots."[25]

Yet Aalto continued to capture the imagination of the more hopeful Italian architects and social critics, who believed in architecture's ability to bring about social change. It was in this cultural climate that Aalto gained several commissions, among them the Riola Church (1966–67), the Villa Erica (1969–72), commissioned by Olivetti's niece, the Cultural Center of Siena (1966), and the San Lanfranco Housing Estate in Pavia (1966–69).[26] Although only the Riola Church got built, it was the housing estate that is most indicative. The commission was to design a satellite town consisting of a town center and housing for eleven thousand people. Aalto proposed a series of serpentine slab buildings in a parklike setting. A diagrammatic drawing depicts rows of continuous serpentine housing blocks forming pod-shaped courtyards in between (fig. 111).

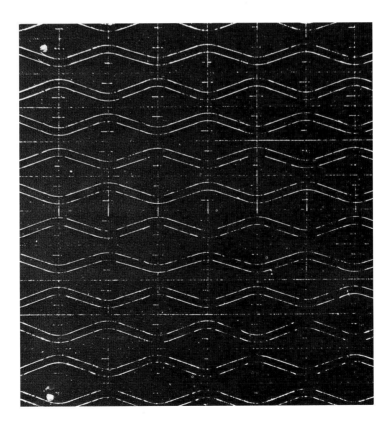

111. Aalto, Pavia, San Lanfranco Housing Estate in Pavia (1966–69). Conceptual diagram.

According to Mosso, who was involved in the project as a design associate, Pavia exemplifies the "synchronic lattice logic of [his] city-house," able to merge multiple programs (for example, house, housing, urbanism, and landscape) and all scales (individual, domestic, communal, and urban).[27] Mosso's enthusiasm for the design was probably influenced by the undulating line—already a trademark of Aalto's work—which here was regulated to be an ideal combination of logic and intuition, so that neither rationality nor irrationality was given full rein. Aalto's proposal was both grounded in real-life problems and poetic enough to trigger the imagination and, thus, hope for the future. An introduction to a portfolio of Aalto's works for *Zodiac* from 1958 by painter and critic Pier Carlo Santini is typical of Aalto's wider Italian reception. In it Aalto's architecture is characterized by a "feeling of space liberated and controlled by form," as a product of "research [that] reaches into the complete bliss of sheer creation." Santini concludes: "With what does it rhyme this strange architecture that escapes any classification in its ultimate greatness? With what indeed, if not with beauty nowadays so oft wronged, so oft denied in a man's life?"[28] The article is accompanied by series of portraits of the aging master sketching at his desk.

Aalto endorsed this reading by celebrating the creative potentials within the human psyche and, in the process, mystifying his own design approach. In the much-quoted article "Architettura e arte concreta" (Architecture and concrete art), commissioned by another Italian friend, Ernesto Rogers, for the Italian magazine *Domus* in 1947 and later published as "The Trout and the Stream," Aalto declared himself a "practicing artist," describing his design process as follows: "This is what I do—sometimes quite instinctively—in such a case. I forget the whole maze of problems for a while, as soon as the feel of the assignment and the innumerable demands it involves have sunk into my subconscious. I then move on to a method of working that is very much like abstract art. I simply draw by instinct, not architectural syntheses, but what are sometimes quite childlike compositions, and in this way, on an abstract basis, the main idea gradually takes shape, a kind of universal substance that helps me to bring the numerous contradictory components in harmony."[29]

He described scribbling ideas intuitively on paper, without a preconception of their outcome, and claimed that this intense creative experience led to an equally intense artistic experience for the beholder. Aalto insisted that reality could not be accessed objectively but required an emotionally invested subject: "Abstract art . . . can be understood purely and solely through feeling, even though ideas about construction and the web of human tragedy often come into it and loom behind it. In this way it is a weapon that can create in us a flow of purely human feeling that the written word has somehow lost."[30] At first, Aalto's statement appears to suggest that art is a way to escape reality; he talked about the "burden" of architects having to deal with "social, humanitarian, economic, and technological requirements combined with psychological problems affecting both the individual and the group."[31] Yet within a postwar context informed by existentialism and phenomenology, Aalto's statements are apt: the revolution was expected to happen from within.

A series of freehand drawings done during trips to the Middle East—a perfect place to escape the mayhem of Cold War Europe—dates from a few years after this essay. They bear a striking resemblance to Joseph Albers' drawings of the early 1940s, done with a single meandering arabesque.[32] Albers considered abstract form powerful precisely because it did not try to represent reality, but was able to create a thoroughly private experience that could shield the viewer from a harsh world. Albers' motto—"Nothing can be one thing but a hundred things, all art is [a] swindle"[33]—shares the ethos that art's power has to do exactly with the ability to trigger the imagination and, in so doing, create new realities. Aalto's drawings of the Middle East can be understood as an endorsement of a particular perceptual process in which the subject matter constantly flickers in and out of focus. The viewer is invited to fill in the gaps. This intense interest in a pure experimentation with technique is most visible in Aalto's 1951 drawing of a human figure riding a donkey in Morocco (fig. 112), which resembles Albers' 1942 drawing *Rondo* (fig. 113). In both works the freehand "curlicue" can be read as a pure idea of drawing that creates richly evolving texture with tactile and spatial effects. Compared to the curvilinear forms from the 1930s, Aalto's draw-

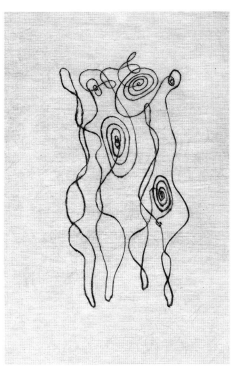

112. Aalto, *Encounter on a Village Street, Morocco*, 1951
113. Josef Albers, *Rondo*, 1942, drypoint 203 × 14 cm. Josef and Anni Albers Foundation, Bethany, Connecticut; Artists Rights Society, New York.

ings of the 1950s appear like compressed bundles of restless scribbles without a sense of even momentary repose or arrival of form.

Aalto's insistence on an intuitive process that would lead to an intense and existential engagement on the part of the viewer can be read both as a sign of discomfort with the world as it was and as an acknowledgment that reality can best be accessed through a symbolic system like art. To be sure, architecture designed after World War II had the immense task of addressing the unfathomable sense of loss and trauma that lingered in Europe. Aalto's emphasis on intuition should therefore not be interpreted simply as an escape from reality but rather as an attempt to tap the deeper layer of the psyche, eliciting a catharsis. The emphasis on large human issues in his writing—"freedom," "universalism," and "harmony"—is symptomatic of the strong existential-humanistic rhetoric common in the immediate postwar era.

Aalto's interest in this quasi-intuitive design method and architectural experience was not devoid of geopolitical content. Therefore, before we explore Aalto's quest for creative "freedom" that resulted in formal exploration without functional or structural considerations, we must be remind ourselves that freedom was, to say the least, a relative term in postwar Finland. One need only recall that the Soviet army even occupied the Porkkala peninsula just west of Helsinki till 1956, an arrangement that was part of the 1945 peace accord. In fact, the notion of freedom had political connotations for Aalto from the beginning. The idea of Finland being a harbinger of a new and presumably free world preoccupied Aalto from the late 1940s. Not only did he start to make frequent claims that Finland was a Western democratic country at this point, but he suggested that freedom and democratic values could become the defining factors in Finland's political and social life, as well as its calling card. The 1949 article "Finland as a Model for World Development" offered a simple recipe: following the logic of nature and its self-generative process will lead to architecture that is equally free. Free architecture will subsequently promote freedom in human society. "Nature is a symbol of freedom. Sometimes it is actually the source of the concept of freedom, and its maintainer. By basing our technical master plans firmly on nature, we have every chance of turning the tide, making our daily work and all its forms increase freedom, rather than reduce it."[34]

Aalto intensified his calls for freedom a year after Finland and the Soviet Union signed the Treaty of Friendship, Cooperation, and Mutual Assistance in 1948, ending a four-year period of uncertainty about whether Finland would succumb to the Eastern Bloc (fig. 114). The events following the World War II had, however, long-term consequences for Finland's future that were caused by unanticipated geopolitical shifts. When America's former ally, the Soviet Union, became its ideological enemy, Europe became divided into West and East. Finland was no longer considered the far corner of Europe but a country caught in the middle of Cold War intrigues and tensions. As a consequence Finland stayed under the Soviet political influence for decades to come.

We have seen how industrialization went hand in hand with the attempt to restructure the Finnish economy after American models in the years during and after the war. These models proved, however, inadequate in addressing the particularly European—and Finnish—need to reinvent its cultural identity long term. Aalto's emphasis on freedom and creativity reflected on a wider shift toward how Europeans started to position themselves vis à vis the new superpowers, the United States and the Soviet Union. Aalto's change of strategy from an interest in large-scale planning to the celebration of the ineffable qualities of architecture can be further linked to the fact that he was, at the time, growing increasingly skeptical about the ever more powerful country across the Atlantic. Writing to Aino during a teaching engagement at MIT in 1945, Aalto paraphrased Frank Lloyd Wright: "My America no longer exists. . . . Democracy has yielded; various fascisms and such have given us a worldwide mobocracy. America has become much more imperialistic than in our days, and so self-sufficient that the civilized people who matter so much to us are no longer as important as they used to be."[35] While once eager to learn American techniques of prefabrication, he now started to see America as the land of rationalization

Countries under U.S. and English influence

Countries under Soviet influence

Countries attempting to stay neutral

114. "Europe Being Divided into Eastern and Western Blocs, 1947," map from a report by the Swedish commander in chief's office. From Pekka Visuri, *Suomi Kylmässä Sodassa* [Finland During the Cold War] (Helsinki: Otava, 2006), 75.

gone amok, where people did not know how to live or feel. Although Aalto never directly criticized the Soviet Union after the war, the ideas about freedom that he put forward in his writings from the late 1940s and 1950s reflected the new geopolitical realities of the Cold War: the Western "free world" against totalitarianism on one hand, and soft European versus hard American values on the other.

Aalto's rejection of America reflects the emergence of the wider European sentiment that, despite their indebtedness to Marshall Plan aid and to American military intervention in the war, Europe should not model its future on America. Aalto's ideas about architecture and its social role were in many ways reflective of this more general thinking about the future of Europe. As historian Tony Judt has noted, there was increasing consensus that Europe had to go beyond the idea that the continent was simply a "geographic expression"—that is, an amalgamation of distinct nations, each with its own autonomous territory.[36] The idea of Europe that started to emerge after the war—of the continent as an increasingly unified social and political entity—was based on socially progressive ideals that would later make the continent, in the words of Judt, both "role-model and magnet for individuals and countries alike."[37] One of Aalto's contributions as a chairman of the Association of Finnish Architecture was to help found the Museum of Finnish Architecture in 1956; its main function was to export Finnish architecture abroad. The first in the series of *Finland Builds* exhibitions was opened in London the following year.[38] It portrayed a country with high standard of living facilitated by quality architecture built in harmony with nature. Finnish architecture and design, with Aalto as its figurehead, became an international standard bearer through the 1960s. It is also the period when Aalto's architectural practice became international, with commissions flowing from different parts of the world.

Apart from Italy, another European country that was a fertile ground for Aalto's architectural ideas, with their political and cultural subtexts, was Germany, which was not only recovering from massive physical destruction but, due to its apportionment, was literally defined by the division between East and West. It is there that we find another locale where the celebration of pure, uninhibited creativity meshes with complex existential and political themes. At the 1951 Darmstädter Gespräche (Darmstadt Discussions), in which Martin Heidegger gave his famous speech "Building, Dwelling, Thinking," the leading German architect-theorist Rudolf Schwarz (1897–1961) put forth ideas about the genesis and experience of form that resonated with Aalto's. Schwarz talked about his "astonishment and wonder [at] how the world exists only in forms, of which each form speaks the truth and does so in an irreplaceable way only to the eye."[39] Schwarz was explicit about why an architect should, at that particular historical moment, start making willful scribbles on paper: he considered it nothing less than a historical responsibility. The open-ended approach to design endorsed an open future. He spoke of the "unplannable" and called for the architect "not [to] overburden himself or the earth with the attempt to eliminate confusion, because the earth and the world require confusion. . . . He must allow space for confusion, enormous free space."[40] Aalto was admired by a group of German architects, including Schwarz, who aimed to steer German postwar architecture away from what they started to consider, somewhat reductively, the rigid Bauhaus legacy, toward a more heterogeneous spatial and formal expression able to trigger deep existential reflection.[41] Poignantly, Aalto's Villa Mairea was included in an exhibition of exemplary buildings that took place in tandem with the Darmstadt Conversations. By the time it had been completed, 1939, Germany had attacked Poland and World War II had begun. In retrospect, the building was a swansong of all the progressive ideals of the modern movement. Retrieving it meant retrieving the ideals it represented and erasing, as it were, what had happened during the war.

Considering the complex political factors and the heavy burden of history, it comes as no surprise that Germany, faced with reinventing its culture, singled out Aalto, who had by the 1950s managed to rid his architecture of any national semantic meanings, as its architect of choice for many significant housing and public projects. The most emblematic of these projects was the Hansaviertel housing block (1955–57, fig. 115), commissioned by the city of West Berlin in response to massive housing developments built along the Stalinallee in Soviet East Berlin. The area contained buildings by the world's leading architects, including Le Corbusier, Gropius, and Oscar Niemeyer, all based on existing modern mass-housing typologies—the slab and the tower in a parklike setting.[42] Aalto's strategy was to envision a whole new typology by designing two low towers consisting of quasi-independent courtyard houses. By emphasizing the individuality of each unit he provided a potent symbol of democratic, anti-Soviet collectivism, while the grouping of the units was communal enough to avoid any reference to extreme individualism. The covered area between the two towers was a perfect metaphor for all new boundaries that had been drawn in Europe,

115. Aalto, Hansaviertel apartment building, Berlin, 1955–57

at times separating families and countrymen from each other (fig. 116). The plan of the Essen Opera House (competition 1959, built posthumously between 1981 and 1988), was, on the other hand, a fitting example of the opposite: a space becoming a kind of "universal substance" without boundaries, in which a "heap," to use Schwarz's term, of different programmatic zones melt inside a continuous skin (fig. 117). Aalto had described just such an approach in the *Domus* article, as had his German colleague, with his conception of "confused" or "free" space.

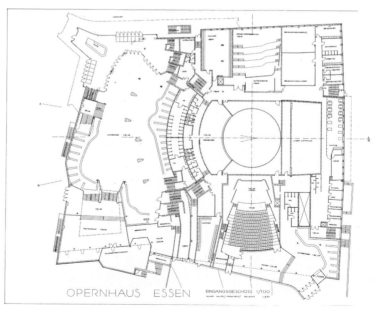

116. Hansaviertel apartment building, entrance area
117. Aalto, Essen Opera House, Germany, 1959–88, first floor plan

Schwarz called for "universal substance" and Aalto started to call for ambiguity just as Europe was being divided into two blocs and, subsequently, when Soviet influence on Finland intensified. Urho Kekkonen (1900–1986), Finland's president from 1956 to 1982, was masterful at dealing with the Soviets, cunningly maintaining Finland's delicate autonomy year after year.[43] The call for ambiguity gains a new meaning against this context.

The convergence of aesthetic strategy and politics leads us to reconsider what Aalto meant by the word *humanism* in the title of the 1955 lecture "Between Humanism and Materialism," given in Vienna. Addressing his Austrian colleagues, who knew something about the relationship between architecture and power (consider, for instance, the baroque buildings of the Habsburg Monarchy), Aalto implied that desire to go beyond mere "humanizing" to consider the visual and symbolic impact of buildings. "I should perhaps devote the last few words of my talk," he said, "to the formal aspects of architecture. Although the solving of architectural problems is a necessary humanizing procedure, the old question regarding form and monumentality remains a reality that architects must still confront, as they have always had to do."[44] Significantly, the speech was published in *Der Bau* magazine in Austria, and then in the German magazine *Baukunst-Werkbund,* whose editorial board included Rudolf Schwarz.

It is interesting to consider the relationship between architecture and power, and, subsequently, to speculate about architecture as power, from this perspective. At the time when Aalto gave the talk he had already gained the unofficial status of "state architect" in his home country. The Helsinki University of Technology (1949–66) and the National Pensions Institute Building (1953–55) are some of his largest commissions. Significantly, these commissions were designed to serve the educational and social infrastructure of the welfare state in the making.

So what were Aalto's own politics? As has already become apparent, the fixed polarities between left and right are insufficient to explain the political map of Finland, let alone the changes in Aalto's political orientations. One could say that Aalto was political in a most common sense, in which being political means responding to a situation in a manner that is beneficial to the particular person or entity, in this case Finland. Therefore even the apolitical stance he occupied later in his career was determined by political realities. His architecture from this period is so free of any contextual associations that we hardly remember the political ghosts hanging over many of his major commissions. The Helsinki House of Culture (1952–58) was, for example, commissioned by the Communist Party, which had until then operated in the shadows. The building demonstrates how architectural form participated in this decontextualization. The brick mullions are the key. Rather than being a product of structural or material considerations, in this case form, in an act of reversal, stretches the limits of material, not settling into a priori ideas about what is an appropriate formal language for brick (fig. 118). Architecture is here made to transcend actual conditions and contingencies, and it is exactly the ambiguity of meaning so created that reflects Finland's political goals: to transcend Russia's political influence and become, at least in people's imaginations, a politically ambiguous neutral zone with no ideological attributes.

Vuoksenniska Church (1955–58), which Aalto began designing the same year he gave the Vienna lecture, can be read as the ultimate outcome of what Aalto himself called architectural "humanism": everything builds on formal and spatial effects that obscure any simple functional or material reading. For example, a functional reading of the sliding walls that divide the space is obscured by the powerful visual effect of their pleated surfaces (fig. 119). Heikki Havas, who photographed most of Aalto's postwar buildings, amplified the design's ambiguous reading by zooming in on details, thereby showing them out of context. These images were disseminated internationally through the *Finland Builds* exhibitions. Rather than giving a comprehensive overview of building activities in the country, the exhibitions created an ensemble of highly abstract close-ups of buildings, which were further detached from their purpose and context by an ultra-abstract exhibition installation consisting of rectangular panels suspended in midair (images that later ended up also in Mosso's exhibition). It's no surprise that, by the late 1950s, foreign critics started to marvel at the "human" and "universal" character of Aalto's architecture.[45] Aalto, who before the war had been considered first and foremost a Finnish architect, was now declared "one of the most important European men" when he arrived at the opening of the London installation in 1957.[46] It seemed that by suspending any explicit social or political

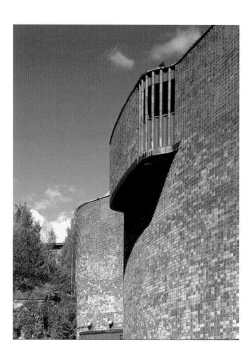

118. Aalto, House of Culture, Helsinki, 1955–58, detail of the facade
[**opposite**] 119. Aalto, Vuoksenniska Church, 1955–57, detail of the windows and of the sliding partition wall

message in favor of formal and spatial ambiguity, Aalto's architecture had, at least momentarily, given hope that Europe could transcend its geopolitical narratives and become united based on shared social and cultural values. Three years later the American magazine *Architectural Forum* went even further in allowing Aalto to transcend geographic locations by declaring in a headline: "Alvar Aalto—Finn Without Borders." Aalto's architecture had universal validity as a "characteristic brand of humanism ... being exported from [his] office in Helsinki."[47]

If we accept the original, Renaissance meaning of the term "humanism," Aalto can indeed be called a humanist architect par excellence—that is, someone who has perfected his art to the level that it became at least as powerful as the political power exercised by the state. The ethos of humanist art could be expressed simply: art was power and it was linked to power. The goal of art was to "delight, to captivate and to convince" an audience, and artists "saw themselves as enfranchised directors and remakers of culture."[48] Due to this ability to sway an audience, an artist was a figure of great authority and influence. "It is not surprising," as Raymond Williams noted, "to find the early 17th century use of 'humanist' to describe someone interested in state affairs and history."[49]

The German philosopher Ernst Cassirer, writing in 1944, building upon the original Renaissance idea of humanism in art, goes even further by observing that human beings depend on such symbolic systems created by man, to access and make sense of reality. He elaborates on man's relationship to the world as follows: "Man does not live in a world of hard facts, or according to his immediate needs and desires. He lives rather in the midst of imaginary emotions, in hopes and fears, in illusions and disillusions, in his fantasies and dreams. . . . Reality is not a unique and homogeneous thing; it is immensely diversified, having as many different schemes and patterns as there are different organisms." Man lives thus "not merely in a broader reality; he lives, so to speak, in a new *dimension* of reality." This affects his interpretation of art, whose function is not to "express thought or ideas, but feelings and affections," which vary from person to person.[50]

We could thus draw two conclusions about the political dimension of Aalto and his architecture. On one hand, his psychologizing, open-ended design method reflected the Finnish Cold War political atmosphere, which was marked by its own share of conceit, ambiguity, and double play. On the other hand we can credit Aalto for transcending this impulse—for not settling to make architecture reflect reality but rather for helping to shape and formulate and imagine a new Finland. Either way, his architecture was successful in both the international and national arenas. Internationally, Aalto contributed to the image of Finland as a free and neutral country, as innocent as its bountiful nature. For Finns, his architecture offered spaces of beauty and harmony in the midst of a complicated geopolitical situation. The emphasis on space was, importantly, primarily experiential, rather than territorial.

The so-called Rautatalo, or Iron Building (1953–55; fig. 120), in downtown Helsinki, built as the Iron Curtain was rising, was perhaps the first spatial manifestation of such an alternative or double play. The building has a reinforced-concrete grid structure that is well within the canon of international modernism. But walking into the marble-clad interior courtyard one feels transported to another world, almost dreamlike, uplifting and light (fig. 121). Nothing on the exterior prepares the visitor for the serenity of the light-filled courtyard. Aalto knew that spatial and aesthetic experience can at times make the most powerful political statement as images and atmospheres. This is not to say that architecture provided a mere escape from reality, but rather that its power resided in its ability to think beyond its surrounding geopolitical coordinates as pure space.

As has been discussed, Aalto's public reception was always tied to questions about Finland's geopolitical role. The renewed interest in Aalto during the late 1970s, including Mosso's, can be viewed against the political backdrop of the end of the Cold War, which officially occurred at the 1975 European Security Conference Summit in Helsinki. Initiated by President Kekkonen, the event also marked Finland's emergence as an officially neutral country able to transcend political conflicts between East and West. As if knowing that he had brought his geopolitical narrative to its conclusion, Aalto died a year later. Appropriately, the summit took place in Aalto's Finlandia House, one of his last designs, which consisted of a concert hall, finished in 1971, and a congress wing, completed in 1975 for the meeting of heads of state (figs. 122, 123). The building can be understood as an open-ended field of meaning and a perfect emblem of Finland's newly gained geopolitical status. References to classical language abounded— the amphitheater-shaped auditorium, the fluted columns—yet it was hard to pinpoint either the geographic or temporal origins of the building. Even the allusions to nature—the quasi-naturalistic zigzagging glass wall in the conference

120. Aalto, Rautatalo (Iron Building), Helsinki, 1953–55
121. Rautatalo, skylit interior hall

wing—seemed to function as generic symbols of freedom. At the same time, the building expressed more specific political messages regarding Finland's geopolitical ambitions: the white walls served as a perfect metaphor for neutrality as an emblem of freedom, in this case freedom from geopolitical constraints.

What should be read as Aalto's political endgame of synthesis and ambiguity has come to be taken for granted by many Aalto scholars. Kenneth Frampton's influential article "Towards a Critical Regionalism: Six Points for an Architecture of Resistance" (1982) led the way by neutralizing the geopolitical dimension in Aalto's architecture. Frampton celebrates Aalto's architecture and Finnish culture for their successful resistance to the dominance of "universal civilization" within twentieth-century culture.[51] Furthermore, he depoliticizes the geographic dimension of Aalto's architecture by referring to the "place-form"—placeness implies geography as pure presence by ignoring historical context.[52]

122. "President Gerald Ford Addresses the European Security Conference Summit at Finlandia House During a Morning Working Session, 15 August 1975"
123. Aalto, Finlandia House, Helsinki, 1962–75, view toward the main entrance of the auditorium

Another, related, critical phenomenon converges criticism with Aalto's own words. This started with Zevi, who cited Aalto's text "Humanizing of Architecture" at length to make a point about the architect's relevance.[53] Tellingly, Aalto's 1998 centennial exhibition at MoMA was entitled after the Vienna lecture as "Alvar Aalto: Between Humanism and Materialism." Aalto criticism has thus come to the point where there is no longer any distance between the author's actions and pronouncements and what we think of those actions and pronouncements. We have come to accept Aalto's ideas about synthesis and in-betweenness without recalling the confrontations and conflicts that brought this strategy into being.

Sigfried Giedion might indeed, in the end, be the first and only critic to acknowledge the political dimension of Aalto's architecture, noting: "Alvar Aalto's active life coincides with the most consistently agitated period of Finland's existence."[54] Yet maybe even he was oblivious to the subtle nuances and potential meanings presented in the Aalto chapter in *Space, Time and Architecture*. In the end, one might consider the image of floating logs used by Giedion the best emblem of Finland's delicate geopolitical situation. The so-called "floating log" theory is, in fact, often used to describe how Finland got sucked into the war in the first place: against its own will, as if caught by a whirlpool nobody could control. In the late 1950s, Aalto was commissioned to design a war monument for Suomussalmi, the site of fierce Finnish resistance to the Soviet invasion during the Winter War (fig. 124). He chose again the undulating line as a motif. In doing so, he made perhaps the most potent image for both Finland and Aalto: perpetually mutable, slightly out of balance, yet striving for stability and harmony during the age of great worldwide turmoil.

124. Aalto, flame monument to the Winter War, Suomussalmi, 1959

This book has placed Aalto and his architecture within the complex web of individual actions, discourse, geography, society, politics, and power. Together, Aalto's architecture, rich in geographic themes, and Finnish national policy, historically based on the interweaving of politics and geography, have laid a ground for what is here called a geopolitics of architecture. As I have indicated, the term *geopolitics* in the title and throughout the text is used to refer to the "combination of geographic and political factors influencing or delineating a country or region"—and, I would argue, Aalto's architecture.[1]

There is no doubt that Aalto was well versed in statecraft. He used architecture as a means to promote and even act out various "geographical scripts" (to use Finnish geographer Anssi Paasi's expression). Three main geographic narratives inform Aalto's work and words: first, that Finns were different from others and had a fundamentally different formal sensibility; second, that Finnish architecture had a particular affinity to—at various times—other Nordic countries, the Baltic States, Western Europe, or America; and third, the national territory could be organized according to different subgroups: Finnish- and Swedish-speakers, members of different social classes, rural and urban Finns, or peoples of different Finnish provinces.[2]

Aalto's "geopolitical" narratives advance strategic spatial responses to internal and external pressures by engaging economic, political, and demographic factors, both nationally and internationally. These narratives aligned with the original definition of the concept of geopolitics as worked out by the Swedish political scientist Rudolf Kjellén in the 1910s: a state is both a *Lebensraum* and a strategic territory; it has a racial conception; it attempts to balance autarky based on land and the pressure of international markets; it is governed through spatial and social governance. He put it succinctly: "Geopolitics sees a nation as a geographical organism or as a spatial occurrence; in other words, a nation as land, territory, area or, perhaps most emblematically, as empire."[3]

While at first I was skeptical about Aalto's ambitions to play a role in shaping Finnish history, I have since grown convinced that he was a master at it. His words and works did not simply reflect geopolitical realities or the official government positions but actively participated in the construction of this reality. Bruno Latour's question is well taken: "Is not society built literally—not metaphorically—of gods, machines, sciences, arts and styles?"[4] Latour argues convincingly that cultural artifacts cannot be reduced to physical objects but are in fact inseparable from a broader cultural and political discourse. The discourse surrounding Aalto's life has involved fellow architects, clients, industrialists, politicians, and critics, and his architecture and objects, their makers, users, and viewers—and all became "coproducers" of Finnish society.

One of the challenges of writing this book has been to hold onto Aalto as a main actor in this geopolitical arena without resorting to psychologizing or over-reading his motivations. I admit being guilty of both. Yet I still believe that a monographic format is well suited to address the very ambiguity and open-endedness of Aalto's geopolitical project. Following Hannah Arendt's notion of "human plurality" I have come to appreciate how, by achieving his self-realization through actions and engagement with other human beings and the world, Aalto's career and persona evolved unpredictably in unpredictable times.[5] I am convinced that the emphasis on the "human dimension" might be the best way to study modern architecture in general.[6]

I ended up seeing Aalto as a *Realpolitiker,* as somebody willing to adjust his works and words to the constantly changing geopolitical landscape of Finland, and, by extension, the world.[7] His architectural anti-idealism can be explained by his sensitivity to Finland's geopolitical situation, which taught him to respect the modest and anti-doctrinaire approach practiced by Finnish politicians. This pragmatic approach helped both Finland and Aalto. It is therefore no surprise that Aalto's ascent from a small-town architect to an international figure is paralleled by Finland's development from a geographically peripheral and economically backward new nation-state in the late 1910s to an economically prosperous welfare state by the time of Aalto's death in the mid-1970s.

Other scholars also have struggled with how to make sense of Aalto, whose work does not settle into easy formulas. Many have come to the same conclusions, albeit from different methodological perspectives. In his 2005 monograph, Nicholas Ray, addressing the difficulty of analyzing Aalto's work, made a similar case by locating Aalto's design approach within an "anti-idealist" tradition that drew upon the works of Aristotle, Ernst Gombrich, Friedrich Nietzsche, and Karl Popper, all of whom favor a piecemeal and pragmatic approach to questions concerning human life and society, imperfections and all.[8] Some have already suggested that it is this aspect of his work and persona that make him so interesting. Roger Connah argues, in the brilliant *AaltoMania: Readings Against Aalto* (2000), for example, that Aalto's cunning and seductive personality was, in fact, an integral part of his professional success. I agree with Connah's assessment that "where we can agree that a knowledge of Aalto's personality (however imperfect) is secondary to his architectural achievements (whatever they are and how they change over the years), it seems clear that Aalto's charisma, his confidence from a very early age, his sheer 'bloody-mindedness,' wetted often by alcohol and his larger-than-lifeness, were responsible for the many commissions he received."[9]

My own emphasis on the geopolitical meanderings is attributable, at least in part, to the fact that this project has a strong autobiographical dimension— one in which geopolitics has played a great role. My father's family comes from Carelia, and wartime events remain painful in our memory. My earliest political recollections are from the late 1960s and early 1970s, watching on television as President Kekkonen boarded the train for yet another trip to Moscow. The geopolitical contingencies were never spoken about.

A seed for this project was planted in the early 1990s as I watched from a distance—first from Austria and later from the United States—as Finland passed through a major political and cultural reorientation. In 1992, having been under heavy Soviet pressure for nearly half a century, the country, without much discussion, made the decision to join the European Union. How fast my countrymen adapted to this change! Suddenly everybody was traveling to European metropolises, listening to Europop, and learning continental manners. The fact that Aalto also loved to travel and was quick to adapt to new milieus made me believe that a love of all things foreign and a certain malleability or responsive flexibility might be the most Finnish characteristic of all.

So if we were to ask how central Finland is to the understanding of Aalto's work, the answer would be that Finland's political and economic situation during its existence has been precarious and fragile, and always mutable, with wide-ranging implications for Aalto's life, career, and public reception. Aalto can be credited for his vision of a better, worldlier future for Finland, and his energetic work toward that dream. I therefore strongly believe that we cannot fully understand either Aalto or his work without taking the geographic context into consideration—and vice versa: we cannot fully understand Finland without Aalto.

Introduction

1. The canonical reading links Aalto's physical distance from the continent to his critical distance from normative modernism. This reading was developed by a group of British historians and critics in the late 1950s, when the tenets of the modern movement started to become questioned. At that moment Aalto began to be seen as a representative of an "other" form of modernism, more authentic and local. Colin St. John Wilson bases this argument, detailed in his book *The Other Tradition of Modern Architecture: The Uncompleted Project* (1995), on Aalto's talk at the 1957 RIBA Discourse, which denounced the "dictatorship" of standard modernism. St. John Wilson visited Aalto's masterpiece Villa Mairea, famous for its subtle quasi-vernacular diversions from international style modernism, a few months after hearing Aalto's talk and started writing on Aalto in 1964. He presented the first paper putting forward his argument in the first international Aalto Symposium in 1979.

Around Aalto's centenary in 1998, a new generation of scholars reassessed Aalto's relationship to continental modernism. Bruno Maurer and Teppo Jokinen's *"Magus des Nordens": Alvar Aalto und die Schweiz* [The Magus of the North: Alvar Aalto and Switzerland] (1998) sheds light on Aalto's contacts in one of his many adoptive lands. Dörte Kuhlman's *Mensch und Natur: Alvar Aalto in Deutchland* (Weimar: Bauhaus Universität, 1999) locates Aalto at the center of French-German debates about the relationship between nature, man, and society, using his housing projects in Germany as examples. See also Eeva Rudberg, "Alvar Aalto and Sweden" and Friedrich Achleitner, "Alvar Aalto in Vienna" in Winfried Nerdinger, ed., *Alvar Aalto: Toward a Human Modernism* (Munich: Prestel, 1999), 91–104, 105, 112.

2. Sigfried Giedion, *Space, Time and Architecture: The Growth of a New Tradition*, 2nd ed. (Cambridge, Mass.: Harvard University Press, 1949), 567.

3. My study has benefited from the recent cataloguing of Aalto's library. Books acquired or given as gifts before 1941, now in the collection of the Aalto Aalto Archive in Helsinki, comprise some 350 items. Unfortunately, the collection was only catalogued recently, some twenty-five years after Aalto's death, and it is impossible to determine what books and journals may have been lost. Most of his architectural books, even old ones, had been kept in the office library. The other part of the collection is still housed in Aalto's nearby residence, which was occupied by relatives until 1998. A complete bibliography of his library dated before 1943 appears in my "Empathetic Affinities: Alvar Aalto and His Milieus" (Ph.D. diss., Columbia University, 2003), appendix 5. A complete bibliography of Aalto's published writings and interviews prior to the Second World War appears in appendixes 1–4.

4. Norberg-Schulz talks about Aalto's desire to give his architecture an "outspoken local character": in his Villa Mairea and Säynätsalo town hall the "Finnish *genius loci* is strongly present." Christian Norberg-Schulz, *Genius Loci: Towards a Phenomenology of Architecture* (London: Academy, 1980), 196.

5. Anthony Giddens, *The Nation-State and Violence* (Berkeley: University of California Press, 1985), 4.

6. See Benedict Anderson, *Imagined Communities: Reflections on the Origin and Spread of Nationalism* (New York: Verso, 1991).

7. See, for example, Heinrich Bünting's illustration *Europa*, from *Itineranum saerae scripturae; Ther är en reesebook* (Stockholm, 1595).

8. See Anssi Paasi's excellent *Territories, Boundaries, and Consciousness: The Changing Geographies of the Finnish-Russian Border* (London: Wiley, 1996), esp. 137–66 and 167–99.

9. My research has also benefited from Louna Lahti's oral history project *Alvar Aalto—ex intimo: Alvar Aalto Through the Eyes of Family, Friends, and Colleagues* (Helsinki: Building Information Center, 2001), as well as Pekka Korvenmaa's extensive research into Aalto's contacts to Finnish industry. See "Aalto and Finnish Industry," in Peter Reed, ed., *Alvar Aalto: Between Humanism and Materialism* (New York: Museum of Modern Art, 1998), 70–92 and "Modern Architecture Serving Modern Production," in Pekka Korvenmaa, ed., *Alvar Aalto, Architect: Sunila, 1936–54* (Helsinki: Alvar Aalto Academy, 2004).

10. Here I would like to refer to Jürgen Habermas' useful distinction between modernization and modernity. The first, he says, "refers to a bundle of processes that are cumulative and mutually reinforcing: to the formation of capital and the mobilization of resources; to the development of the forces of production and the increase in the productivity of labor; to the establishment of centralized political power and the formation of national identities; to the proliferation of rights of political participation, of urban forms of life, and formal schooling; to the secularization of values and norms; and so on." See *The Philosophical Discourse of Modernity: Twelve Lectures* (Cambridge, 1992), 2.

11. Anthony Giddens, *Modernity and Self-Identity: Self and Society in the Late Modern Age* (Stanford: Stanford University Press, 1991), 1. Giddens' study emphasizes the link between the psychology of self and the cultural phenomenon of modernity and thus provides an important intellectual context for my study.

12. Giddens writes: "The self is not a passive entity, determined by external influences; in forging their self-identities, no matter how local their specific contexts of action, individuals contribute to and directly promote social influences that are global in their consequences and implication." Ibid., 2.

Chapter One. In Search of a National Style

1. Armas Lindgren, "Något om Vår Medeltida Konst" (A Few Words About Our Medieval Art), *Ateneum: Internationell, Illustrerad Tidskrift för Konst, Literatur och Sporsmål af Allmänt Intresse* (Ateneum: International, Illustrated Magazine of Art,

Literature, and Issues of General Interest) (1901), 81.

2. Lindgren, quoted by Riitta Nikula, in *Armas Lindgren, Architect, 1874–1929* (Helsinki: Suomen Rakennustaiteen Museo, 1988), 18.

3. Matti Klinge's *Vihan veljistä Valtiososialismiin: Yhteiskunnallisia ja Kansallisia Näkemyksiä 1910—ja 1920-luvuilta* (From Brothers in Hatred to State-Socialism: Societal and National Attitudes from the 1910s and 1920s) (Porvoo: WSOY, 1972) offers an excellent overview of Finland's internal politics between the two world wars, highlighting the problem of national unity.

4. Aalto fought in Länkipohja in February 1918 and was involved in the capture of Tampere. For more on his involvement with the events of the civil war, see Göran Schildt, *Alvar Aalto: The Early Years* (New York: Rizzoli, 1984), 93–96.

5. Juhani Vikstedt, *"Pikkukaupunkiemme myöhemmässä rakennustyylissä ilmenevien epäkohtien poistamisesta"* (Concerning the Removal of Defects in Recent Building Styles of Our Small Towns), *Rakennustaito* (Building Art) (1920), 211–15, quoted by Riitta Nikula, "The Inter-War Period: The Architecture of the Young Republic," in Marja-Riitta Norri et al., eds., *Finland: Twentieth-Century Architecture* (Helsinki: Museum of Finnish Architecture, 2000), 41.

6. Carolus Lindberg, "Vanhempaa Rakennustaidetta Suomessa" (Older Building Art in Finland), *Arkkitehti* 6 (1926): 72.

7. Aalto, "Maalarit ja Muurarit" (Painters and Masons), *Keski Suomi*, 23 December 1923. English trans. slightly modified from Göran Schildt, ed., *Alvar Aalto in His Own Words* (New York: Rizzoli, 1998), 31.

8. Armas Lindgren, "Något om Vår Medeltida Konst," 81. English trans. partly modified from P. E. Blomstedt's 1929 "Armas Lindgren Rakennustaiteen Opettajana: Luonnekuvan Ääripiirteitä Vanhan Kirjoitelman

Ympärillä" (Armas Lindgren as a Teacher of Building Art: A Sketch for a Character Portrait around an Old Essay) and Yrjö Lindegren, ed., *P. E. Blomstedt, Arkkitehti* (Helsinki: Suomen Arkkitehtiliitto, 1951), 181–82.

9. Aalto, "Maalarit ja Muurarit," 32.

10. Aalto, "Miten Kaupungintaloa Rakennetaan" (How to Build a City Hall), *Iltalehti*, 12 November 1921, 8; English trans. from Schildt, *Aalto in His Own Words,* 113.

11. Ibid.

12. See Juhani Paasivirta, *Finland and Europe: The Early Years of Independence, 1917–1939,* trans. Peter Herring (Helsinki: Finnish Historical Society, 1988), 308. The hostility between the two countries can be traced to the civil war and the continuing cultural conflict between Finnish and Swedish speakers. Despite increased cultural collaboration, resistance remained strong among many prominent politicians. See *Finland and Europe,* chapters 4 and 5, on Finland's relationship to Scandinavian countries.

13. Aalto, "T. K. Sallinen," 3.

14. See Kaufmann, *Toward a Geography of Art,* esp. chapter 1.

15. Aalto, "T. K. Sallinen," 5.

16. I have adopted the characterization from Paasivirta, *Finland and Europe,* 321.

17. Erik Ahlman quoted by Päivi Huuhtanen, *Tunteesta henkeen: Antipositivismi ja suomalainen estetiikka, 1900–1939* (From Psychological Emotionalism to the Philosophy of Spirit: The Development of Antipositivist Tendencies in Finnish Aesthetic and Art Philosophy) (Helsinki: Suomalaisen Kirjallisuuden Seura), 169. My discussion on Finnish aesthetic debates has been informed greatly by Huuhtanen's pioneering study.

18. A collection of essays entitled *Finns in the Shadow of the "Aryans": Race Theories and Racism,* edited by Aira Kemiläinen (Helsinki: Suomal-

aisen Kirjallisuuden Seura, 1998) discusses how debates on race and ethnicity influenced the perception and self-perception of Finns.

19. Aalto, *"Menneitten aikojen motiivit"* (Motifs from Past Ages), *Arkkitehti* 2 (1922): 25; English trans. from Schildt, *Aalto in His Own Words,* 33.

20. Ibid.

21. Ibid.

22. Ibid.

23. Heinrich Wölfflin, *Renaissance and Baroque* (Ithaca: Cornell University Press, 1966), 79.

24. It is therefore no coincidence that the beginning of the debate about style and historicism, as Wolfgang Hermann has pointed out, coincides with Romanticism. See his introduction to *In What Style Should We Build? The German Debate on Architectural Style* (Santa Monica: Getty Center for the History of Art and the Humanities, 1992), 2.

25. Hirn formulates this thesis in his dissertation, "Förstudier till en konstfilosofi pa psyckologist grundval" (A Preliminary Study for a Philosophy of Art Based on Psychological Criteria) (1896), which was translated into English under the title *The Origins of Art: A Psychological and Sociological Inquiry* (London: Macmillan, 1900).

26. Hirn, *Origins of Art,* 98.

27. Ibid., 33.

Chapter Two. Toward Cultural Revival
1. See Raymond Williams' definition of the word *culture* in *Keywords: A Vocabulary of Culture and Society* (New York: Oxford University Press, 1985), 87–93.

2. Ibid.

3. See Friedrich Nietzsche, *On the Advantage and Disadvantage of History for Life,* trans. Peter Press (Indianapolis: Hackett, 1980), 69.

4. "Motifs from Past Ages," 25.

5. See Aino Niskanen, *Väinö Vähäkallio ja hänen toimistonsa: Arkkitehdin Elämäntyö ja Verkostot* (Väinö Vähäkallio and His Office: An Architect's Lifework and His Networks), Ph.D. diss., Teknillisen Korkeakoulun Arkkitehtiosaston Tutkimuksia, Helsinki, 2005, 22.

6. The idea of Finns as fierce, somewhat primitive people equipped with strong emotions and able to prevail through hard work was further propagated in novels, such as the first Finnish-language novel, *The Seven Brothers* (1868–70) by Aleksis Kivi, a Bildungsroman about how education turned semibarbarian brothers into law-abiding citizens.

7. Topelius, journalist, author, and the dean of Helsinki University, is best known for depicting Finnish history in narrative form for children. The publication of *Maamme Kirja* (The Book of Our Land) coincided with the spread of elementary-school education during the 1870s, which guaranteed its success. During Topelius' lifetime the book was published in eight Swedish and fourteen Finnish editions. Its success continued through the twentieth century, and by the 1960s an estimated 2.5 million copies had been sold, which makes it one of the most widely read books ever published in Finland.

8. Zacharias Topelius, *Maamme Kirja* (Helsinki: Otava), 124.

9. Ibid., 14.

10. Oswald Spengler, *The Decline of the West*, trans. Charles Francis Atkinson (abbreviated one-volume edition, New York: Modern Library, 1962), 182.

11. Ibid., 133–34.

12. Aalto, "En barnsage vid brasan" (A Fireside Story), *Kerberos* 4 (1921): 11–12; English trans. modified from Schildt, *Aalto in His Own Words*, 13: "You people who read books, don't you give a damn about German philosophers and the decline of Western Civilization [*Untergang!*]. When I

go home to the country I go up to the attic and get out a pile of detective stories. That surely helps. I am almost convinced that Nick Carter is a good detective. . . . He is definitely the man for 1921. I will ask him for help when Oswald Spengler starts seriously threatening Europe."

13. Ibid, 182.

14. Aalto, "Our Old and New Churches," *Iltalehti*, 14 December 1921; English trans. from Schildt, *Aalto in His Own Words*, 36.

15. The latter book bears an inscription: "Aino Aalto. Acquired in Berlin 1921," a sign not only that Aino visited Berlin before Aalto, but that she may have been instrumental in introducing him to the German debate about cultural revival.

16. Since the copy was in German, published in 1924 by Bruno Cassirer, a Berlin publisher, I speculate that Aalto acquired it during his honeymoon, which took the couple to Italy via Poland, Germany, and Austria.

17. Aalto, "Motifs from Past Ages," 24; English trans. from Schildt, *Aalto in His Own Words*, 33.

18. Aalto, "Oma Talo: Miksi sen täytyy olla kaunis," *Taide-Käsiteollisuus* 2 (1922): 17.

19. Ibid., 20.

20. Ibid. Italics in the original.

21. Aalto and Taito Oy, advertisement placed in the 31 December 1921 issue of *Sisä-Suomi*, repr. in Schildt, *Early Years*, 126.

22. Several of these had preceded him to Italy: Bryggman, Ekelund, P. E. Blomstedt. See *Matkalla! En Route!* (Traveling!) (Helsinki: Museum of Finnish Architecture, 1999).

23. See, for example, Timo Tuomi, "Välimeren Maiden Kutsu: Hilding Ekelunding Suuret Matkat 1920-luvulla" (Lure of the Mediterranean: Hilding Ekelund's Great Trips During the 1920s), in *Hilding Ekelund: Arkkitehti*

(1893–84) (Helsinki: Suomen Rakennustaiteen Museo, 1997), 64–73.

24. See Schildt, *Early Years*, 135–36.

25. See Goethe's *Versuch die Metamorphose der Pflanzen zu Erklären* (Gotha, 1790), translated as "An Attempt to Interpret the Metamorphosis of Plants," in Frans Verdoorn, ed., *An International Collection of Studies in the Method and History of Biology and Agriculture* 10, no. 1 (1946): 98–124. The drawing by Goethe on 96–97 shows the influence of altitude on plants.

26. Nikolaus Pevsner, *An Outline of European Architecture* (London: Penguin, 1983), 107.

27. "Ylös Ateenasta" (Rise from Athens), *Sisä-Suomi*, 9 January 1924; "Katukulttuuria" (Street Culture), *Sisä-Suomi*, 11 January 1924; "Kukkosh-khaa," *Sisä-Suomi*, 13 January 1924; "Kaksi kaupunkia" (Two Cities), *Sisä-Suomi*, 27 February 1924; "Kauppatori— Kauppahalli—Kauppakuja" (Market Square—Market Hall—Market Street), *Keskisuomalainen*, 11 November 1924; "Kaupunkikulttuuri" (Urban culture), *Sisä-Suomi*, 12 December 1924; "Eräs kaupunkimme kaunistustoimenpide ja sen mahdollisuudet" (One Attempt to Beautify Our Town and Its Changes to Succeed), *Keskisuomalainen*, 22 January 1925; "Eräs asemakaavakysymys" (One zoning issue), *Sisä-Suomi*, 5 June 1925; "Keskisuomalaisen maiseman rakennustaide" (Landscape in Central Finland), *Sisä-Suomi*, 28 June 1925.

28. Aalto, "Keskisuomalaisen maiseman rakennustaide" (Architecture in the Landscape of Central Finland), *Sisä-Suomi*, 26 June 1925; English trans. adapted from Schildt, *Aalto in His Own Words*, 21–22.

29. Aalto, "Maiseman rakennustaide" (Architecture of the Landscape), *Taide-Käsiteollisuus* 3 (1926): 42.

30. Aalto's distaste for pure nature is here identical to Schultze-Naumburg's in *Die Gestaltung der Landschaft durch den Menschen* (1928): "The primeval forest differs radically from what we today consider the most beautiful

kind of German forest." Pure nature is less important as a signifier of "Germanness" or of innately German culture than a nature in which architecture and design have intervened, so that nature becomes a part of national consciousness.

31. Spengler, *Decline of the West*, 245.

32. Aalto, "Eräs kaupunkimme kaunistustoimenpide ja sen mahdollisuudet," *Keskisuomalainen*, 22 January 1925, 3.

33. Ibid.

34. Aalto, "Kaupunkikulttuuri" (Urban Culture), *Sisä-Suomi*, 12 December 1924, 1; English trans. from Schildt, *Aalto in His Own Words*, 20.

35. The idea of a city-region was first put forward by the Scottish urban planner Patrick Geddes in his famous Valley Section study of 1909. Aalto's thinking bears some resemblance that of Geddes, especially in the links drawn between geographic conditions and social relations and development. See Volker M. Welter, *Biopolis: Patrick Geddes and the City of Life* (Cambridge, Mass.: MIT Press, 2002), esp. chapter 3.

36. Aalto, "Porraskiveltä arkihuoneeseen" (From Doorstep to Living Room), *Aitta* 1 (1926): 63; English trans. slightly modified from Schildt, *Aalto in His Own Words*, 50.

37. *Aitta* was published 1926–30. It covered a wide range of issues, from art, fashion, and lifestyle to politics, cultural criticism, and short stories by leading intellectuals of the time.

38. Aalto, "Porraskiveltä arkihuoneeseen," 63.

39. Ibid., 69; English trans. from Schildt, *Aalto in His Own Words*, 55.

40. Gustaf Strengell wrote this series of books addressing the aesthetic dimension of the built environment: *Staden som Konstverk* (The City as a Work of Art) (Helsinki: Holger Schildt, 1922); *Hemmet som Konstverk* (The Home as a Work of Art) (Helsinki: Holger Schildt, 1923); and *Byggnaden som Konstverk* (The Building

as a Work of Art) (Helsinki: Holger Schildt, 1928). All were translated into Finnish from Swedish. Aalto owned copies of all three volumes.

41. Gustaf Strengell, *Rakennus Taideluomana; Luonnos Arkkitehtuurin Ilmaisukeinoista* (Building as a Work of Art: A Sketch Toward Architectural Expression) (Helsinki: Otava, 1929), 44.

Chapter Three. National Identity in the Age of Mass Culture
1. See Sinikka Uusitalo, *Turun kaupungin historia, 1918–1970* (History of the City of Turku, 1918–1970) (Turku: Turun Sanomat, 1982).

2. University of Jyväskylä was not founded until 1960.

3. Bryggman's library, now at the Library of the Museum of Finnish Architecture, bears witness to an intellectual versatility that extended into the areas of psychology, philosophy, and sociology, suggesting his interest in linking aesthetic and social ideas. Bryggman's collection includes several early histories and critical essays on modern architecture, such as Adolf Behne's *Eine Stunde Architektur* (1928); Walter Curt Behrendt's *Der Sieg des neuen Baustils* (1927); Sigfried Giedion's *Bauen in Frankreich, Bauen in Eisen, and Bauen in Eisenbeton* (1928); Gregor Paulsson's *Den nya arkitekturen* (1916); Richard Neutra's *Wie baut America* (1927); Erich Mendelsohn's *Amerika: Bilderbuch eines Architekten* (1926); Alberto Sartoris' *Gli elementi dell'architettura funzionale* (1935); Ludwig Hilberseimer's *Internationale neue Baukunst* (1928); and all of Le Corbusier's books. Bryggman also subscribed to several magazines, including the French *Cahiers d'art;* the Danish *Arkitekten* and *Kritisk Revy;* the German *Stein, Holz, Eisen;* and *Svenska Slöjdföreningens Tidsrift*. His collection also included books by leading Finnish and western European intellectuals, such as the literary critic Rolf Lagerborg, the art critic Olof Enckell, the sociologist Edward Westermarck, and the French philosopher Henri Bergson.

4. "Aurajoen Oxford-Cambridge" (Oxford-Cambridge on the Aura

River), *Aitta*, 29 October 1928, 40.

5. Aalto, "Pienasunnot—sosiaalinen ja taloudellinen kompastuskivi" (Minimum Dwelling—A Social and Economic Hurdle), *Sosialisti*, 10 December 1927.

6. Bryggman had visited Frankfurt in early 1928.

7. Aalto, "Uusimmista virtauksia rakennustaiteen alalla: Taiteen olemuksen ydinkysymyksiä ja meidän aikamme probleemeja; Mihin uusi realismi rakennustaiteessa pyrkii" (On the Latest Trends in Architecture: The Key Questions Concerning the Essence of Art and the Problems of Our Times; What Is the Aim of the New Realism in Building Art?), *Uusi Aura*, 1 January 1928, 12.

8. Henningsen's magazine can be credited with introducing its Scandinavian readership to a wide range of phenomena associated with modernity, often in a critical and satirical light.

9. Aalto modeled his argument after Henningsen's, as expressed in his article "Tradition og Modernisme" (Tradition and Modernism), *Kritisk Revy* 3 (1927): 30–46. Aalto subscribed to the magazine between 1926 and 1928. His annotations suggest that he was particularly interested in Hennigsen's ideas about "traditionalism," "modernism," and "realism." Despite his obvious debt to Henningsen, he did not cite this article in his own text.

10. The working drawings were completed in May 1928.

11. I owe this latter observation to Markku Norvasuo, "Skylit Room: Lighting Thematics in Alvar Aalto's Architecture, 1927–1956," Ph. diss., Helsinki Technical University, 2008, pp. 27–28.

12. *Tulenkantajat* was first issued in 1924 and went to wider circulation in 1928.

13. I owe my discussion of the operating-room lighting in Paimio Sanatorium to Norvasuo, "Skylit Room," 81–82.

14. Detlef Mertins has shown that similar debates about national expression are part of the history of the Neues Bauen movement. See his introduction to Walter Curt Behrendt, *The Victory of the New Building Style* (Los Angeles: Getty Research Institute, 2000), esp. 58–59.

15. Benedict Anderson discusses the role of media in the formation of national identity in *Imagined Communities: Reflections on the Origin and Spread of Nationalism* (London: Verso, 1983), esp. chapter 3.

16. Aalto, "Itsenäisyyden Muistomerkki—Stadion" (Independence Monument—A Stadium), *Uusi Suomi*, 25 November 1927, 12.

17. Bruno Taut put forth the idea of Stadtkrone in his book of the same name (Jena: Eugen Diederichs, 1919), which includes contributions by Paul Scheerbard, Eric Baron, and Adolf Behne.

18. Iain Boyd Whyte's landmark book *Bruno Taut and the Architecture of Activism* (Cambridge: Cambridge University Press, 1982) serves as the best guide to Taut's ideas in this respect.

19. Alvar Aalto, "Rationel Biograph" (Rational Cinema), *Kritisk Revy,* 3 October 1928, 70; English trans. from Schildt, *Aalto in His Own Words,* 71.

20. Ibid., 66; English trans. from Schildt, *Aalto in His Own Words,* 67.

21. Aalto was able to build a version of the slatted wall when one of the rooms in the Civil Guard Building was converted into a movie theater.

22. The Finnish reaction to Phoebus cartel was first discussed by Juho Jännes in his book *Suomen sähkölamppusota* (Finland's Electric Bulb War) (1933). I am indebted to Norvasuo's "Skylit Room" for this information (227).

23. Aalto, "Rationel Biograph," 67.

24. Alvar Aalto in "Nykyajan Arkkitehtuuria: Alvar Aallon Haastattelu" (Contemporary Architecture: An Interview with Alvar Aalto), *Tulenkantajat* 3 (1929): 36.

25. Aalto, "Rationel Biograph," 67–68.

26. *Tulenkantajat,* for example, published more articles on theater than all other arts combined, and the Turku theater scene was frequently reviewed in its pages.

27. See Ernst Stern and Heinz Herald, *Reinhardt und seine Bühne: Bilder von der Arbeit des Deutschen Theaters* (Reinhardt and His Stage: Pictures Documenting the Work of the German Theater) (Berlin: Dr. Ensler, 1919), 5. Stern and Herald celebrate Reinhardt's theater as a truly German phenomenon.

28. Erwin Piscator, *Das Politische Theater* (Political Theater) (Berlin: Adalbert Schultz Verlag, 1929), 45.

29. László Moholy-Nagy, "Theater, Zirkus, Varieté" (Theater, Circus, Variety), in Oskar Schlemmer, László Moholy-Nagy, and Farkas Molnár, *Die Bühne im Bauhaus* (Stages at the Bauhaus) *Bauhaus Book 4* (Munich: Albert Langen, 1924), 51.

30. Ibid., 54–55, my translation.

31. Aino Marsio-Aalto wrote: "Huomattava vieras messuilla eilen" (Important visitor to the fair yesterday). See *Uusi Aura,* 23 June 1929, 3. Quoted by Norvasuo, "Skylit Room," 22. Marsio-Aalso reports on Gunnar Asplund's visit to the fair.

32. It is also likely that Aalto had consulted Strengell's book, *Contemporary Advertisement: Its Character and Means of Effect* (1924), which paid particular attention to the instantaneous psychological effect of the medium. His was the earliest Finnish study of mass culture and one of the first responses to American culture among Finnish intellectuals and academics.

33. Kerstin Smeds and Timo Mäkinen's *Kaiu, Kaiu Lauluni: Lauluja Soittojuhlien Historia* (Echo, Echo My Song: The History of Singing Festivals) (Helsinki: Otava, 1984) gives an excellent overview of the cultural context of the singing festivals from the turn of the century. Annual national singing festivals were established in 1922 and often took place in tandem with major exhibitions. They are still popular today.

34. Aino Aalto reports on Asplund's visit and impressions in her article "Huomattava vieras messuilla eilen."

35. Gunnar Asplund et al., *Acceptera* (1931; repr. Stockholm: Berlings, 1980). Later edition with commentary by Anders Åman; all quotations are from this edition.

36. English translation from Lucy Creagh, Helena Kaberg, and Barbara Miller Lane, eds., *Modern Swedish Design: Three Founding Texts* (New York: Museum of Modern Art, 2008), 143.

37. See Peter Kropotkin, *Mutual Aid: A Factor in Evolution* (New York: Knopf, 1902).

38. Aalto, "Tukholmannäyttely" (Stockholm Exhibition), *Arkkitehti* 8 (1930): 120.

39. Scheffler, quoted in Asplund et al., *Acceptera,* 173; English translation from Creagh, Kaberg, and Miller Lane, *Modern Swedish Design,* 313.

40. See Maurice Tuchman, ed., *The Spiritual in Art: Abstract Painting, 1890–1985* (New York: Abbeville, 1986), esp. 33.

41. William James, *Varieties of Religious Experience* (1902; repr. New York: Penguin, 1982), 407. Quoted by Tuchman, *Spiritual in Art,* 34.

42. Gustave Le Bon, *Psychologie des Foules* (Paris: Felix Alcan, 1895). The book was translated into Finnish as *Joukkosielu* (1912) and into English as *Crowd: A Study of the Popular Mind* (1913).

Chapter Four. Pan-European Aspirations
1. Erik Allardt, "Bilingualism in Finland: The Position of Swedish as a Minority Language," in William R. Beer and James E. Jacob, eds., *Language

Policy and National Unity (New Jersey: Rowman & Allanheld, 1985), 81.

2. Georg Brandes, "Thoughts on the Turn of the Century" (1900), repr. in *Tanker ved Århundredskiftet* (Thoughts on the Turn of the Century) (Copenhagen: Forlaget Geelmuyden, 1998), 102.

3. Ibid., 100.

4. Sigurd Frosterus and Gustaf Strengell, *Arkitektur: En Stridskrift Våra Motståndare Tillägnad af Gustaf Strengell och Sigurd Frosterus* (Helsinki: Eutarpe, 1904); translated as "Architecture: A Challenge," in *Abacus* 8 (Helsinki: Museum of Finnish Architecture, 1983), 75.

5. Frosterus worked with van de Velde in Weimar between 1903 and 1904. In his autobiography, *Geschichte meines Lebens* (The Story of My Life) (Munich: R. Piper, 1962), the Belgian master writes fondly of his Finnish intern and his offer to make him a partner in the firm. Instead, Frosterus returned to Finland and formed a brief partnership (1904–6) with Strengell, after which he became a successful architect in his own right. The 1916 Stockmann Department Store, still standing in the heart of Helsinki, is his best-known work. On the founding and design of the Nietzsche archive, see Ole W. Fischer, "Nietzsche-Archive in Weimar: A Retroactive *Studiolo* of Henry van de Velde," *Threshold* 32 (2006): 42–56.

6. Friedrich Nietzsche, *Beyond Good and Evil: Prelude to a Philosophy of the Future*, trans. Judith Norman (Cambridge, Eng.: Cambridge University Press, 2002), sec. 240; quoted in Luke Smith, "Towards Critical Cosmopolitanism: Nietzsche and the National Question," master's thesis, Central European University, Budapest, 2002, 16.

7. *Beyond Good and Evil*, sec. 13; quoted in Smith, "Towards Critical Cosmopolitanism," 17.

8. Ibid., sec. 244; quoted in Smith, "Towards Critical Cosmopolitanism," 17.

9. Manfredo Tafuri has pointed out that the Werkbund idea about how forms came into being had as its origin Alois Riegl's notion of *Kunstwollen,* or will-to-art, which called for a creative individual to synthesize the general ethos of the era into form. See Manfredo Tafuri and Francesco Dal Co, *Modern Architecture* (New York: Rizzoli, 1986), 1: 82.

10. Aalto, "Alt Riga och bi-ba-bo" (Old Riga and Bi-Ba-Bo), *Kerberos* 8 (1921): 8, my translation.

11. Ibid.

12. Ibid.

13. "Political Agreement Between Estonia, Finland, Latvia, and Poland, signed in Warsaw on March 17, 1922." Accessed digitally on 1 May 2008.

14. Nietzsche, *Birth of Tragedy,* sec. 256.

15. Ibid., sec. 242.

16. Richard N. Coudenhove-Kalergi, *Pan-Europa* (New York: Knopf, 1926), 7.

17. Ibid., 12–13.

18. Ibid., 10.

19. Ibid., 89.

20. Ibid.

21. Barbusse's most famous novel, *Le Feu* (Fire) (1916), gave an account of his horrific experiences as a foot soldier during World War I, which turned him into a pacifist and a crusader for international brotherhood. Barbusse was also an Esperantist.

22. The Swedish chapter of Clarté had a strong following among the Scandinavian intelligentsia and political class. From Sweden the organization spread to other Scandinavian countries; Georg Brandes became a member of the Danish chapter. The Finnish Clarté was founded in 1926 by a group of young writers and artists and one university professor, but it evaporated soon after the first meeting.

23. Lissitzky used the term in "Kunst und Pangeometrie," in Carl Einstein and Paul Westheim, eds., *Europa Almanach: Malerei, Literatur, Musik, Architektur, Plastic, Bühne, Film, Mode* (Europe Datebook: Painting, Literature, Music, Architecture, Sculpture, Stage, Film, Fashion) (Potsdam: G. Kiepenheuer, 1925), 103–13.

24. For discussion of Lissitzky's ideas of visual aperceptions, see Leah Dickerman, "El Lissitzky's Camera Corpus," in Nancy Perloff and Brian Reed, eds., *Situating El Lissitzky* (Santa Monica: Getty Research Institute, 2003).

25. Gilles Deleuze and Félix Guattari, "The Smooth and the Striated," in Deleuze and Guattari, *A Thousand Plateaus: Capitalism and Schizophrenia* (London: Athlone, 1988), 266. "Then there is altogether different plane, or altogether different conception of the plane. Here, there are no longer any forms or developments of forms; nor are there subjects of the formation of subjects. There is no structure, any more than there is genesis. There are only relations or movement and rest, speed and slowness between unformed elements."

26. Hagar Olsson, "Terveisiä Tukholmasta" (Greetings from Stockholm), *Tulenkantajat* 1 (1930): 10.

27. "Det Intellektuelle Sveriges Grepp på Herr Medelssvensson: Alvar Aalto Karaktäriserar Utställningen I Stockholm" (Intellectual Sweden's Idea of Mr. Average Swede), *Åbo Underrättelser,* 22 May 1930, 1; English trans. from Schildt, *Aalto in His Own Words,* 72.

28. Ibid.

29. Aalto, "Tukholmannäyttely," 120; English trans. slightly modified from Schildt, *Aalto in His Own Words,* 75.

Chapter Five. Being International

1. Francis Delaisi, *Les Deux Europes* (The Two Europes) (Paris: Payot, 1929), 227–28. Other countries in B-Europe were Greece, Ireland, Portugal, Italy, Spain, and all the eastern European countries.

2. Aalto's 1930 and 1931 trips are well

documented; see Göran Schildt, *Alvar Aalto: The Decisive Years* (New York: Rizzoli, 1986), 65–78.

3. Olavi Paavolainen, *"Sinisen oven kynnyksellä"* (On the Threshold of the Blue Door), *Ylioppilaslehti* 11 (1927): 226.

4. Paavolainen mentions "spending the evening at 'Cigogne' with Aalto, who arrived on an airplane." *Nykyaikaa Etsimässä, Esseitä ja Pakinoita* (In Search of the Modern: Essays and Columns) (Helsinki: Otava, 1929), 148.

5. The journal *I 10* was edited by Arthur Müller Lehning and included contributions by van Eesteren, Stam, Oud, Brinkman, van der Vlugt, Moholy-Nagy, Kurt Schwitters, Ernst Kallai, Adolf Behne, Ilya Ehrenburg, and Wassily Kandinsky. The magazine of the Dutch CIAM group, *De 8 en Upbouw,* was edited by Ben Merkelbach. It drew contributions from Stam and van Eesteren, among others. Ideologically, it focused on the actual functional, social, and economic tasks facing the modern architect. After this trip Aalto kept contact with A. Boeken, secretary of the Dutch CIAM delegation and of De 8 group.

6. "Nykyajan Arkkitehtuuria," 36.

7. "Mitä arkkitehti Aallolle kuuluu?" (What's New with Architect Aalto?), *Sisä-Suomi,* 18 August 1928, 3.

8. Walter Gropius, *Internationale Architektur* (International Architecture) (Munich: Albert Langen, 1925), 1.

9. Walter Curt Behrendt, *The Victory of the New Building Style,* trans. Harry Francis Mallgrave (Santa Monica: Getty Research Institute Publications and Exhibitions Program, 2000), 89.

10. Ibid., 107.

11. Ibid.

12. Ludwig Hilberseimer, *Internationale Neue Architektur* (International New Architecture) (Stuttgart: Julius Hoffmann, 1928), 5.

13. "Nykyajan Arkkitehtuuria," 36.

14. Ibid.

15. Ibid.

16. Separate branches of the Nordic Association were founded in Denmark, Norway, and Sweden in 1919 and in Iceland in 1922. The goal of the association, which is still in operation, is to foster Nordic cooperation in all areas of culture.

17. Elsa Enäjärvi, "Suomalainen—Eurooppalainen,"' *Tulenkantajat* 1 (23 November 1928): 11.

18. Göran Schildt chronicles these trips in *Alvo Aalto: The Mature Years* (New York: Rizzoli, 1989), 65–68.

19. Aalto to Walter Gropius, postcard, 23 October 1930, written in Turku, Alvar Aalto Archive (hereafter AAA) document.

20. Aalto to "Ellen and Moholy," letter, Helsinki, 1931, AAA document.

21. Franz Muller-Lyer wrote widely translated books such as *Familie* (1912) and *Formen der Ehe* (Forms of Matrimony, 1911). For further discussion of CIAM, see Eric Mumford, *The CIAM Discourse on Urbanism, 1928–1960* (Cambridge, Mass.: MIT Press, 2000); for discussion of Gropius' lecture, see 36–37.

22. For a full set of drawings, see *The Architectural Drawings of Alvar Aalto, 1917–1930* (New York: Garland Architectural Archives, 1994), 123–36.

23. Alvar Aalto, "Asuntomme-probleemina," *Domus* 8–9 (1930): 176; English trans. modified from Schildt, *Aalto in His Own Words,* 78.

24. Ibid., 77–78.

25. Henri Bergson, *Creative Evolution,* Arthus Mitchell, trans. (London: Macmillan, 1913), 134.

26. Oskar Schlemmer, "Mensch und Kunstfigur," in Schlemmer, Moholy-Nagy, and Molnár, *Bühne im Bauhaus,* 15.

27. Schlemmer developed his Bauhaus theories about the relationship

between the human body and built space in theatrical performances. Aalto saw him perform one of these, his *Ursonata,* consisting of what he called *Urlauten,* or "primal sounds," in an evening event at the Frankfurt CIAM conference. See program to the Frankfurt conference in Martin Steinmann, ed., *CIAM Documente, 1928–1939* (Basel: Birkhäuser, 1979), 46–47.

28. Henri Bergson, *Matter and Memory* (1896; repr. New York: Zone, 1988), 208.

29. See Moholy's photo essay "Dynamik der Gross-stadt" (Dynamism of the Metropolis), in *Malerei, Fotografie, Film* (Painting, Photography, Film), *Bauhaus Book* 8 (Munich: Albert Langen, 1925), 20–22. Aalto's library includes this and two other of Moholy's books published in the *Bauhaus Book* series: *Die Bühne im Bauhaus, Bauhaus Book* 4; and *Von Material zu Architektur* (From Material to Architecture), *Bauhaus Book* 14 (Munich: Albert Langen, 1929).

30. Naum Gabo's and Antoine Pevsner's manifesto, quoted by Eleanor Hight, in *Picturing Modernism: Moholy-Nagy and Photography in Weimar* (Cambridge, Mass.: MIT Press, 1995), 189.

31. László Moholy-Nagy, "Dynamisch-Konstruktives Kraftsystem" (Dynamic-Constructive System of Forces) *Der Sturm* 12 (1922): 186, English trans. from Oliver Árpád István Botar, "Prolegomena to the Study of Biomorphic Modernism: Biocentrism, László Moholy-Nagy's 'New Vision' and Ernõ Kállai's *Bioromantik,*" Ph.D. diss., University of Toronto, 1998, 405.

32. Naum Gabo and Anton Pevsner, "Realist Manifesto," printed 5 August 1920 in a Soviet state printing plant; repr. in Herbert Read, ed., *Gabo: Constructions, Sculpture, Paintings, Drawings, Engravings* (Cambridge, Mass.: Harvard University Press, 1957), 152.

33. Moholy-Nagy, *Von Material zu Architektur,* 195.

34. Ibid.

35. Ibid., 111.

36. Siegfried Ebeling, *Der Raum als Membran* (Dessau: Duennhaupt, 1926). English trans. Kathryn Schoefert and Spyros Papapetros, in *Pidgin* (New York: Princeton Architectural Press, 2006), 6. I thank Spyros Papapetros for making the article available to me.

37. The issue also included texts by Sven Markelius, the editor, Gregor Paulsson, Sven Wallander, Gunnar Myrdal, Roul Henningsen, Gotthard Johansson, Stig Odeen, and Viking Göransson.

38. Asplund et al., *Acceptera,* 16.

39. Ibid., 187. The definition comes close to Behrendt's in *Victory of the New Building Style:* "The city should now be conceived for what it in reality is—namely, a *living organism* whose supporting framework and structure are to be designed to handle as thoroughly and efficiently as possible the many *functions of life* they must fulfill" (134).

40. Quoted in Botar, "Prolegomena to the Study of Biomorphic Modernism," 445.

41. Alvo Aalto, "Bostadsfrågans Geographie" (The Geography of the Housing Question), in Sven Markelius, ed., *Arkitektur och Samhälle* (Stockholm: Bröderna Lagerström Boktryckare, 1932), 88; slightly modified from Schildt, *Aalto in His Own Words,* 87; emphasis in the original.

42. Justus Buekschmitt, *Ernst May* (Stuttgart: A. Koch, 1963), 64.

43. Alvo Aalto, "Bostadssystem i USSR" (The Housing System in the USSR), *Granskaren,* July–August 1932, 104.

44. In *Victory of the New Building Style,* Behrendt discusses large German regional plans that similarly used rivers as infrastructure to connect industry and the small towns along them. See, e.g., 137–38, discussing the master plan for Rühl in Magdeburg.

45. Aalto, "Bostadsfrågans Geographie," 87.

46. Erkki Vala, "Uusi Vuosi—Uusi Aika" (New Year—New Era), *Tulenkantajat* 1 (1929): 11.

47. The Lapua Movement aimed at rooting communism from Finland. One of their tactics was to kidnap members of the Communist Party and take them over the border to the Soviet Union. For further discussion on the hostilities between left and right in interwar Finland, see Paasivirta, *Finland and Europe,* esp. 378–85. While the rise of extremist right wing groups was widespread throughout the world in the 1930s, Paasivirta locates the origin of these movements in a popular bitterness and disappointment with the parliamentary system that had been brewing among members of the White Army since the civil war, parallel in some respects to the tensions between Weimar democracy and right wing movements in the same period in Germany.

48. Here I am referring to the competition that was held to design the Palace of Soviets, intended to be the world's largest building, opposite the Kremlin. The Italian-trained Russian Boris Iofan won with a revivalist design for a monumental neoclassical megabuilding, consisting of several receding tiers, which featured a large, unbuildable sculpture of Vladimir Lenin at the top of its spire. Le Corbusier and Gropius were among the competitors.

49. Otto Korhonen died in 1935, after which his son Paavo continued the company. For more information on the founding of Artek, see Pekka Suhonen, *Artek: Alku, Tausta, Kehitys* (Artek: Beginning, Background, Development) (Helsinki: Artek, 1985). See also Paavo Korhonen's interview in Lahti, *Alvar Aalto—ex intimo,* 223–31.

50. Passage quoted from "Manufacture of Alvar Aalto Furniture at the Huonekalutehdas Korhonen OY Furniture Factory in Liittoinen," *Alvar Aalto as a Designer* (Jyväskylä: Alvar Aalto Museum, 2002), 211.

51. During his first visit to London, Moholy-Nagy helped Aalto to arrange the exhibit. Philip Morton Shand organized the exhibition under

the auspices of the *Architectural Review* magazine. I owe this information to Terence A. Stenter, "Moholy-Nagy: The Transitional Years," in Achim Borchardt-Hume, ed., *Albers and Moholy-Nagy: From the Bauhaus to the New World* (London: Yale University Press, 2006), 86.

52. The founding meeting was held 15 October 1935 at a Helsinki restaurant. Present were Aino and Alvar Aalto, Maire Gullichsen (1907–1990), heir to Finland's largest paper company, and Hahl. Alvar Aalto and Gullichsen became the main shareholders, Hahl the director of day-to-day operations, and Aino Aalto director of the design department and author of many of its products (for example, children's furniture).

53. My discussion is informed by Suhonen's observations of the founding manifesto. See Suhonen, *Artek: Alku, Tausta, Kehitys* (Helsinki: Artek, 1985), 66–67.

Chapter Six. Regional Plans

1. Finnish industrial production increased an average 7 percent during the interwar years. For more about Finland's economic policies during that time, see "Nationalism and Industrial Development in Finland," *Business and Economic History,* 2nd ser. (Helsinki: Business History Conference, 1992), 21: 343–53. Accessed online 15 April 2008.

2. I have borrowed the concept *patriotic manager* from two Finnish historians at the University of Helsinki who have written extensively on Finnish industry, Karl-Erik Michelsen and Markku Kuisma. See their article "Nationalism and Industrial Development in Finland," *Business and Economic History* 21, 2nd ser., 1992. Accessed online 15 July 2008.

3. The most famous practical application of Virtanen's work, fresh fermented fodder, was, like the advanced products of the forest industry, based on maximizing nature's resources through technological processes. The so-called AIV-method preserves the nutritional values of fresh pasture for winter use.

4. See also Sirkka Soukka, "The Journey of the Wood," Momoneco website, section on the Sunila pulp mill, http://momoneco.kotka.fi/sunila_nayttely_uk.html (accessed 3 March 2007). For a complete history of the Sunila Pulp Mill, see Pekka Korvenmaa, ed., *Alvar Aalto, Architect: Sunila, 1936–54* (Helsinki: Alvar Aalto Foundation, 2004).

5. Aalto, Sunila Sulphate Pulp Mill Project Description," reproduced in Korvenmaa, *Alvar Aalto, Architect,* 52.

6. Established already in the 1920s by the Regional Planning Association of America (RPAA), the planning principles were based on the study and coordination of the use of material and human resources, and the distribution of industry and human settlement. For an excellent discussion about MacKaye's planning ideas, see Keller Easterling, *Organization Space: Landscapes, Highways, and Houses in America* (Cambridge, Mass.: MIT Press, 1999), esp. 54–66.

7. Perry Anderson, *The Invention of the Region, 1945–1990* (Florence: European University Institute, 1994), esp. 6–8.

8. Lewis Mumford, *Technics and Civilization* (New York: Harcourt, Brace, 1934), 206.

9. Petr Kropotkin, *Fields, Factories, and Workshops; or, Industry Combined with Agriculture and Brain Work with Manual Work* (1901; repr. New York: Benjamin Blom, 1968), 22.

10. Mumford, *Technics and Civilization,* 232–33.

11. Ibid., 231.

12. Sweet's Catalog of Building Construction started publishing in 1906, and new editions come out annually. It was issued by a New York- and Chicago-based company, the Architectural Record Company, and is still in print. I thank Rosamond Fletcher for sharing her research on Sweet's Catalog with me.

13. Richard Neutra, *Wie Baut Amerika?*

(How Does America Build?) (Stuttgart: Julius Hoffmann, 1927), 74.

14. On the way to San Francisco Aalto stopped to see the 1928 Gregory Farm House in Scott's Valley, the most famous of Wurster's earlier buildings, exemplifying his interest in the vernacular. The compound consists of a three-story water tower, an L-shaped house proper, a mud-brick wall with a wide gate, and a courtyard.

15. See Greg Hise, "Building Design as Social Art: The Public Architecture of William Wurster, 1935–1950," in *An Everyday Modernism,* 141. Wurster and Aalto were by no means the only modernists doing prefabricated housing. However, their interest arose somewhat earlier than did others'. It was shared by Walter Gropius and Konrad Wachsmann, among others, in the 1940s. Also, they can be credited for tying the debate of prefabrication to regionalism. On Albert Farwell Bemis' contribution to standardization, see Rosamond Fletcher, "Negotiating the Interface: Communication and Collaboration in Building Technology, from Graphic Manuals to Software," master's thesis, Yale University, New Haven, 2005.

16. Aalto to Wurster, letter written in Helsinki, 13 June 1939; Alvar Aalto Archive document, 4.

17. Ibid.

18. Aalto in an interview in *Nya Pressen,* 23 June 1939. Quoted in Schildt, *Decisive Years,* 179.

19. Lecture in Gothenburg, October 1939; transcript, 2–3; AAA document.

20. On Mumford's response to the Soviet attack on Finland, see Serge Guilbaut, *How New York Stole the Idea of Modern Art* (Chicago: University of Chicago Press, 1983), 39–40.

21. For further discussion about Mumford's planned contribution to the magazine, see Schildt, *Mature Years,* 184–85.

22. Aalto in a memorandum attached

to the documents regarding the *Human Side* magazine; AAA document. Quoted by Pekka Korenmaa in "Modern Architecture Serving Modern Production," in Korenmaa, *Alvar Aalto, Architect,* 13.

23. Aalto to Frank Lloyd Wright, letter, 8 January 1940; AAA document.

24. Ibid.

25. Ibid.

26. Quoted in Schildt, *Mature Years,* 17.

27. Schildt, *Mature Years,* contains detailed information about Aalto's 1940 trip to America.

28. Aalto, "Finland," *Architectural Forum,* June 1940, 399.

29. Ibid.

30. Ibid.

31. Ibid.

32. Ibid.

33. Aalto, *Post-War Reconstruction: Rehousing Research in Finland* (New York, 1941), 15.

34. Bemis, who studied low-cost prefabricated housing at MIT and published The *Evolving House* in three volumes between 1933 and 1936, particularly influenced this aspect of Aalto's approach.

35. Olavi Paavolainen, ed., *Karjala Muistojen Maa* (Carelia: Land of Memories) (Helsinki: Werner Söderström, 1940).

36. Aalto was exposed to American prefabricated housing through *Architectural Forum,* to which he subscribed from 1937 on, among other sources.

37. Aalto, "Karjalan Rakennustaide" (On Carelian Architecture), *Uusi Suomi,* 2 November 1941, 12.

38. See the cover of the *A-Talo* brochure published by the A. Ahlström Company in 1941; AAA document.

39. See, for example, Maunu Häyrynen, "The Kaleidoscopic View: The Finnish National Landscape Imagery," in *National Identities*, vol. 2, no. 1 (London: Taylor and Francis): 5–19.

40. "Finland" includes two aerial views of the Finnish lake district. Aalto also used this type of image in a lecture given at the Eidgenössische Technische Hochschule in Zurich in 1941, which was published as "Euroopan Jälleenrakentaminen Tuo Pinnalle Aikamme Rakennustaiteen Keskeisimman Probleemin" (The Reconstruction of Europe Is the Key Problem for the Architecture of Our Time), *Arkkitehti* 5 (1941).

41. Schildt, *Aalto in his Own Words*, 131.

42. Aalto, "Intellectual Background of American Architecture," English trans. in *Aalto in His Own Words*, 132. Orig. "Amerikkalaisen Arkkitehtuurin Henkinen Sisältö," *Arkkitehti* 1 (1945): 2.

43. Aalto, "Valtakunnan Sunnittelu ja kulttuurimme tavoitteeet" in *Suomalainen Suomi*, no. 5 (1949): 262. My translation.

44. Ibid., 263.

45. See also Pekka Korvenmaa's discussion on Aalto's regional plans in "Aalto and Finnish Industry" in *Alvar Aalto, Between Humanism and Materialism* (New York: Museum of Modern Art, 1998), 71–92.

Chapter Seven. Organic Lines
1. Aalto to Gropius, postcard 23 October 1930; AAA document.

2. Aalto to Moholy, undated letter, 1931; AAA document.

3. Moholy-Nagy, *Von Material zu Architektur* (1929; repr., Mainz: Florian Kupferberg, 1968), 17.

4. Walter Gropius, "Programme of the Staatliches Bauhaus in Weimar" (1925), repr. in Ulrich Conrads, *Programs and Manifestoes of Twentieth-Century Architecture* (Cambridge, Mass.: MIT Press, 1991), 49.

5. Ibid.

6. Olavi Paavolainen, *Suursiivous eli kirjallisesta lastenkamarista* (Helsinki: Otava, 1932), 140. He also condemned modernist writers for their ignorance of the psychological theories of Bergson and Freud.

7. Raoul Haussmann, Hans Arp, Ivan Puni, and Lázló Moholy-Nagy, "Aufruf zur elementaren Kunst," *De Stijl* 10 (October 1921); quoted and translated by Botar, "Prolegomena to the Study of Biomorphic Modernism," 405.

8. Quoted in Botar, "Prolegomena to the Study of Biomorphic Modernism," 425.

9. Moholy-Nagy, *Von Material zu Architektur*, 12–13.

10. Ibid., 60.

11. Jean (Hans) Arp, "Looking," in *Arp* (New York: Museum of Modern Art, 1958), 14–15.

12. See Harriet Watts, "Arp, Kandinsky, and the Legacy of Jacob Böhme," in Tuchman, *Spiritual in Art*, 240.

13. Hans Arp, "Signposts" (1955), in Jean Arp, *Arp on Arp: Poems, Essays, Memories*, Marcel Jean, ed., Joachim Neugroschel, trans. (New York: Viking, 1972), 242.

14. She used this term for the first time in describing Arp and Brancusi in her 1934 article "Neue Wege der heutigen Plastik." See Botar, "Prolegomena to the Study of Biomorphic Modernism," 141, n. 153.

15. Carola Giedion-Welcker, "Hans Arp: Dichter und Maler," repr. in *Carola Giedion-Welcker: Schriften, 1926–71* (Cologne: M. Dumont Schenbert, 1973), 249.

16. Ibid.

17. Carola Giedion-Welcker, "Arp: Appreciation," in *Arp*, 22.

18. The idea can be traced to the "*Empiriokritizismus* of Ernst Mach and Richard Avenarius, who proposed individual subjectivity as the source of perception." See Botar, "Prolegom-

ena to the Study of Biomorphic Modernism," 321.

19. Aalto, "Rationalismen och Människan" (Rationalism and Man) in *Form* (Stockholm: Svenska Slöjdföreningen, 1935), 16–170; English trans. from Schildt, *Aalto in His Own Words*, 90.

20. Freud's theories gained wide attention in Finland only in the 1930s.

21. Paavolainen, *Suursiivous*, 137.

22. See Henri Focillon, *The Life of Forms in Art* (New York: Zone, 1992). First published as *Vie des formes* (Paris, 1934).

23. See Yve-Alain Bois' excellent discussion of the work of two Polish avant-garde artists, Wladyslaw Strezeminski and Katarzyna Kobro, in *Painting as Model* (Cambridge, Mass.: MIT Press, 1993), 133.

24. Aalto's drawings demonstrate awareness of contemporary acoustic research, such as Helge H. Finsen's article "Akustik" in the 1928 issue of *Kritisk Revy*, in which Aalto had published his article "Rational Cinema." Relying on Floyd Rowe Watson's 1923 book *Acoustics of Buildings*, the article put forward the idea that acoustics should be studied by drawing the rays of sounds and their reflections, a method Aalto used in Viipuri. I owe this information to Norvasuo's "Skylit Room," 69.

25. Founded by the Frenchman Émile-Jacques Dalcroze, eurythmics was a movement that blended dance with pedagogy. It was hugely popular in Finland in the 1930s and discussed in the magazines *Aitta* and *Tulenkantajat*. See, for example, Hilma Jakkanen, "Uuden Naisvoimistelun Periaatteita" [Principles of New Women's Gymnastics] in *Aitta* 6 (1930): 8–15.

26. Émile-Jacques Dalcroze, *Le Rhythme, la musique, et l'education* (Paris: Librairie Fischbacher, 1920), 60.

27. Jean-Marie Guyau, *L'Art au point de vue sociologique* (Paris: Alcan,

1889), 8. Guyau was widely during the 1920s. In Finland, Guyau was cited by Gustaf Strengell in *Rakennus Taideluomana*. Strengell refers to Guyau's "Les problèmes de l'esthetique contemporaine," in which Guyau breaks away from the dominating idea of *l'art pour l'art* and reconnects art to the principle of life. Strengell summarizes Guyau's aesthetic theory as follows: "Art's function is to serve life, to make it richer and stronger. Art has to serve as the integrating substance of all moral and material life" (136).

28. See Nina Lara Rosenblatt's illuminating essay "Photogenic Neurasthenia: On Mass and Medium in the 1920s," *October* 86 (Fall 1998): 55.

29. See Adolf Behne, *Der moderne Zweckbau* (Munich: Drei Masken Verlag, 1926), published in English as *The Modern Functional Building,* trans. Michael Robinson (Santa Monica: Getty Research Institute for the History of Art and the Humanities, 1996). Behne writes: "The social sphere, after all, must lie in the primeval elements of the aesthetic," 137.

30. Ibid., 121.

31. Ibid., 123.

32. Botar, "Prolegomena to the Study of Biomorphic Modernism," 406.

Chapter Eight. Geopolitics of Fame

1. Although MoMA was a new institution, it already was playing a significant role as a kingmaker in the field of art and architecture; inclusion in the show certainly played a significant part in launching Aalto's international fame. The story of how individual architects were selected for it has yet to be told, but Aalto's inclusion indicates that the modern movement, aside from being a uniform style of sorts, was grounded in a network of friends, colleagues, and mentors who promoted one another. Although Johnson and Aalto did not meet until 1939, Uno Åhren introduced Aalto's work to Johnson for inclusion in the exhibition. See Johnson to Aalto, letter, 15 July 1930, requesting material for the exhibition and for a book

on international style modernism; AAA document.

2. Sigfried Giedion, "Über finnische Architektur" (On Finnish Architecture), *Bauwelt* 25 (1931): 34.

3. Ibid.

4. Giedion, "Produktion Paris, 1930: Malerei und Plastik," in *Produktion Paris, 1930: Werke der Malerei und Plastik* (Zurich: Kunstsalon Wolfsberg, 1930).

5. Philip Morton Shand, "Stockholm, 1930," *Architectural Review,* August 1930, 69.

6. Ibid., 69, 46, 71.

7. Philip Morton Shand, "The Work of Alvar Aalto," *Architectural Review,* September 1931.

8. Henry-Russell Hitchcock and Philip Johnson, *International Style: Architecture Since 1922* (New York: Museum of Modern Art, 1932), first photo insert. The exhibition catalogue, which bore a slightly different title, *Modern Architecture: International Exhibition* (New York: Museum of Modern Art, 1932), preceded the book.

9. Alfred H. Barr, Jr., "Foreword," *Modern Architecture: International Exhibition,* 16.

10. For a history of the Museum of Modern Art's early exhibition programs, see A. Conger Goodyear, *The Museum of Modern Art: The First Ten Years* (New York, 1943).

11. Hahl, "Kongressen Reser" (Congress Travels), *Hufvudstadsbladet,* 10 September 1933, 13. English trans. from Schildt, *Decisive Years,* 91–92.

12. Hahl's description of the boat and its passengers exemplifies what Foucault called "counter-utopias": "real arrangements that can be found within society which are at one and the same time represented, challenged, and overturned: a sort of place that lies outside all places and yet is actually localizable." Foucault, "Espaces Autres," *Architecture Movement Continuité* 5 (1984),

repr. as "Of Other Space: Utopias and Heterotopias," in Joan Ockman and Edward Eigen, eds., *Architecture Culture, 1943–1968: A Documentary Anthology* (New York: Rizzoli, 1993), 422.

13. Hahl, "Kongressen Reser," 13.

14. Fernand Legér, "Discourse to Architects," repr. in Steinmann, *CIAM,* 130–32. The lecture made a passionate plea for the architects to integrate color, particularly into public buildings. "The Wall, the Architect, the Painter," another lecture given the same year, restates this message: "The masses are full of good intentions, more perhaps than you think. Get in touch with them. You are members of society, my dear architects, and that enlarges enormously your position as artists: when one says social, one says human. . . . I repeat, the 'public building' is more than social; it is for the people" (repr. in *Functions of Painting,* trans. Alexandra Anderson, ed. and intro. by Edward F. Fry [New York: Viking, 1973], 91–99. Orig., *Functions de la Peinture* [Paris: Editions Gonthier, 1965]). My discussion on Legér has been informed by Romy Golan's essay "From Monument to Muralnomad: The Mural in Modern European Architecture" in Karen Koehler, ed., *The Built Surface: Architecture and the Pictorial Arts from Romanticism to the Twenty-First Century* (London: Ashgate, 2002), 186–208, which discusses the ideological implication of the mural debate around the CIAM Athens meeting, the Milan 1933 Triennale, and the Paris Exposition des Arts et Techniques de la vie Moderne of 1937. French and Italian artists and architects were vocal in calling for the revival of the Latin tradition of painted architecture and condemned the northern aesthetic modernism of bare walls.

15. Aalto, "Nykyaikaiset arkkitehtuuripyrkimykset lähtevät ehdottomasti yhteiskunnalliselta pohjalta" [Contemporary Architecture Is Based on Societal Concerns], *Tulenkantajat* 31 (1933): 3; English trans. from Schildt, *Decisive Years,* 94–95.

16. Giedion to Aalto, postcard, 3 July

1933; AAA document. Giedion had made the same point in another card to Aalto, written during the Milan Triennale on 27 June, calling Aalto's chairs an exception in the Finnish section of the show.

17. Giedion to Aalto, postcard, written in Zurich, 6 August 1933; AAA document.

18. See Werner Oechslin, introduction to Teppo Jokinen and Bruno Maurer, eds., *Magus des Nordens: Alvar Aalto in der Schweiz* (Magus of the North: Alvar Aalto in Switzerland) (Zurich: Eidgenössische Technische Universität, 1998), 9.

19. Henry-Russell Hitchcock, "Paris Exhibition," *Architectural Forum*, September 1937, 160.

20. John McAndrew, foreword to *Architecture and Furniture: Alvar Aalto*, exh. cat. (New York: Museum of Modern Art, 1938), 3.

21. Alfred Barr, Jr., *Cubism and Abstract Art* (New York: Museum of Modern Art, 1936), 19.

22. Hitchcock's favorite, Oud, and Johnson's favorite, Mies van der Rohe, might have been more likely candidates.

23. Barr, *Cubism and Abstract Art*, 200.

24. On the *Circle* exhibition, see Foster, *Art Since 1900*, 286–89.

25. Clement Greenberg, "Avant-Garde and Kitsch," *Partisan Review*, Autumn 1939, 34–49.

26. John McAndrew to Aalto, letter, 16 April 1938; AAA document.

27. See Goodyear, appendix, in *Museum of Modern Art: The First Ten Years*.

28. Simon Breines, "Architecture," *Architecture and Furniture: Alvar Aalto*, 9.

29. Aalto, interview in *Helsingin Sanomat*, 23 June 1939, 12.

30. Aalto, "Maailmannäyttelyt: New York World's Fair, The Golden

Gate Exhibition" (World Exhibitions: New York's World's Fair, The Golden Gate Exhibition), *Arkkitehti* 8 (1939): 113; English trans. from Schildt, *Decisive Years*, 121.

31. See Romy Golan, "A 'Discours aux Architectes'?" *Rivista de architectura* 5 (June 2003): 153; and Roland Barthes, "The Reality Effect," in Tzetan Todorov, ed., *French Literary Theory Today: A Reader* (Cambridge, Eng.: Cambridge University Press, 1982), 131–35.

32. My discussion owes a debt to Golan's interpretation of the vernacular.

33. The building was de facto an elaborate stage set, a wooden frame covered with plasterboard made to look like masonry. Ornamental motifs based on Finnish flora and fauna were used here, as in other of their buildings, to communicate that the essence of Finnishness lay in nature.

34. Aalto, "Comments on the 1939 World's Fair in New York," a speech given at an event organized by the American Federation of Art in Washington, D.C., in June 1939. See "Maailmannauttelyt," 113–15; English trans. from Schildt, *Aalto in His Own Words*, 121.

35. Giedion, "Irrationalität und Standard," 2.

36. Elizabeth Mock, introduction to *Built in USA: 1932–1944*, exh. cat. (New York: Museum of Modern Art, 1944), 20.

37. Catherine Bauer to Aalto, letter, 27 February 1950; AAA document.

38. Edgar Kaufmann to Aalto, letter, 29 March 1946; AAA document.

Chapter Nine. Ambiguity
1. Robert Venturi, *Complexity and Contradiction in Architecture* (New York: Museum of Modern Art, 1977), 16.

2. Ibid.

3. Umberto Eco, *Open Work* (Cam-

bridge, Mass.: MIT Press, 1989), 3. Orig. *Opera aperta: Forma e indeterminazione nelle poetiche contemporanee* (Milan: Bompiani, 1962).

4. Leonardo Mosso, *alvar aalto: systematic and structural reading* (Turin: Alvar Aalto Institute, 1982), portfolio section.

5. Ibid., part 1.

6. Leonardo and Laura Mosso, "Self Generation of Form and the New Ecology," *Architectural Asociation Quarterly* (Winter 1971): 8–27. I thank Britt Eversole for bringing this article to my attention and for sharing his research on Mosso with me.

7. Ibid., 10.

8. I have borrowed the concept *renationalization* from Renate Holub's informative essay "Post-War Italian Intellectual Culture: From Marxism to Cultural Studies" (Paper at the Department of Interdisciplinary Studies, University of California, Berkeley). Accessed on line 22 May 2008.

9. Mosso, "alvar aalto, architect of social and cultural communication," part 1.

10. Ibid, part 3.

11. Aalto, "Asuntomme-probleemina" [The Housing Problem], *Domus* 8–9 (1930): 176. "Eri tilaisuuksissa, eri henkilöitten ja yhteiskuntaluokkien käyttäminä merkitsevät usein samat sanat miltei täysin eri käsitettä, joskus niille annetaan suorastaan vastakkaisiakin merkityksiä."

12. Aalto, "Rationalismen of Människan, 90.

13. Ibid., 93.

14. British ecologist Arthur Tansley coined the term "ecosystem" in 1935. Ecology thus became the science of ecosystems.

15. Aalto, "Rakenteitten ja Aineitten Vaikutus Nykyaikaiseen Rakennustaiteeseen." The text was later published in *Arkkitehti* 9 (1938);

English trans. from Schildt, *Aalto in His Own Words.*

16. Ibid., 98.

17. Ibid., 99.

18. Aalto, "The Humanizing of Architecture: Functionalism Must Take the Human Point of View to Achieve Its Full Effectiveness," *Technological Review,* November 1940, 15.

19. Mosso wrote on Aalto also for *Zodiac* as early as 1958, also published by Olivetti's Communità press. See, for example, "La luce nell'architettura di Aalto," *Zodiac Revue internationale d'architecture contemp-oraine,* no. 7 (Milan: Edizione di Communità 1960), 19.

20. APAO's magazine *Metron: Rivista Internazionale di Architettura,* which was founded in 1945, published Aalto already in 1946. See Alvar Aalto, "Fine della 'Machine à Habiter,'" Luici Piccinato, "La Finlandia ricostruisce," and "Rovaniemi," Metron 7 (1946): 2–5, 11–21. Issue 10 from the same year reports that Frank Lloyd Wright and Aalto have been made honorary members of APAO.

21. Bruno Zevi, *Towards an Organic Architecture* (London: Faber & Faber, 1949), 57.

22. Ibid., 71.

23. Ibid., 145.

24. See Manfredo Tafuri's discussion on Zevi and APAO in *History of Italian Architecture, 1944–85* (Cambridge, Mass.: MIT Press, 1990), 8–9.

25. Manfredo Tafuri and Francesco Dal Co, *Modern Architecture* (New York: Rizzoli, 1986), 2: 338.

26. For further discussion about Aalto's contacts and commissions in Italy, see Schildt, *Mature Years,* 214–30.

27. I owe this information about Mosso's involvement in the project to Markku Lahti, the longtime director of Alvar Aalto Museum. He also told

me that the model of Pavia project, as well as the original drawings, are in Mosso's possession. Markku Lahti in interview with the author, 18 August 2008.

28. Pier Carlo Santini, "Alvar Aalto from Sunila to Imatra: Ideas, Projects and Buildings," *Zodiac 3* (1958): 27–28.

29. Aalto, "Architettura e arte concreta," *Domus* 225 (1947): 108; English trans. from Schildt, *Aalto in His Own Words,* 108.

30. Ibid.

31. Ibid.

32. Contact between Aalto and Albers can be traced to the early 1930s. They probably met during Aalto's visit to Berlin in summer 1931. Albers was close to Moholy: they had been hired by Gropius to teach at the same time in 1923, and Albers took over Moholy's *Vorkurs* in 1928.

33. In *Art Since 1900* the authors describe Albers' project: "Part of [his] education of the eye was fooling the eye," thus revealing the "discrepancy between the physical fact and the psychic effect," 346. Vincent Katz uses the word *curlicue* in "Black Mountain College: Experiment in Art," 46.

34. Alvar Aalto, "Finland as a Model for World Development," *Suomalainen Suomi* 5 (1949): 1; English trans. from Schildt, *Aalto in His Own Words,* 171.

35. Aalto to Aino Aalto, letter, 15 December 1945, quoted in Schildt, *Mature Years,* 103.

36. I borrow this concept and phrase from Tony Judt's illuminating book *Postwar: A History of Europe Since 1945* (New York: Penguin, 2005), 8.

37. Ibid.

38. See Petra Ceferin, *Constructing a Legend: The International Exhibitions of Finnish Architecture, 1957–1967* (Helsinki: Suomalaisen Kirjallisuuden Seura, 2003) for further discussion of the traveling exhibitions that ce-

mented the reputation of Finnish architecture. Hildi Hawkins has written on the export of Finnish design in Nina Snitzler-Levine, ed., *Finnish Modern Design* (New Haven: Yale University Press, 1998), 232–51.

39. Rudolf Schwarz, "Das Anliegen der Baukunst," in Otto Bartning, ed., *Darmstädter Gespräch, 1951: "Mensch und Raum"* (Darmstadt: Neue Darmstädter Verlagsanstalt, 1951), 60; English trans. in Lynnette Widder, "The 'Darmstadt Conversation': On the Reconstruction of Meaning and the Construction of Dwelling," paper presented at the conference "Architecture + Art: New Visions, New Strategies," 2nd International Alvar Aalto Research Conference on Modern Architecture, 12–14 August 2005, Jyväskylä, Finland; repr. in conference proceedings (Helsinki: Alvar Aalto Academy, 2005), 133. My discussion on Schwarz is greatly indebted to Widder's illuminating paper.

40. Rudolf Schwarz, "Das Unplanbare," *Baukunst und Werkform* (1947/48), repr. in Ulrich Conrads, ed., *Die Städte Himmeloffen: Reden und Reflexionen über den Wiederaufbau des Untergangenen und die Wiederkehr des Neuen Bauen, 1948–49* (Berlin: Birkhäuser, 2003), 97–99; English trans. in Widder, "'Darmstadt Conversation,'" 134.

41. This reduced reading of Bauhaus that eliminated the mystical and artistic dimension of Bauhaus education was put forward by no other than Walter Gropius in his 1935 book *New Architecture and the Bauhaus.* The book emphasized "rationalization" and "standardization" as dominant Bauhaus legacy. This reading is clearly in stark contrast with Gropius' own early affinities with expressionism, as well as of many of those he hired to teach, such as Moholy-Nagy and Johannes Itten.

42. For further discussion of the politics behind the Hansaviertel, see Francesca Rogier, "The Monumentality of Rhetoric: The Will to Rebuild in Postwar Berlin," in Sarah Williams

Goldhagen and Réjean Legault, eds., *Anxious Modernisms: Experimentation in Postwar Architectural Culture* (Cambridge, Mass.: MIT Press, 2000), 165–89.

43. For further discussion of Finnish foreign policy after the war, see Jorma Kallenautio, *Suomi Katsoi Eteensä: Itsenäisen Suomen Ulkopolitiikka, 1917–1955* (When Finland Looked Forward: The Foreign Policy of Independent Finland, 1917–1955) (Helsinki: Tammi, 1985), esp. "Välirauhasta Avunantosopimukseen—Puolittaista ja Epävarmaa Itsenäisyyttä" (From Ceasefire to Collaboration Treaty—Halfhearted and Insecure Independence).

44. Aalto, "Between Humanism and Materialism" ("Zwischen Humanismus und Materialismus"), *Der Bau* 7–8 (1955): 174–75, repr. in *Baukunst und Werkform* 6 (1956): 298–300; English trans. from Schildt, *Aalto in His Own Words,* 179.

45. Ceferin's *Constructing a Legend* discusses the international reception of the *Finland Builds* exhibitions at length; see 117–39.

46. Robert Wraight, "One of the Great Men of Europe Comes to London," *Sunday Times,* 14 April 1957, facsimile repr. in Petra Ceferin, "In Pursuit of Finnishness: The Foreign Press on Finnish Architecture, 1957–1967," *Arkkitehti* 1 (2004): 22.

47. "Alvar Aalto–Finn Without Borders," *Architectural Forum,* July 1960, 116. The article does not name the author.

48. Robert Grudin, "Humanism," in *Encyclopaedia Britannica,* 15th ed. (London: Encyclopaedia Britannica, 2002), 20: 675.

49. Williams, *Keywords,* 150.

50. Ernst Cassirer, *An Essay on Man: An Introduction to a Philosophy of Human Culture* (New Haven: Yale University Press, 1944), 24–25.

51. See Kenneth Frampton, "Towards a Critical Regionalism: Six Points for an Architecture of Resistance," in Hal Foster, ed., *Postmodern Culture* (London: Pluto, 1985), 16–30.

52. Ibid., 28–29.

53. See Zevi, *Towards an Organic Architecture,* 63–64.

54. Giedion, *Space, Time and Architecture,* 566.

Conclusion

1. See "Geopolitics" in Stuart B. Flexner, ed., *The Random House College Dictionary,* rev. ed. (New York: Random House, 1988), 552.

2. See Paasi, *Territories, Boundaries, and Consciousness,* 14, on "statecraft."

3. See Rudolf Kjellén, *Staat als Lebensform* [State as a Living Form] (Berlin-Grunewald: K. Vowinckel, 1924), 45.

4. Bruno Latour, *We Have Never Been Modern,* trans. Catherine Porter (Cambridge, Mass.: Harvard University Press, 1993), 54.

5. Hannah Arendt, *The Human Condition,* 2nd ed. (Chicago: University of Chicago Press, 1998), 176.

6. Literary historian Hans Robert Jauss goes so far as to argue that "only when this 'active life-process' is represented 'does history stop being a collection of dead facts'" (Hans Robert Jauss, quoting Werner Krauss in *Toward an Aesthetic of Reception,* trans. Timothy Bahti [Minneapolis: University of Minnesota Press, 1982], 10). For him, it is exactly this capacity to react to one's surroundings, or what he calls the "human appropriation of the world," that makes human beings human. Jauss argues that those who reductively argue that a work "reflects" the reality within which it was conceived have often overlooked this "human" dimension. A modern biography should therefore avoid succumbing to the same danger, seeing an individual as either fully autonomous or merely a product of personal events.

7. The term was coined in the nine-teenth century when it came to refer to a moderate alternative to extreme nationalism. Realpolitik characterizes also American foreign policy of the postwar era—for example, allowing support for suspect governments, as in South America, in order to secure political and economic interests.

8. See Nicholas Ray, *Alvar Aalto* (New Haven: Yale University Press, 2005), 182–88.

9. Roger Connah, *Aalto MANIA: Readings Against Aalto* (Helsinki: Building Information Center, 2000), 9.

Index

A. Ahlström Company, 117–18, 132, 134

Aalto, Aino (née Marsio): and the Artek furniture company, 214(n52); background, 29, 32; books owned, 36, 209(n15); and the Finnish Pavilion at the N.Y. World's Fair, 171–72 (figs.); in Italy, 39; marriage, 29, 209(n16); and the *Minimum Apartment Exhibition*, 99, 100–101 (figs.), 102, 104, 105(fig.); on the Turku Exhibition, 64

Aalto, Alvar: Association of Finnish Architects chaired, 192; in Athens, 162–63; Bryggman's partnership with, 52; and CIAM, 97–98, 162–63; design process, 188–90; drawing, 153–55, 154(fig.); education and student years, 11–12, 16, 32, 80–84; European travels (generally), 16, 19, 93, 97; family background, 16, 31–32, 76; as historicist, 17–18; in Italy, 39–44; in Jyväskylä, 29, 31–32, 38, 44–47 (*see also* Jyväskylä, Finland); languages, 16, 31, 32; library, 2–3, 62, 85, 95, 207(n3), 213(n29); marriage, 29, 209(n16) (*see also* Aalto, Aino [née Marsio]); move to Helsinki, 117; in Paris, 93–95; in Riga, 80–84, 83(fig.); in Turku, 49, 51 (*see also* Turku, Finland); in the U.S., 122–25, 127, 129–30, 176, 178, 215(n14); wartime activities, 117, 125–27; writings on geography, 1–2. *See also specific buildings, artistic works, and publications*

AaltoMania: Readings Against Aalto (Connah), 204

AA-System of houses (Aalto), 132, 133(fig.), 134, 137(fig.)

Åbo Underrättelser (newspaper), 51

"About Our Medieval Art" (Lindgren), 14, 14(fig.)

abstract art, 168–69, 188

Acceptera (Asplund et al.), 3, 68–71, 69–70(figs.), 106, 107(figs.)

acoustics, 155–56, 155(fig.), 216(n24). *See also* Viipuri Library (Aalto)

advertisements: Aalto on, 172; for Aalto's architectural firm, 38; for Artek, 114, 115(fig.); Turku Exhibition, 64, 64(fig.). See also Finnish Pavilion (Aalto; New York World's Fair, 1939); Finnish Pavilion (Aalto; Paris Exposition, 1936–37)

Agricultural Cooperative Building,

Turku (Aalto), 52, 62, 63(fig.)

Ahlberg, Håkon, 39

Ahlman, Erik, 21

Åhren, Uno, 66, 93–94, 217(n11). See also *Acceptera* (Asplund et al.); Stockholm Exhibition (1930)

Aitta (magazine), 48, 52, 210(n37)

Albers, Josef, 189, 189(fig.), 219 (nn32–33)

Alberti, Leon Battista, 42

Alexander, Christopher, 182

"Alvar Aalto: Between Humanism and Materialism" (MoMA exhibition, 1998), 201

Alvar Aalto Museum, Jyväskylä, 182, 183(fig.)

alvar aalto: systematic and structural reading (Mosso), 182–83

Alvar Aalto: The Decisive Years (Schildt), 7, 144

ambiguity, and Aalto's architecture: Aalto on, 184; Aalto's design approach, 188–90; in popular perception, 181; postwar buildings, 194–97, 194(fig.), 196–97(fig.); Venturi on, 181. See also confusion, need for; humanism, in Aalto's thought and works

America. *See* United States

America Builds exhibition, 137

"An American Town in Finland" (Aalto), 1

Amerika (Neutra), 123–24

Amphora (Arp wood relief), 151, 151(fig.)

Anderson, Perry, 120

The Annunciation (Fra Angelico fresco), 47–48

apartments: Hansaviertel apartment building, Berlin (Aalto), 193–94, 194–95(figs.); "minimum dwelling" projects, 99–102, 100–101(figs.), 104, 105(fig.), 113; Tapani apartment building, Turku (Aalto), 53–54, 53(fig.). *See also* housing: mass housing

Architectural Forum (magazine), 197

architectural research, 124

"Architecture: A Challenge to Our Opponents" (Frosterus and Strengell), 76–77

Architecture and Furniture: Aalto (MoMA catalog), 166–67

"Architecture of Landscape" (Aalto), 43

"Architettura e arte concreta (Architecture and concrete art)" (Aalto, published in *Domus*), 188, 194

Arendt, Hannah, 204

Arp, Hans (Jean): drawing process, 153; exhibited, 160, 177; on form and elementalism, 148; McAndrew on, 167; wood reliefs, 150–52, 151(fig.)

Artek furniture company, 113–15, 214(n52). *See also* furniture of Aalto

Asplund, Gunnar, 39; *Acceptera*, 3, 68–71, 69–70(figs.); MoMA's 1938 exhibition visited, 170; and the Stockholm Exhibition, 66–68, 89, 90(fig.)

Association of Finnish Architects. *See* SAFA

Athens CIAM meeting, 162–63

The Attack (Isto painting), 11, 12(fig.)

automatic drawing process, 153–55, 154(fig.). See also design process(es) of Aalto

"Avant-Garde and Kitsch" (Greenberg), 170

Baker House dormitory, MIT (Aalto), 181

Barbusse, Henri, 86, 212(n21)

Baroni, Ernesto, 183

Barr, Alfred H., 161–62, 168–69, 168(fig.), 177

Barthes, Roland, 173

Bassi, Charles, 21–23, 22(fig.)

Bauentwurslehre: Handbuch für den Baufachmann, Bauherren, Lehrenden und Lernenden (Neufert), 104

Bauer, Catherine, 178

Bauhaus school, 101, 147, 219(n41). *See also* Gropius, Walter; Moholy-Nagy, László; *and other individuals*

"A Beautifying Measure Undertaken in Our Town, and Its Chances of Success" (Aalto), 44

Beethoven, Ludwig van, 90

Behne, Adolf, 156–57, 213(n5)

Behrendt, Walter Curt, 95, 214(nn39, 44)

Bergson, Henri, 101, 103

"Between Humanism and Materialism" (lecture; Aalto), 195

Bildung, 29. *See also* culture

biocentrism, 143–44, 152, 155, 185. *See also* organic line

biodynamism, 99–103. *See also* dynamism

Biotechnik, 150, 155

Blomstedt, Aulis, 147

Book of Our Land (Topelius), 32–33, 209(n7)

Brandes, Georg, 3, 48, 76

Brinkman, J. A., 94, 213(n5)

Brunelleschi, Filippo, 40–42

Illustration Credits

Cover image: National Board of Antiquities, Helsinki; fig. 3: Kalervo Ojutkangas; fig. 6: Max Plunger; fig. 7: Atelier Laurent; fig. 9: Jukka Romu; fig 10: Signe Brander; figs. 12, 14, 21: Päijänne; figs. 13, 123: Kari Hakli; fig. 15: Göran Schildt; figs. 16, 18, 19: P. O. Welin; fig. 17: Hannu Aaltonen; fig. 26: Martti Kapanen; fig. 27: Alvar Aalto; figs. 29, 35, 37–40, 83, 95: Gustaf Welin; fig. 41, 54: C. G. Rosenberg; fig. 47: Board of Antiquities photo archive, Helsinki; fig. 50: Maija Holma; fig. 56: Heinrich Iffland; fig. 70: Eino Veljekset Karhumäki Oy; fig. 80: I. K. Inha, Vienna; figs. 84–86: Kolmio; fig. 87: Haus und Garten; fig. 89: Weltspiegel; fig. 92: Walter Klein; figs. 98, 100, 105, 120, 121: Eino Mäkinen; fig. 101: Artek; figs. 104, 106: Ezra Stoller, © ESTO; fig. 108: Collection of the author; fig. 115, 119: Heikki Havas; fig. 118: Rune Holma; fig. 122: David Hume Kennerly © The White House/ UPI/Lehtikuva